D1800967

THE EUROPEAN COMMUNITY AND THE DEVELOPING WORLD

The European Community and the Developing World
The Role of the Lome Convention

MARJORIE LISTER
University of York

Avebury
Aldershot · Brookfield USA · Hong Kong · Singapore · Sydney

©Marjorie Lister 1988

All rights reserved. No part of this publication may be reproduced, stored in a retrieval system, or transmitted in any form or by any means, electronic, mechanical, photocopying, recording, or otherwise without the prior permission of Gower Publishing Company Limited.

Published by
Avebury
Gower Publishing Company Limited
Gower House
Croft Road
Aldershot
Hants GU11 3HR
England

Gower Publishing Company
Old Post Road
Brookfield
Vermont 05036
USA

British Library Cataloguing in Publication Data

Lister, Marjorie, *1955*–
 The European Community and the developing world : the role of the Lome Convention.
 1. Foreign trade. Treaties : ACP. EEC Convention of Lome
 I. Title
 341.7'54

Library of Congress Cataloging-in-Publication Data

Lister, Marjorie, 1955–
 The European Community and the developing world.
 Bibliography: p.
 Includes index.
 1. European Economic Community—Developing countries.
 2. Lome Convention (1975)   I. Title.
 HC241.25.D44L57   1988   337.40172'4   88–6189

ISBN 0 566 05609 7

Printed and bound in Great Britain by
Athanaeum Press Limited, Newcastle upon Tyne

Contents

List of tables	viii
Acknowledgements	x
Introduction: The creative development of a traditional Association	xii
Notes	xv

1 Association: The legacies of colonialism and the Treaty of Rome — 1
    Association policy — 2
    The French Union — 3
    The French Community — 6
    Continuities in the system: Treaty of Rome Association — 10
    Negotiations leading to the Treaty of Rome Association — 13
    Objectives of the Association — 18
    Major provisions of the Association — 19
    Accomplishments of the Association — 20
    The results of Association — 29
    Notes — 31

2	**Association under the Yaounde Conventions**	34
	Yaounde I negotiations	35
	Objectives of the Yaounde Association	38
	Major provisions of Yaounde: Stability with change	40
	Aid provisions	42
	Trade provisions	43
	Yaounde II	45
	Yaounde II negotiations	46
	The changing context of the Association	47
	Yaounde II aid	48
	Yaounde II trade	52
	Conclusion	55
	Notes	56
3	**Lome: The new Association**	58
	Introduction	58
	British entry into the European Community	61
	The AAMS view	64
	The Commonwealth: Unprepared	66
	Intra-ACP negotiations	69
	Guinea and the EEC: A case of policy reversal	70
	ACP–EEC negotiations	74
	Industrial cooperation	89
	The institutions of the Lome Convention	96
	The new language	103
	Notes	106
4	**The results of the Lome Convention**	110
	Trade results	110
	Aid results	131
	Conclusion	155
	Notes	162
5	**ACP unity in theory and practice**	167
	The history of ACP cooperation	169
	ACP cooperation in practice	174
	Conclusion	183
	Notes	184

6 The discreet entente	186
The non-political alliance	189
Political issues in the Lome entente	192
French policy and Lome policy	201
Superpower attitudes to Lome	203
The Lome Convention and neo-colonialism	208
The prospects for Lome	216
Notes	219
Selected bibliography	224
EEC documents	224
ACP and other documents	225
Other sources	226
Index	233

Tables

1.1 Total exports of French West Africa and French Equatorial Africa in 1957; French and EEC tariffs
1.2 Exports by LDCs to the EEC: regional shares 1953–68 (in per cent)
1.3 Aid to the Associated states by the EEC (in million US dollars)
1.4 Contributions to the first three European Development Funds (1 unit of account = 1 dollar)

2.1 Rates of common customs tariff (for non-Associated non-member countries) (percentages)
2.2 EDF aid: Yaounde I and II
2.3 Aid and GNP of selected EEC Associates
2.4 EEC trade with major developing areas (millions of units of account)

3.1 List of Associable countries mentioned in the Treaty of Brussels
3.2 Main differences between CFF and STABEX
3.3 Utilization of the first three EDFs (cumulative position 31.12.80) (millions of units of account)
3.4 Net sectoral disbursements of EDF IV (at the end of 1979)
3.5 Share of manufactures in exports 1978 (per cent)

4.1 Development of ACP–EEC trade (compared with the development of trade between the EEC and third countries and the EEC and developing countries) (1,000 million units of account)

4.2 EEC imports from the ACP states: classification in descending order of average volume for 1976–8 (ten largest exporters)
4.3 EEC states' shares of ACP exports to the Community (per cent)
4.4 EEC–ACP trade balance (millions of units of account)
4.5 ACP allocation of STABEX over five years
4.6 Reduction of STABEX transfers by year of application (millions of units of account)
4.7 Aggregate STABEX transfers for the financial years 1975–9
4.8 Rankings in Lome I indicative programme allocation (disbursements 31.12.79)
4.9 Sectoral distribution of regional cooperation activities (as of 31.1.80)

Acknowledgements

Thanks are due to the many people who assisted me in my work on this study, some of whom are listed below. All the opinions expressed here are solely the responsibility of the author.

Those who assisted me include: the European Commission which allowed me to work in its Development Directorate as a 'stagiaire'; many of the Commission staff, including M.H. Ferraton, M. Parmentier, Mr P. Roscow, Mr John Scott, M.F. Thurmes, the staff of *The Courier*, and Ms Trudy Beeching of the London office; the staff of the Secretariat of the European Council of Ministers, including M. Gonzague Lesort, Co-Secretary of the ACP–EEC Council of Ministers, Mlle Bonnelle, and M. Schweiga; the information office of the European Parliament, Mr Derek Enright, MEP, Mme Carla Ferrari, and Mr James Pond; the UK Permanent Representation to the European Community, including Mr K. Bloomfield, Mr J. Rollo and Ms Margaret Vowles, and Ms Marion Bywater of the Hong Kong Government Office; the ACP General Secretariat, including Secretary-General Carrington, Mme G. Bernard, and Dr Clement Tibazawa; Dr Akinerere, Deputy Director of the Centre for Industrial Development, and Mme Wilson; ACP diplomats including Ambassador Monyake of Lesotho, Miss A. Clarke of Jamaica, Mr D. Hales of Guyana, Dr C. Twesigye and Mr H. Nyakoojo of Uganda; the Commonwealth Secretariat, including Deputy Secretary-General David Anderson, Dr Bishnodat Persaud and other officials; the staff of the US Mission to the EEC; Mr Adrian Hewitt and Dr Christopher Stevens of the Overseas Development Institute; Dr C. Twitchett; Mr C.R. Hill and Dr P.G. Cerny of the University of York;

Mrs Kaye Kneen who typed the first manuscript; and my family who made this undertaking possible.

Introduction: The creative development of a traditional Association

The relationship between the European Community and the 66 developing countries which comprise the African, Caribbean and Pacific (ACP) Group of States has been much discussed in academic and political circles. Judgements ranging from the laudatory to the scathing have been and continue to be passed on the Lome relationship. Although many commentators perceived the Lome Convention as arriving full-blown on the international scene in 1975, this was far from the case. The continuity and stability of the Lome entente were among its most outstanding features. The legacies of colonialism, particularly French colonialism, were crucial in shaping the relationship between the European Economic Community (EEC) and the ACP states.

Another main theme of this study is that the Lome Convention's success lay in its ability to distance itself from its colonial heritage as well as to draw on its traditional ties. Although fundamentally conservative, the Lome association managed to adapt itself to changing times and to appear 'progressive', 'innovative' or even 'revolutionary'.

The Treaty of Rome Association founded in 1957 was the first direct predecessor of the Lome Convention. It united the six EEC member states and their dependencies in a formal association. Like the later Lome Convention, it had a treaty basis, concentrated on Europe and Africa, offered trade preferences and financial aid to the developing countries, and was an unequal relationship.

Although the subsequent associations were negotiated with independent African states rather than imposed by the colonial powers, as was the case in the Treaty of Rome Association, their economic results were similar. Problems of delay in aid-giving and the lack of improved export performance by the developing countries were continuing themes of the EurAfrican associations.

The decade of the two Yaounde Conventions, in force from 1964 to 1975, saw the continuation of the entente between the European Community and eighteen independent, francophone African states. The biggest change in the relationship from the Treaty of Rome Association was the new, legal equality of the signatories. Nevertheless, in practice, the EEC member states were more equal than the others.[1]

In 1975 the signing of the Lome Convention caught the imagination of many of those interested in constructing a new international economic order. Lome, however, was not designed to bring about a radical restructuring of the international political or economic systems. It was the creative development of a traditional policy.

Like the first Yaounde Convention, the Lome Convention made strenuous attempts to distance itself from its antecedents. It referred neither to the Yaounde Associations nor to the Treaty of Rome. This pretence of newness was a convenient fiction which suited both the ACP and EEC parties to the Convention, helping them to avoid the stigma of neo-colonialism.

The appeal of the Lome Convention was especially remarkable in the case of Guinea (Conakry). Since 1958 Guinea's leader, Ahmed Sekou Toure, rejected any form of association with Europe, fearing that it would compromise Guinea's independence. However, by 1975 Guinea abandoned its anti-European stance and joined the Lome Convention. The reasons for this policy reversal are analysed in Chapter 3.

The Lome Convention set out to become a 'model' for North–South relations. However, the innovations it contained, such as the provisions for export earnings stabilization and industrial cooperation, failed to bring real development to the ACP. Beneath the new rhetoric of the Convention was a politically and economically conservative relationship.

One significant but little-known aspect of the Lome Convention was the quest for ACP unity. A large degree of solidarity among the African, Pacific and Caribbean states was achieved during the Lome I negotiations. Its philosophical basis was rooted in pan-Africanism and in the new international economic order's call for collective self-reliance. However, the obstacles to ACP unity proved, in general, stronger than their will to cooperate. The ACP failed to implement their own proposals to strengthen their secretariat, create a trade and development bank or even publish a newsletter.

Another interesting aspect of the Lome Convention was its political identity. The Lome Convention created a unique, sophisticated political image which has largely escaped scrutiny. The European Commission presented the Lome Convention as a non-political organization. As a politically neutral association, the Convention seemed to offer developing countries a safer, middle way between alliances with the superpowers.

In fact, the Lome Convention was not politically neutral, just politically discreet. It did encounter political problems over its policy of creating a regional bloc or sphere of influence in the ACP, over relations with the socialist countries, and over questions of human rights. Nevertheless, the Convention's low political profile helped it to avoid many political issues and to survive those it could not avoid.

Lome was part of the traditional international system in which the United States primarily interested itself in Latin America and the Europeans primarily concerned themselves with Africa. The Lome relationship was a part of, not a threat to this system. The European Community's expanding interest in Latin America, rather than intermittent US concern with Africa, could be expected to produce at least a partial challenge to the old political and economic order.

Finally, this study examines the charges of neo-colonialism which have been made against the EurAfrican relationship. After a survey of the principal reasons which have been advanced as to why the Lome Convention was not neo-colonial, it is concluded that these are unconvincing and that the relationship was an example of European neo-colonialism. Because of the softening of the Lome Convention with financial aid, trade concessions and apparent equality for the ACP, the Lome Convention is here termed 'welfare neo-colonialism'.

It is always difficult to assess a political relationship still in progress,[2] but the prospects for the continuation of the Lome alliance appear bright. Since the signing of the Lome Convention in 1975, two more Lome agreements have been negotiated. Lome II and Lome III were signed in 1979 and 1984 respectively, and these, which are briefly examined in Chapter 5, showed a continuation and incremental development of the relationship. Although these later agreements are mostly beyond the scope of this study, they followed the basic pattern of EurAfrican associations established by Lome I and its predecessors. The prospects, however, for the Lome relationship to live up to its ambitious ideals of equality and partnership or to make a real change in the impoverished condition of the now 66 African, Caribbean and Pacific countries are less hopeful.

The themes introduced here are more fully explained in the following chapters. The framework for analysis has been a realistic one, examining the often idealistic aspirations and pronouncements of the states involved in the light of actual political and economic experience. Direct contact with many senior European and ACP officials, the opportunity to attend private meetings of the Convention's decision-making bodies, and access to many published and unpublished sources have made it possible to take an in-depth look at the Lome Convention and the attitudes of those party to it.

Notes

1. A phrase used by Brogan, D.W., 'The Post-Imperial Age', *New Republic*, 17 December 1956.
2. As noted by Krause, L. (ed.), *The Common Market: Progress and Controversy*, New Jersey, Praeger, 1964, 'Preface'.

1 Association: The legacies of colonialism and the Treaty of Rome

At the most basic level, continuity in the Lome relationship lay in the fact that most of the ACP states were once colonies of either France or Britain. Their administrations were fashioned by the Quai d'Orsay or Whitehall, their indigenous policy-makers could converse in French or English, and Christianity was frequently their religion. The former colonies owed their organization as sovereign states and their entry into the modern international state system to their colonial experience.[1]

On the developing countries' side, the roots of the Lome Convention lay in Africa. This was because most of the original dependencies of the European Six and later the majority of the Lome signatories were African. Africa was at the centre of the European colonialist theories which led to the Lome Convention.

Just as connections between colonial history and the Lome Convention centred on Africa (particularly sub-Saharan Africa), they also centred on France. It was due to French insistence that the Community's original colonial policy was adopted. The relationship between France and its African colonies was the seed of the present Lome alliance between the European Community and over sixty developing countries.

These broad continuities or legacies of the colonial past, as well as the more specific legacies canvassed later in this chapter, reveal that the Lome relationship was not built upon a *tabula rasa*. In the wake of the signing of the Lome Convention in 1975, one European political analyst wrote, 'The EEC thus demonstrates that it has inaugurated a new policy toward the third world.'[2] Although this opinion of Lome has been often expressed, one of the main contentions of this book is that it is untenable. What the European Community demonstrated in the Lome Convention was not a totally new policy, but its desire to preserve as much as possible of the international prestige and other benefits which had accrued to its members as colonial powers. At the same time as trying to maintain some of its members' former status as metropoles, the Community was realistic enough to allow the colonial relationship established under the Treaty of Rome to evolve in a manner consistent with changing political and economic realities.

Association policy

One policy in particular of the French colonial empire had an important role in shaping the Lome relationship. The policy of association was a pragmatic answer of the late nineteenth and early twentieth century to the difficulties of assimilation. Assimilation was a policy or rather an ideal of fully integrating the colonized peoples into the French political system and French culture. Black Africans under French rule were to become black Frenchmen, speaking French, imbued with French ideas, culture and rights, and owing allegiance to France. However, assimilation proved difficult to practise upon Muslim and black Africans whose own culture and traditions were not easily abandoned even when the reward of French citizenship was offered. The assimilationists' insistence on re-making Africans in the French image, an image they believed superior to the African one, is now widely denigrated as cultural imperialism.

The policy of association, in contrast, recognized that African societies were too different to French society to be assimilated easily. Instead of imposing all things French upon the Africans, association sought to accommodate existing African structures and customs within French rule. To Jules Harmand, the leading advocate of this policy, association for Africa meant 'the scrupulous respect of their customs, indirect administration, economic aid, and intellectual and technical development'.[3]

Association policy, like British indirect rule,* allowed the Africans to have more control over their own affairs than earlier policies. Association involved the French in working through indigenous institutions rather than trying to abolish them. According to the theory, both sides were to benefit from the policy of association. The French would give economic aid and assist economic and technical development in the colonies. African traditions would be respected. In return

---

* British indirect rule was a more pragmatic, less theoretically articulated policy than association.

the French would reap the rewards of unopposed rule and the enlightened exploitation of African resources.

But association did not mean giving Africans rights equal to the French. Unlike assimilation it did not envisage the Africans becoming equal to the French through the civilizing influence of French rule. To quote Harmand:

> The policy of association . . . does not at all attempt to prepare and achieve an equality forever impossible, but rather it attempts to establish a certain equivalence or compensation of reciprocal services. Far from letting the domination weaken, the policy wants to reinforce it by making it less offensive and repugnant.[4]

Under association, Africans were to be recognized as different from Europeans, but not equals. The policy intended Africans to benefit from its liberality, but it did not intend them to acquire any influence over the decisions of the metropole. The sphere of autonomy allowed to Africans by the association policy was limited to local matters; it did not include questioning the activities of the colonizing power.

In practice, the policy of association became blurred. Instead of a clearly defined policy, association was only a set of ambiguous ideas.[5] While association was practised, assimilation was never completely abandoned. Not until Algerian independence in March 1962 marked the final failure to create an *Algérie française* was the assimilationist view laid to rest.

Unlike assimilation, the policy of association was adaptable to the changes of independence. The policy practised by the European Community towards its member states' dependencies and the states which attained independence derived from the colonial theory of association. Until 1975 the developing countries affiliated to the EEC were known as 'Associates'. Although the name 'Associates' was altered to 'partners', elements of association policy have persisted up to the present. These comprised: Europe's interest in maintaining links with former colonies in Africa; its interest in access to African resources; its interest in African social and economic development; and the maintenance of an unequal relationship while striving to overcome its most 'offensive and repugnant' elements.*

The French Union

Having uncovered in association a large part of the theoretical

---

* The concept of 'EurAfrica', discussed later in this chapter, complemented association as a theoretical basis for the Lome Convention.

foundation of the Lome Convention, the historical antecedents of the Convention can be considered. The French Union was in many ways a model for the European Community's development policy.

The French Union was established by the French constitution of 1946. The previous French constitution of 1875 had made no reference to the dependencies. This was changed in the 1946 constitution which named the overseas dependencies of France, not as colonies, but as Overseas Departments and Territories and Associated States and Territories.

The institutions of the French Union were the President, High Council and Assembly. However, these institutions were largely superfluous. The Union President was the Republic's President; the High Council existed only in theory and the Assembly had no statutory powers. In practice, the French president and cabinet governed the French Union as they governed France.

The French Union was short-lived; it lasted only until the French Community superseded it in 1958. Nevertheless, the French Union established in practice many of the themes carried through in the association policy of the European Community as well as in the French Community. Three major aspects of the French Union which appeared in the European Community's association policy were the multinational structure, political structure and terminology.

The French Union accommodated a wide variety of territories. It united disparate nations from Caribbean islands to Africa and Indochina. Like the EEC's Lome Convention, it brought together European and non-European peoples under a common legal umbrella. Thus, in the policy of establishing a multinational organization of European states and overseas territories in various stages of dependency, the French Union was a progenitor of the Lome Convention.

Within this multinational organization, France did not insist on having one pattern of colonial government for all its dependencies from Algeria to Indochina. The spectrum of arrangements France had with its overseas dependencies, ranging from department to Associated State, was in this respect similar to the arrangements made by the European Community in its relations with developing countries. That is, the Community offered Association, and later 'partnership' to sub-Saharan African and other selected ldcs as well as concluding a variety of agreements with developing countries from Asia to Latin America. This EEC policy of different agreements for development cooperation was set out in the Community's 1974 'Fresco' document.[6] It proposed that different ldcs with different development problems (and varying importance to the Community) should be treated differently. Just as France in 1946 felt that a diversity of dependencies required a diversity of approaches, the European Community in its proliferation of agreements with North Africa, sub-Saharan Africa, Latin America and Asia believed that different approaches were required.

The political structures of the French Union also resembled and influenced those of the later French Community and the Lome Convention (through its predecessors: the Treaty of Rome Association and the two Yaounde Conventions). Like the Lome Convention, the French Union provided for a tripartite governing structure. The French Union's President, High Council and Assembly can be compared to the Lome Convention's Council of Ministers, Committee of Ambassadors and Consultative Assembly.

Differences, of course, existed between the institutional structures of the French Union and the Lome Convention, but the similarities were striking. The President of the Union and the Council of Ministers sat at the top of their respective hierarchies, exercising wide powers. On the next level of structure, the French Union's High Council's functions were performed by French ministers; in the Lome institutions the Committee of Ambassadors was composed of diplomats rather than ministers, but it was also an influential body responsible for many decisions. In the assemblies of the two organizations, similarities of function were notable. The assemblies shared the characteristic of being advisory bodies, without legislative powers.*

Both systems, the French Union and the Lome Convention, created a semi-federal structure. The French Union came the closer to being a federation, an effective political entity, by assigning a greater scope of powers to the 'federal' institutions. The French Union was a union of non-self-governing territories. The Lome Convention, in contrast, united sovereign states in its quasi-federal institutions. Its scope for decision-making at a central level was therefore more limited.

But despite having federal-type institutions, neither the French Union nor the Lome Convention operated as a federation. The French Union was metropolitan France writ large. It was more like the French empire than the United States of France and Associated Peoples to which it aspired. In the Lome relationship, the quasi-federal structures showed its inheritance from the French Union and reflected also the tripartite division of the European Community into Council, Commission and Parliament. But these quasi-federal structures were of questionable value to the Lome relationship. (See also Chapter 3.)

The terminology used in the French Union was echoed in the early treaties of the European Community with its affiliated developing areas. Most striking was the use of the term 'Association'. 'Association' meant the French theory of indirect rule and it was applied in the French Union to 'Associated States and Territories'. The term was

---

* This was also the case for the European Community's Parliament whose statutory powers were extremely limited.

adopted by the European Community and applied to all the dependencies 'Associated' with the Community under Part IV of the Treaty of Rome and known collectively as the 'Associates'.

The French constitution of 1946 contained two basic principles which were further developed in the Yaounde and Lome Conventions. There were references to 'equality of rights and obligations' and 'nations and peoples who put in common or coordinate their resources and their efforts to develop their respective civilizations'.[7] These themes of equality and development have remained primary concerns of the EurAfrican relationship.

In summary, a list of the policies and structures of the Lome relationship which can be traced to French colonialism is given below:

1   The policy and terminology of association.
2   The multinational structure bringing disparate nations into a single legal structure centred on Europe.
3   The policy of having different kinds of relationships with different developing countries.
4   The creation of tripartite, quasi-federal political structures.
5   The expressed principles of equality and development.

The French Community

The French Community was not constituted until after the Treaty of Rome had been signed (25 March 1957). Thus the French Community came into being after the Treaty of Rome Association which was the basis of the Lome relationship. Therefore, unlike the French Union, the French Community was not in the direct lineage of the Lome alliance. It was a parallel but abortive development. Nevertheless, an examination of the French Community reveals similarities to the Lome relationship and policies which foreshadowed later policies.

The French Community, established under the 1958 constitution of the Fifth Republic, bore many resemblances to the French Union. Like the Union, it attempted to create a central organization uniting metropolitan France and its dependencies. The Community's governing organs were the President, Executive Council and Senate, with a Court of Arbitration to solve judicial disputes.[8]

The 1958 constitution gave the French president wide powers 'to preside over and represent' the French Community. The French Community's Executive Council was composed of the French prime minister, the heads of government of the constituent areas, and 'the Ministers responsible on behalf of the Community for common affairs'.[9] The functions of the Executive Council were vaguely defined and all the ministers responsible for common affairs were French.

In the tradition of the institutional systems discussed earlier, the French Community's Senate, composed of delegates from France and the member territories, had only an advisory role. French domination of the Community was evident in its judicial institution, the Court of Arbitration, whose functions were performed by the French supreme court. The representation of the dependencies in the Executive Council and Senate only thinly disguised the fact that the French Community was again France writ large.

Given the preponderance of powers allotted to the French president, ministers, and parliament, the Community in the later 1950s and early 1960s was unable to accommodate the growing dissatisfaction of the Africans. By allocating France too great a role, the Community could not evolve into a federation of equals. The Africans' nationalistic aspirations could not be expressed within an organization so completely dominated by France.[10]

Unlike its Belgian counterpart, the French Community did come into existence.[11] Accession to the Community was by referendum. On 28 September 1958, the populations of the French African territories were to vote 'oui' or 'non' to accepting the new 1958 constitution. If they voted to accept the constitution, they agreed to participate in the French Community. Rejecting the constitution meant rejecting the Community and choosing a quick (and in the French view ill-advised) path to independence.

The atmosphere surrounding the referendum was heavy. On the one hand, the Community as it was offered was not entirely to the Africans' liking. Even relatively conservative leaders such as Senghor feared the Community would imprison the Africans in an internal autonomy preventing full independence.[12] Further qualms were expressed by the heads of government of Niger and Guinea.[13]

On the other hand, the Africans' choices were limited. De Gaulle and the French leadership were determined that the Africans should accept or reject the Community as it had been proposed. The details were not negotiable. De Gaulle made it clear that for a territory to vote 'non' meant losing the goodwill and support of France. On 8 August 1958, he broadcast his message on Radio Dakar:

> But one cannot conceive that France would continue to aid an independent territory. The [independent] government would take the economic or other consequences that would follow the demonstration of such a decision.[14]

The French colonies were presented with a Community they could take or leave. However, if they chose to decline the offer of Community membership, France assured them that unpleasant consequences would follow.

The 'take it or leave it' approach adopted by the metropole showed that the dependencies had very little bargaining power. The French made the rules of the Community and the Africans had either to acquiesce or go away empty-handed. In the end, most acquiesced.

The 1946 French constitution spoke of French commitment to leading the African colonies to self-government:

> Faithful to her traditional mission, France intends to conduct the peoples of whom she has taken charge to the liberty of self-administration.[15]

But far from having equipped the Africans for self-rule, the French in 1958 were proposing a Community whose field of competence included foreign policy, defence, currency, economic and financial policy, supervision of justice, higher education, transport and telecommunications. Without powers in these areas, African self-administration was meaningless. Yet France intended that these fields of action should not be devolved to local governments but put under the control of the Community apparatus, or effectively under French control.

In the referendum 13 of France's 14 African colonies voted by majorities of over 95 per cent to accept the 1958 constitution and its provisions for the French Community. This result was interpreted by France as a triumph for its policies. Although it had been expected that Senegal and Niger might also vote against the Constitution, only Guinea actually voted 'non'. Ninety-five per cent of Guinea's voters rejected the new constitution and chose instead the complete independence France had warned them against. Guinea's leader, the late Ahmed Sekou Toure, had been offended by French pressure to vote in favour of the Community. Sekou Toure considered 'my self-respect for the dignity of Africa has been shocked'. He contended that the consequences of voting no would be felt in France as well as in Africa.[16]

After the referendum the French precipitately abandoned Guinea. They stopped all bank credits, prevented technicians and supply ships from arriving, withdrew administrative personnel, light bulbs and telephone wires, offered aid to enemies of the regime, and refused to recognize the new state.[17] De Gaulle believed that without French support the Guinean government would soon collapse and serve as a good example to other Africans too eager for independence. In fact, it was the French Community and not the small state of Guinea (Conakry) which soon disintegrated.

De Gaulle later wrote that the French Community had played a 'supporting and transitional role' in helping the African territories to reach independence.[18] But the Community had not been designed as a stepping stone to independence. Originally, a state could not become independent and remain within the Community, although this was later altered. The French Community had been intended to stem the tide of independence, not to facilitate it.

The French Community had little effect on the ultimate course of African independence. It did allow the French a short period between Guinean independence and the independence of their other sub-Saharan African colonies to get used to the idea of losing their African empire.

Failure of the French Community

The French Community was almost immediately a failure. It failed to convince the African colonies that they needed it. Instead of serving as a warning to other African independence seekers by its collapse, Guinea was an incentive to them by its success. Guinea succeeded in receiving international recognition, foreign aid, and admission (approved unanimously except for France) to the United Nations. It showed that a poor, new, independent African state could survive in the international system even without the support of the former colonial power.

Cracks in the French Community's structure became apparent when in 1959 the Mali Federation objected to excessive French interference in the Community.[19] In early 1960 Madagascar and the Mali Federation asked for and received independence. At the same time they successfully negotiated to continue their Community membership, henceforth as 'Associates'. But by the summer of 1960, Mauretania, Ivory Coast, Upper Volta, Dahomey and Niger became independent outside of the Community. The French Community withered away as the colonies became independent.

Under the French Community, sub-Saharan French Africa (excluding Madagascar) achieved independence peacefully. But the piecemeal way in which the colonies attained independence militated against the emergence of a pan-African polity. The Parti du Regroupement Africain had hoped in 1958 'to negotiate with France the creation of a multinational federation of free and equal peoples, without in any way renouncing its wish to federate all the former colonies into a United States of Africa'.[20] The French and later the French Community failed to create a workable federal governing structure for the African colonies. This made it more unlikely that such a federal African government could be created after independence.

One theme which emerged in the French Community and later in the Lome relationship was the development of African regional organizations. De Gaulle credited French policy with the regional groupings which it 'helped to create and foster'.[21] Although France was never keen on the Mali Federation, it did permit bodies such as the Council of the Entente (Ivory Coast, Dahomey, Niger and Upper Volta) to exist within the French Community. The Lome Convention, too, fostered some regional organizations such as the Economic Community of West African States while falling short of creating a pan-African federation.

The French Community proved much less durable than the Treaty of Rome (later Lome) Association. Both systems grew out of the French colonial experience, but they differed in important respects. Only the Treaty of Rome relationship survived African independence.

The ability of the European Community to distance itself from the colonial era and to maintain a low political profile gave it advantages over the French Community. To remain linked to the French Community after independence, as Madagascar and the Mali Federation tried to do, was to remain affiliated with the old colonial master. Association with the European Community seemed to be free from the taint of colonialism. The European Community was not itself a colonial power. Member states like Luxembourg or Germany after 1914 were not colonial powers and the Netherlands had not been a colonial power in Africa since 1872.[22] Because the EEC had fewer associations with colonialism than the French Community, it was a more acceptable partner for the new African states.

Developing countries found it easier to align themselves with an ostensibly economic organization than with the French Community which openly concerned itself with the highly political areas of defence and foreign policy. The EEC's Association was less overtly involved with politics, less ambitious in scope, and less tainted by the colonial past.

The success of the EEC–African relationship compared to the French Community cannot be attributed to the prospect of greater financial benefits for the African states. French aid in 1958 to French Africa totalled approximately 350 million dollars. Based on a four-year average for 1958 to 1962, EEC aid to French Africa was only 150 million dollars or less than half as much.[23] French Africa was also heavily dependent on its trade with France. However, the Africans' wish to secure French trade and aid did not prevent the break-up of the French Community.[24]

Continuities in the system: Treaty of Rome Association

The rest of this chapter is devoted to the first direct predecessor of the Lome Convention, the Treaty of Rome Association. Before turning to this Association in detail, the persistence of certain distinguishing features from the Treaty of Rome Association to the Lome Convention will be examined. The persistence of these features from the 1957

Treaty of Rome Association to the 1975 Lome Convention shows that the Lome relationship was fundamentally conservative.

Jacqueline Matthews noted four characteristics which differentiated the EEC's Association system from the Commonwealth.[25] The fourth characteristic, the greater age of the Commonwealth, is of little analytical value, but the other three are revealing. The first distinguishing characteristic related to the diversity of economies found within the Commonwealth. These ranged from industrial Britain to the newly developed economies of Australia and Canada and the struggling economies of Africa and Asia. The Lome relationship, however, consisted of two broad types of economies: the developed economies of the EEC member states and the underdeveloped economies of the Associates.

For the European Community, limiting the Lome relationship to only two types of economies was deliberate. The EEC's 1963 Declaration of Intent had offered Association with the Community only to countries at a similar level of economic development to those already Associated with it under the Treaty of Rome.[26]

The second distinguishing characteristic of the EEC's association policy was its ability to encompass countries which were not, as well as those which were, former colonies. Although colonies were the first Associates of the Community under the Treaty of Rome and former colonies continued in 1975 to form the core of the ACP, the Community by 1963 offered its Association to any country 'which has an economic structure and production comparable to those of the Associated States'.[27]

The EEC's 'open door' policy for selected developing countries can be traced back to the Treaty of Rome which contained declarations that the EEC was willing to contemplate association agreements with countries of the franc zone, and after independence with Somalia, with Surinam and the Netherlands Antilles.[28] The EEC's eagerness to sign up new Associates was particularly notable in Africa. The Community's regional strategy called for it to encourage all of black Africa to join the Lome Convention. This policy of the European Community could be called a new scramble for Africa.* This was not a scramble for outright conquest, but for a sphere of political and economic influence.

The third distinguishing characteristic of the Lome relationship was its formal, legal basis compared to the informal, customary basis of the Commonwealth. This difference reflected the British attachment to common law in contradistinction to the French predilection for codified, civil law. The basis of the European Community's relationship with the developing countries, beginning with the Treaty of Rome

---

* This scramble was particularly clear in the cases of Mozambique and Angola, described in Chapter 6.

Association, was formalized and legal, as were the bases of the French Union and the French Community.

The treaty basis of the Lome relationship had the advantage of setting out the rights and obligations of both sides. The fact that the Conventions of Association (other than the first, the Treaty of Rome) ran for five years allowed changes to be included in each new treaty.* The Community's 'Fresco' document emphasized the importance of the legal basis of EurAfrican relations:

> The Associations, moreover, are the result of contractual Acts. Once the Conventions are signed, our Associates are assured of Community aid in all its forms: we have the right neither to revoke nor to modify our undertakings for the duration of the contract; this is a valuable stabilizing factor for development.[29]

The legalistic approach of the EEC's development policy was emulated by the African, Caribbean and Pacific States in 1975. The Community's developing country partners often adopted policies similar to those of the Community. Thus, the ACP, like the EEC member states, based their relations with each other on a formal treaty, the Georgetown Agreement. (For this treaty, see Chapter 5.)

The three characteristics of economic diversity, openness to non-colonies, and legalism persisted from the Treaty of Rome Association to the Lome Convention signed nearly two decades later. The persistence of these characteristics demonstrates that although modifications were made in the EurAfrican relationship, its fundamental characteristics were not altered. It remained a relationship between the 'have' countries which set its parameters and the 'have-nots' which sought its benefits.

The Treaty of Rome did not specify that its terminology of 'Association' derived from French colonial theory.[30] Nevertheless, it was clear that the Association established by Part IV of the Treaty of Rome arose from the colonial rather than the general meaning of the word. The term 'Associate' had earlier been applied within the French Union to the dependencies of France; it was then used by the European Community in much the same way to refer to the affiliated dependencies of the member states. As discussed earlier, the French concept of association was a general orientation rather than a detailed policy, and the European Community's use of 'Association' was similarly general.

The essence of Association under Part IV of the Treaty of Rome was to establish special relations between the European Community and the

---

* The EEC Commission wanted a permanent treaty basis for Lome but the ACP preferred the freedom to renegotiate every five years.

dependencies of France, Belgium, Italy and the Netherlands. These numerous Associated 'countries and territories' comprised French West Africa, French Equatorial Africa, St Pierre and Miquelon, the Comoros, Madagascar and dependencies, New Caledonia and dependencies, the French territory of Afars and Issas, French Southern and Antarctic territories, (excluding French departments), Togoland, the French Cameroons, the Belgian Congo, Ruanda-Urundi, Italian Somaliland, and the Netherlands Antilles.

The Treaty of Rome did not declare the Associated dependencies to be the equals of the European Six, just as French colonial association had not made the dependencies the equals of metropolitan France. The Associates were not involved in the decision-making system of the Treaty of Rome and indeed had no choice over whether to join the Association. Like the role envisaged for the associated territories by French colonial theorists, the EEC's Associates were expected passively to accept the political, economic and social benefits given to them.

The Treaty of Rome Association never had a theoretical exponent like Harmand or Lyautey to propound its principles. Nevertheless, it did make an addition to the theory of association. The Treaty of Rome couched its enumeration of the benefits of Association in terms not only of the interests of the dependencies, but also in terms of their expectations.[31] This was an advance over the colonial theory of Association which had not tried to take into account the actual desires of the colonized peoples. However, despite the promulgation of this advanced view, no procedures for assessing and accomplishing the wishes of the indigenous people were instituted.

Negotiations leading to the Treaty of Rome Association

The broad debate

After the Second World War the question of future relations between Europe and Africa and, more broadly, between metropoles and colonies was at issue. Through the establishment of the French Union and then the French Community, France tried to reassert French influence in Africa and its other dependencies. The rest of Europe was also concerned with future relations between Europe and the colonies. Prior to the negotiations which resulted in the Treaty of Rome Association, a variety of discussions were held and proposals put forward dealing with the future of EurAfrican relations.

These included the European Economic Conference of 1949 (Westminster Conference),[32] the 1952 Strasbourg Plan,[33] debates in the Commonwealth and in the Organization for European Economic

Cooperation. Thus, in the post-war period even non-colonial powers participated in the debates over the colonies' future. Just as the Berlin West Africa Conference of 1884 to 1885 had subjected colonial relations to international scrutiny, the post-war period saw an international debate on colonialism.[34] But while the Berlin West Africa Conference formulated an authoritative policy on colonialism in Africa, the post-war debates were less conclusive.[35] Nevertheless, the idea that Europe should develop a common policy towards the dependencies was widely mooted before the creation of the Treaty of Rome Association.

In the context of the European Community, the issue of the overseas dependencies was raised as early as 1953 in the Ad Hoc Assembly set up by the European Coal and Steel Community (ECSC).[36] But after the French scuttled the European Defence Community in 1954 and the subsequent attempts to create a European Political Community foundered, interest in the overseas dependencies diminished. Community-builders adopted a less ambitious approach and finally succeeded in establishing the European Economic Community in 1957.

African input into the post-war debates on colonial relations was limited. As representatives of France d'outre mer, Africans did participate in the Consultative Assembly of the Council of Europe and the Ad Hoc Assembly of the ECSC.[37] But the Africans, and these assemblies, had little power. Because some Africans did have a chance to express their views, this was an improvement over the Berlin West Africa Conference where Africans were not consulted about their future. Nevertheless it was still possible, as in the case of the Treaty of Rome Association, for major policy decisions to be made by Europeans without reference to the Africans affected by their decisions.

The negotiations on Association

The Treaty of Rome Association was imposed on the dependencies 'in a fashion which could not have been more colonial in spirit'.[38] The Association of 'the overseas countries and territories' was accomplished by the governments of the six original EEC states: France, the Federal Republic of Germany, Italy, Belgium, Luxembourg, and the Netherlands. Although a few African voices such as that of Senghor, who was a member of the French parliament, had been heard in the debates over the future of EurAfrican relations, in the lengthy negotiations which produced the Treaty of Rome Association, none of the Associates-to-be was allowed to participate. Some Africans had qualms that the Association could make independence more difficult to achieve, but such views got no hearing.[39] There was no opportunity for the Six's dependencies to veto the result of the Europeans' decisions, nor to withdraw from the Association.[40]

The 1956 Spaak Committee Report, which formed the basis of the European Economic Community, concentrated on issues of European integration to the exclusion of colonial questions. With the exception of France, the governments of the Six were prepared to embark on the European Economic Community without having provisions for their dependencies included. The French first introduced the idea of association for the dependencies in May 1956, just one month after the Spaak Report had been submitted to the governments of the Six.[41] The initial reaction of the other European governments was cool.

The French managed to persuade the Belgians and Italians in favour of their proposal. The dependencies of Belgium and Italy — the Belgian Congo and Ruanda-Urundi and the Italian Trusteeship Territory of Somalia — would be treated on an equal basis to the French dependencies. The Germans, who lost their colonies after World War One, and the Dutch, who ceded their last African colony to Britain in 1872, were less readily persuaded.[42]

It soon became apparent that France was determined to make the Association a *sine qua non* of joining the EEC.[43] In October 1956 France and Belgium, which often followed the French lead in development matters, issued a joint memorandum calling for the Association of the overseas dependencies of all EEC member states.

In February 1957 Association was the last outstanding issue of the negotiations on the EEC. By 20 February, agreement was reached on the Association of the dependencies. France had conceded Germany special provisions to import Latin American bananas and consented to allowing all the EEC states equal rights of establishment for businesses in the Associated territories. But overall France had gained a major victory.

It seems probable that France would not have joined the EEC if it had not got its way regarding the dependencies. France placed great emphasis on maintaining close ties with its dependencies. The French rejection of the European Defence Community showed that France was willing to take unilateral action to achieve its goals.

Two schools of interpretation of French motives for wanting the Association can be distinguished. The first emphasized French economic ties with the colonies; the second focused on broader political motives. An exponent of the first school, David Wall of Sussex University maintained that the intention of France was to continue the benefits of the franc zone and to provide:

> compensation for the expected losses accruing to the associates with the gradual phasing out (required by the Treaty of Rome) of the managed market schemes of guaranteed prices for imports into France from her associates.[44]

W.A. Ndongko similarly concluded that the reason for France's desire to associate its dependencies with the EEC lay in the extensive nature of Franco-African trading and economic ties.⁴⁵

French economic links with the colonies were important, more so to the colonies than to France. Trade with Africa was only a small proportion of French trade, but it was vital to the colonies. In 1953, 85 per cent of French West Africa's imports came from France and nearly all of its exports went to France. In that year French West Africa's imports were one-third greater than its exports, but this was only a small trade surplus for France. France paid about 15 per cent above world market prices for African agricultural products, while they charged a premium on French goods imported by Africans. This premium price varied from product to product: wheat was sold at 80 per cent above the world market price and French trucks cost 100 per cent more than comparable American ones.⁴⁶ The French system allowed relatively inefficient African producers to survive because the French protected them from competition.

As well as depending on the French to buy their products at inflated prices, the Africans depended on French capital (from 1947 to 1956, 70 per cent of public capital investment in French West Africa came from France).⁴⁷ Even the stability and convertibility of the African currencies was guaranteed by participation in the French franc zone. Any sudden change in the economic relations of the colonial African economies and France would have seriously damaged the Africans. The EEC's application of its common external tariff to the colonies' exports to France would have been such a detrimental change.

Before France presented its demands for the Association of the overseas countries and territories, it was generally believed that existing preferential relations and colonial responsibilities would be continued under the Treaty of Rome.⁴⁸ Article 234 of the Treaty guaranteed that pre-existing conventions between one or more members and one or more third countries 'shall not be affected by the provisions of this Treaty' though incompatible arrangements were to be phased out.

The French were not satisfied with an informal understanding that colonial preferences would be continued. A formal, legal Association in the Treaty would commit the Community to trade preferences for the Associates, put the dependencies' role on a firmer footing, and satisfy the French penchant for codified documents. Association would not just be a temporary derogation from the principles of the Treaty, to be abolished as soon as possible. As an Association concluded for an indefinite, i.e. long-lasting if not permanent period, it would be an integral part of the EEC. The treaty basis of the Association also allowed more detailed measures on aid and trade to be included than an *ad hoc* understanding could have incorporated.

As well as guaranteeing the continuance of trade preferences for the French dependencies, the Association was more in keeping with the 'Principles' set out in the Treaty of Rome than were existing colonial trading systems. The freer access of Associates to the markets of the Six was in accordance with the EEC's objective of reducing restrictions on world trade. The aid-giving provisions of the Association were in keeping with the Community's stated objective of fostering development.[49]

A further economic interpretation of French motives concerning Association was that France sought Association not only to preserve existing colonial trading arrangements, but to obtain financial help from the EEC. The Germans feared that Community aid to the Associated French colonies would free French resources for prosecuting the war in Algeria.[50] But whether or not France intended to use freed resources for the Algerian war, the financial aid from its European partners to the Associates of 381.25 million European units of account from 1958 to 1963 was a significant economic benefit.[51]

Although the economic interpretation of French insistence on Association correctly identified the close economic links between France and its overseas territories, it overlooked the underlying reasons for the French desire to maintain economic links. For example, paying higher than world market prices for African agricultural products (which sometimes competed with French agricultural products) was not of economic benefit to France. The tropical African colonies had never been especially profitable, and the reasons for France's interest in maintaining close ties with them must be sought outside solely economic considerations. France had a political commitment to maintaining the colonies' orderly social and economic development. Cutting off France's special economic ties with them would mean economic stress, possible socialist revolution or breaking ties with France.

At the root of France's interest in Africa was a deep-seated belief that France and Africa were ideal complements for one another. This complementarity was not only economic; it was political, social and cultural as well. What the Africans lacked in political and technical expertise, in social and cultural development, Europe could provide. What Europe lacked in manpower, land and natural resources could be got from Africa. This vision of a EurAfrican partnership was widely held in France. The EurAfrican relationship, with Europe intellectually and managerially at the helm, was not seen as ending with outright colonialism. The 'EurAfrica' it wanted was based on '[the symbiosis] which is the permanent coexistence of organisms of different natures which sustain each other mutually'.[52]

There was also an element of the *mission civilisatrice*, of moral responsibility toward the welfare of the colonies which prompted

French action.[53] But the main French concern was to ensure that nothing, no economic vicissitude visited on Africa through French membership of the EEC, could weaken Franco-African ties. The intensity of France's desire to maintain 'familial' relations with its dependencies was shown by its resistance to the Guinean, and later Algerian, path to independence.

Objectives of the Association

The purposes of Association set out in Part IV of the Treaty of Rome and in the related Implementing Convention were in keeping with the economic complexion of the European Economic Community. They primarily referred to economic and, to a lesser extent, social development in the Associated countries and territories.

Article 131 of the Treaty (Part IV) stated that the Association would 'permit' (rather than practise) measures which would further 'the interests and prosperity of the inhabitants of these countries and territories in such a manner as to lead them to the economic, social and cultural development they expect'. The most crucial type of development which the Associates were likely to have expected in 1957, that is, the political development of independence, was not mentioned. And, as noted earlier, no means of ascertaining what the Associates did expect, or for achieving their expectations was established.

The 'Implementing Convention relating to the Association with the Community of the Overseas Countries and Territories' (which was appended to the Treaty of Rome) also stated its general aim for the Association. Article 1 of the Implementing Convention called for the EEC:

> by means of efforts complementary to those made by the responsible authorities of the countries and territories listed in Annex IV to this Treaty, participate in any measure suitable for the promotion of social and economic development of those countries and territories.

The Implementing Convention mentioned the need for EEC actions to complement the policies pursued by the member states. It went further than the Treaty in obliging rather than just permitting actions to foster the social and economic development of the Associates.

In summary, the expressed objectives of the Association emphasized the benefits, particularly economic ones, to be reaped by the Associates. Neither the political motives for Association nor the expected benefits for the Community states were mentioned.

Major provisions of the Association

Part IV of the Rome Treaty which established the EEC contained a complex set of provisions for freer trade between the Six and the Associates and for financial aid. The provisions for fostering freer trade can be separated into those which spread the benefits of the colonial relationship equally among the Six and those which gave the Associated countries and territories freer access to a wide European market. Under the first category of provisions, each Associate was obliged by Article 132 (2) of the Treaty of Rome to apply the same rules it applied to its trade with the colonial power to the other EEC states' Associates. Thus, preferential tariffs and trading arrangements were (in accordance with the progressive rate of abolition provided for in the treaty) to be enjoyed equally by the Six. Fiscal duties to raise revenue and tariffs deemed necessary to promote development were permitted to the Associates as long as they were applied equally to the members of the EEC.

The Six were also given the right for their enterprises to tender for Community-financed development projects on an equal basis. The Associated countries and territories had to grant the right of establishment within their boundaries to companies and nationals of the EEC member states equally, without discriminating in favour of the colonial power. Article 135 of the Treaty of Rome stipulated that workers from the member states and the dependencies should be treated alike, subject to conventions unanimously agreed by the Six.

Provisions to benefit the Associates in their trade with Europe were included in Article 135 of the Treaty. It provided for free entry for the Associates' products into the Community market through the gradual abolition of tariffs.

The financial aid allocated to the Associates by the new Community was channelled through the European Development Fund (EDF). The Fund was administered by the European Commission, with important decisions about finance being referred to the Fund council. The member states were represented on the council and allotted a number of votes based on the size of their contribution to the EDF.[54] France and Germany had 33 votes each; Belgium, Italy and the Netherlands each had 11 votes, and Luxembourg had 1 vote. The total resources of the Fund for its five-year development programme amounted to 581.25 million units of account, equal to the same amount in US dollars.[54]

The Association provisions of Part IV of the Treaty of Rome were concluded for an unlimited period. But the Implementing Convention which gave the details of the contributions to and administration of the EDF, and allowed special duty-free third country imports of bananas and coffee was concluded for only five years.[55] The EEC's Council of Ministers was empowered, before the five years elapsed, to 'determine the provisions to be made for a further period'.[56] This procedure for concluding a new Implementing Convention did not call for any consultation with the Associates.

In summary, the major provisions of the Association were determined and implemented without any effective input from the dependencies. The Europeans, nevertheless, tried to create a system which would work to the benefit of the Associates, through trade liberalization and aid, as well as to the benefit of the Community.

Accomplishments of the Association

Trade

The record of the Treaty of Rome Association was mixed. Aid-giving was plagued by problems of delay. The provisions for liberalizing trade were implemented gradually, but did not have the beneficial effects that had been anticipated. Although this initial phase of Association was a transitional period in which the full repercussions of the Treaty were not yet experienced, it did reveal many of the trends which were to continue under later conventions, for example, slow aid dispersal and lack of improvement in the Associates' export performance. Themes of criticism of the Association also emerged.

GATT discussions from 1957 to 1958 exposed fears held by third countries about the effects of the Association. A working party established to report on the Association to the 13th session of the GATT concluded that Association did not mean the creation of a free trade area, but an expansion of existing discriminatory trade provisions. For this reason the Association infringed Article XXIV of the General Agreement on Tariffs and Trade.[57]

Although the Six claimed they were creating a free trade area through the Association, the Latin American, African, Asian and British members of the working party (the US did not concur) disagreed. They reckoned that the Associates would become the major suppliers to the EEC of commodities for which a common external tariff was fixed, displacing other countries. The Associates could export to the Six at prices above the world market price because of their tariff preferences. Thus, the Associates would increase their production of commodities to satisfy EEC demand and thereby cause a decline of world market prices for other exporters.

The Latin American countries, which were excluded from the EEC's preferences, and Secretary-General Prebisch of the United Nations

Conference on Trade and Development (UNCTAD), also objected to the Association preferences. Negotiations within UNCTAD resulted in a lowering of the Community's common external tariff (CET) against tropical products.[58] (Reductions also occurred under the Dillon and Kennedy rounds of the GATT negotiations.)

The Six responded to criticisms of the Associates' preferences by arguing that world consumption of primary products was growing and thus the Associates' increased production could be absorbed without depressing prices. Effects of the Association on other producers, the Six maintained, were minimal. The GATT declined to take strong action against the EEC and the Six made a conciliatory statement that if there were, contrary to expectations, proven deleterious effects on third countries from the Association, they would consider action to alleviate those effects.[59] That there were substantial negative effects on the trade of third countries caused by the Association was not conclusively proven for the period of the first Association, or for later Associations.

Inter-Associate trade The Six argued that the Association under the Rome Treaty created a free trade area. This meant free trade among the Associated countries and territories as well as among the Six and between the Six and the Associates. However, inter-Associate trade was minimal: most of the Associates produced competing primary materials rather than complementary goods.[60] The low level of trade among the Associates led the International Monetary Fund's economist Ouattara to write, 'Trade relations among the associated countries were not affected by the association arrangement'.[61] Thus, although the Treaty of Rome provided for freer trade among the dependencies, lacking a tradition of trade relations, lacking complementary products and the appropriate trade and transport infrastructure, the effects of the trade liberalization were minor enough to discount. Indeed, no provision for an inter-Associates customs union featured in the succeeding Yaounde Conventions, showing that developing inter-Associate trade was given little importance.

Rights of establishment and freedom of movement During the Treaty of Rome Association period, the implementation of equal rights of establishment for companies of the Six in the Associated countries and territories was slow. French companies continued to receive favoured treatment in many of the French colonies. Whether the Associates had rights of establishment in the Six was not explicit in the Treaty and no test case was put forward, so the point remained academic.[62]

The provisions in the Rome Treaty for negotiating the freedom of movement of workers were not put to work during the first (or second) five years of Association. Freedom of movement was more of a long-term objective than a provision to implement, as its neglect in the first two Associations demonstrated.[63]

Associate—Community trade The application of the trade provisions of the Treaty of Rome was flexible. The European Commission had to struggle with the governments concerned to get the principles of equal rights of establishment recognized. The EEC's first Development Commissioner, Robert Lemaignen, observed that France continued to extend preferences to Morocco and Tunisia which were contrary to the letter of the Treaty of Rome.[64] He accepted that existing preferences could not immediately be abolished.

Owing to differences and gaps in data collection, trade data for the Associates before 1960 are not entirely comparable with post-independence data. French colonies' trade data were not reported by country before 1960 and data for the Belgian colonies were given only as an aggregate until 1959. But, allowing for some inaccuracies, general comparisons can be made.[65]

According to the economic theory of customs unions, by supplying the EEC with goods previously produced internally, the Associates would create more trade. However, this substitution of Associates' for Community products did not generally occur. Because the Associates' and the Community's products were complementary rather than competitive, preferences tended to result in trade diversion rather than trade creation. The only areas of competition between the Community and the Associates were in a few agricultural products, the simple processing of agricultural products, and simple manufactures.[66]

In terms of economic theory, trade creation could be measured in increased levels of Associate—EEC trade; trade diversion would be reflected in increased levels of Associate—EEC trade while at the same time trade with other, unpreferred developing countries declined. However, no clear gains were observed for the largest group of Associates, the French colonies, and no clear losses were sustained by other developing countries during the Treaty of Rome Association.[67] Thus, neither trade creation nor trade diversion were definitely attributable to the special trading system of the Association.

A number of reasons for this lack of dramatic changes can be adduced. As noted earlier, the 'tariff disarmament' of the Rome Treaty occurred only gradually. But even after the common external tariff was in full operation after mid-1964, it did not greatly affect these conclusions.

The French Associates exchanged a higher level of preferences in the French market for a smaller (and declining in line with international negotiations in GATT and UNCTAD) level of preference in the larger EEC market. In theory this exchange could result in more trade for the Associates. But, especially in cases where France was the main importer of a commodity from a French dependency, the reduced margins of preference could mean a loss of trade for the Associates. (See Table 1.1.) Other reasons for the lack of trade creation included inelasticities of supply owing to a long growing season, which made it hard for an Associate to expand production to Europe to counteract the loss of the generous guaranteed French price. The lack of market information, transport and credit infrastructure also made it difficult for the Associates fully to exploit the EEC's preferences.

Table 1.1 Total exports of French West Africa and French Equatorial Africa in 1957; French and EEC tariffs

Product	Value (millions of CFA francs)	French Tariff %	EEC Tariff %
Unroasted coffee	16,139	20	9.6
Shelled peanuts	14,918	10	–
Cocoa beans	6579	25	5.4
Cattle	271	–	–
Crude oil	480	–	–
Unprocessed wood	7064	10	–
Processed wood	1475	15	10
Cotton	4398	–	–
Diamonds	424	–	–
Fresh bananas	1839	20	20
Palm nuts	1839	10	–
Crude peanut oil	7315	18	10
Refined peanut oil	1196	18	15
Oil cake	1759	10	–
Other	9479	4.4	2.7
Total	75,175		
Weighted average (all items)		8.1	4.8
Weighted average (preference items)		8.7	5.1

Source: Lawrence, R., 'Primary Products, Preferences and Economic Welfare: the EEC and Africa', in Robson, P. (ed.), *International Economic Integration*, Harmondsworth, Penguin, 1972, p. 366.

As the European Commission admitted, for EEC—Associate trade, 'the figures seem fairly disappointing'.[68] From 1953 to 1958 the EEC took an average of 72 per cent per annum of the Associates' exports. But from 1959 to 1964, when the Association system was operating, the EEC share fell to 71 per cent instead of rising as had been predicted.[69] EEC trade grew less rapidly with the Associates than with other ldcs. The Associates supplied 14 per cent of EEC imports yearly from 1953 to 1958, but only 12 per cent from 1959 to 1964. Although the Associates' absolute level of trade with the Community did not decline, they had a smaller market share. (See Table 1.2.)

Table 1.2 Exports by LDCs to the EEC: regional shares 1953—68 (in per cent)

Year	LDCs	Latin America	Asia	Middle East	Africa	North Africa	AACs*	Competing Africa	Other Africa	Other LDCs
1953	100	24	16	20	40	12	15	3	9	—
1954	100	25	15	21	39	11	14	4	9	—
1955	100	23	16	22	39	12	14	4	9	—
1956	100	26	15	20	39	12	14	5	9	—
1957	100	25	15	20	40	13	14	5	8	—
1958	100	23	11	28	35	14	13	5	3	3
1959	100	24	12	27	34	11	13	6	4	3
1960	100	24	13	26	35	13	12	5	5	3
1961	100	24	12	26	36	14	12	5	4	3
1962	100	26	11	25	35	15	11	5	4	3
1963	100	25	10	26	37	16	11	5	5	3
1964	100	24	11	25	38	16	12	5	5	2
1965	100	24	11	25	38	17	11	5	5	2
1966	100	24	11	24	40	17	12	5	6	2
1967	100	23	10	26	38	18	11	4	5	2
1968	100	21	9	27	39	19	12	3	5	4

* Associated African countries

Source: Ouattara, A., p. 512. See note 73.

Some of the Associates' most important exports were not given preferences over the exports of third countries. The single most important Associate export, copper from Zaire, accounting for 15 to 20 per cent of the value of the Associates' exports, was not given preferred status.

Neither were exports of timber or other minerals. Of the important Associate exports, coffee, cocoa, bananas, groundnut oil, and palm oil, only cocoa and groundnut oil benefited significantly from the EEC trade regime from 1959 to 1964.[70]

As noted above, the Associates' share of EEC imports fell from the periods 1953–1958 to 1959–1964. But EEC exports to the Associates fared better, benefiting from the reduction of discriminatory tariffs. From 1953 to 1958 the annual average share of the Community in the Associates' imports was 66 per cent, rising to 68 per cent for 1959 to 1964.[71]

The trade results of the Treaty of Rome Association were embarrassing for the EEC. Under the trade provisions of the Association, the EEC fared better in terms of increasing exports than did the Associates for whose economic and social benefit the Association ostensibly existed.

Although the economic results of the Treaty of Rome Association were very limited, some changes did occur. Overall EEC—Associate trade did not expand impressively, but trade between the Associates and the EEC states other than France and between France and the non-French colonies grew more rapidly. Some commodities — cocoa and groundnut oil — benefited from the Association preferences. Another result of the Association was that France was relieved of the sole responsibility of supporting its colonies' agricultural export earnings.

The preferences in the Treaty of Rome did not fully compensate the Associates for the loss of higher French preferences, but they did prevent the disruptions which free competition on the world market would have caused. The failure of the Associates to expand their exports to the EEC as rapidly as other countries highlighted the problems of these underdeveloped economies. Without the preferences given them by the EEC, the Associates would probably have fared even worse.

Financial aid

Despite the problems encountered by the EEC aid programme in its first five years, it was considered by the European Commission to have achieved more than the trade programme.[72] Insofar as Community aid represented a supplement rather than a substitute for bilateral aid from the Six, it was a net gain for the Associates. From the Commission's point of view, there was no doubt that Community aid supplemented and not substituted for bilateral aid.[73] One former EEC development official 'insisted' that Community aid was a supplement of about 3 US dollars per capita to the Associated countries.[74]

However, although the official Community view was that European aid was additional to bilateral aid, there was clearly some aid substitution in the case of France. Whereas bilateral aid from Germany, Belgium and Italy to the Associates increased from 1962 to 1968, bilateral aid from France decreased during this period (Table 1.3).* French bilateral aid to the Associates fell from 288.1 million dollars in 1962 to 241.8 in 1966 and 269 in 1968. The total bilateral aid of the EEC member states also decreased from 358.8 million dollars in 1962 to 358.2 million in 1968 owing to the French reduction.[75] Assuming that — in the absence of the EDF — French bilateral aid to the Associates would have remained constant (if not increased), the diversion of French bilateral aid to the European Development Fund amounted to as much as 40 million dollars in one year (1966).

Table 1.3 Aid to the Associated states by the EEC (in million US dollars)

	1962	1964	1966	1968
Bilateral aid	485.5	450.3	421.5	412.1
of which:				
Germany	6.5	18.9	26.2	17.6
Belgium	53.4	66.1	59.7	60.6
France	288.1	277	241.8	269
Italy	10.8	8.6	6.8	11
EEC as a whole	358.8	370.6	334.5	358.2
USA	94	71	72	43
Multilateral aid	96.4	95	111.7	135.6
of which EEC	50.7	76	100	101.3
UNO	15.3	32.1	22.5	25.3
Others	30.4	13.1	10.8	9
Total aid	581.9	545.3	533.2	547.7
of which EEC	409.5	446.6	434.5	459.5

Source: *European Development Aid*, Brussels, EEC, (undated), p. 30.

As well as diverting bilateral to multilateral aid, as noted in the case of France, the EDF was an additional source of funds or aid creator for

* Figures here begin with the end of the Treaty of Rome Association (1958—62) and refer to trends continuing through the first and second Yaounde Conventions, signed in 1963 and 1969 respectively.

the Associates. Increased bilateral aid from the other EEC countries, notably Germany, meant that bilateral aid from the EEC as a whole decreased only slightly during this period (Table 1.3). EDF aid, which rose rapidly from 581.25 million dollars in 1958 to nearly 1000 million dollars for the third EDF of 1970–75 (Table 1.4), more than compensated for the decrease in bilateral aid.

Table 1.4 Contributions to the first three European Development Funds (1 unit of account = 1 dollar)

in millions of units of account	Rome Treaty		Yaounde I		Yaounde II	
Belgium	70	12.04%	69	9.45%	80	8.89%
Germany	200	34.41%	246.5	33.77%	298.5	33.16%
France	200	34.41%	246.5	33.77%	298.5	33.16%
Italy	40	6.88%	100	13.70%	140.6	15.62%
Luxembourg	1.25	0.22%	2	0.27%	2.4	0.28%
Netherlands	70	12.04%	66	9.04%	80	8.89%
Total European Development Fund	581.25	100%	730	100%	900	100%
European Investment Bank	–		70		100	
Total	581.25		800		1000	

Source: European Development Aid, Brussels, EEC, (undated), p. 30.

Although the European Development Fund did elicit new aid funds from the EEC member states, the use to which it put those funds was less than ideal. From its inception, delays in the EDF's activities were apparent. All activities of the European Development Fund were held up for one year after the coming into force of the Treaty of Rome because of the Council of Ministers' delay in setting out the regulations governing the operation of the Fund.[76] The first project of the EDF was not financed until 7 April 1959.

Robert Lemaignen, the European Commissioner in charge of the development directorate, acknowledged that the EDF continued to experience problems after its delayed start.[77] Lemaignen cited problems of slow disbursement of money and the difficulty of getting the representatives of the Six to agree on projects. By the end of 1961, only 43 per cent of the EDF's money was committed (not disbursed) to projects although four-fifths of the duration of the Fund had elapsed.[78]

Political exigencies and practical problems burdened the aid-giving programme of the Treaty of Rome Association. One problem was the difficulty of sharing out EDF contracts equitably among the European member states. Commissioner Lemaignen admitted that up to 1963 French companies, to the dismay of the other Europeans, won most of the contracts for EDF projects. The procedures established by the Commission for overseeing the execution of projects were particularly tortuous. They included nominating a 'Technical Control Officer' of a different nationality to the contractor to supervise works.

Although the European Commission claimed that the EDF 'took from the experience of each national and international association dealing with aid whatever seemed good from the point of view of the Africans', this was certainly an overstatement.[79] In fact, until the African Associates became independent, the Commission found it difficult even to contact them directly to ascertain what, in their view, 'seemed good'.[80]

The colonial authorities of the Associates often had difficulty in preparing and presenting to the Commission feasible and technically satisfactory proposals for EDF projects. By 31 December 1962 the EDF had only accepted 39 per cent of the projects submitted for the Associates. Thus, the Association provision that projects were to be chosen by the Associates rather than by Brussels appeared to give great freedom to the Associates (or the colonial authority), but in fact presented many problems for administrations ill-equipped to select development projects.

Despite the problems of bureaucracy, delay, and lack of favourable response to the majority of project proposals, the accomplishments of the first European Development Fund (EDF I) were not altogether negligible. According to Commissioner Lemaignen, the results of the EDF's brief for fostering social and economic development during the five years of EDF I compared favourably to the achievements of other organizations. During this period, primary classes in the Associates increased by 7 per cent, secondary classes by 16 per cent; public health funds increased by 9 per cent and the length of paved roads by 30 per cent. Improvements in transport, agriculture, education, ports and public health were obtained.[81] Nevertheless, as the EEC Commission recognized, EDF projects did not create a new Africa:

> All the roads are not as good as these, and all the secondary schools are not like the one in Bamako; there are still too few hospitals, and the peasants are still poor.[82]

As aid donors, the Six were relatively generous compared to other industrialized countries. In 1969 they gave bilateral and multilateral aid to the value of 1.03 to 1.32 per cent of GNP per country whereas US aid was 0.49 per cent and UK aid was 0.83 per cent of GNP in that year.[83] From 1962 to 1968, Table 1.3 shows that EEC multilateral aid was consistently greater than US or other multilateral aid to the Associates. Therefore, excepting the bilateral aid of the Six, EEC aid was the major source of development aid for the Associates. The small population of the Associates (fewer inhabitants at the time of the first Association than Germany), meant that EEC per capita aid amounted to 8 dollars, or roughly twice the world per capita average of overall official aid.[84] Although the EEC did not have quick, non-political procedures for funding projects, by virtue of the amount of aid it controlled, it was of great importance to the Associates. Some of the problems of delay and rigidity of procedures noted in the first EDF could be attributed to the inexperience of the Fund, but many of the same criticisms continued to be applicable to later EDFs.

The results of Association

The EEC's trade and aid programme for its Associated countries and territories did not produce fundamental economic or social changes in the Associates. The trade preferences helped to prevent the loss of markets and of confidence for the Associates when French trade preferences were withdrawn, but they did not create a dynamic upsurge in EEC–Associate trade. Aid provided by the Community also contributed, though slowly, modestly and often inefficiently, to improving the welfare of the Associates. However, the real successes of the Treaty of Rome Association lay in the political rather than the economic sphere.

Although the Treaty of Rome was not specific on this point, the European Commission held that any Associated state which became independent still remained Associated with the Community through the Treaty of Rome.[85] Even Guinea was considered by a European Parliamentary Committee to remain legally an Associate because it did not formally renounce the Rome Treaty after independence.[86]

The Commission's view on the continuing validity of Association was in accordance with the wishes of the Associates, all of whom, except Guinea and Togo, wrote to the Commission in late 1958 saying that they would honour the terms of their Association up to the expiration date of the Implementing Convention.[87] The majority of the Associates never wavered in their desire to be affiliated with the European Community. Not only were they willing to fulfil the terms of the first

Association, they wanted to extend the arrangements for a further five years. Negotiations held throughout 1961 resulted in the initialling of a new Association agreement, known as the Yaounde Convention (Yaounde I), on 20 December 1962.

In the opinion of Commissioner Lemaignen, the Associates' choice of staying with Europe was an adventure because the ultimate results of the new Yaounde Association could not be known beforehand.[88] Commission publications, too, expressed this idea.[89] But in fact, the Treaty of Rome Association was not the result of an adventurous leap into the future by either the Community or the Associates. The Community (particularly France) wished to maintain a position of influence in the colonies and former colonies; the Associates wished to avoid the uncertainties of absolute independence. They were reluctant to venture into the international political system without any economic or political support from Europe.

Association with the European Community appealed to the conservative, Europe-oriented feelings of many African leaders. In 1959 de Gaulle had appealed to the newly independent states of the French Community saying, 'Abide with us. The day is far spent. Night is falling upon the world.'[90] The European Community similarly appealed to the Africans' desire for protection from the potential dangers of independence.

The conservative nature of the Treaty of Rome and then Yaounde Associations was in clear contrast to the radical approach of Guinea (Conakry). After becoming independent from France in 1958, Guinea did not participate in the Association. (Although Sekou Toure made it clear that Guinea did not want to be an Associate, the Commission continued to regard Guinea as one.) Sekou Toure felt that Guinea had the ability to prosper without the aid, preferences or interference of the European Community.[91] Because of its confidence in its economy, its policies and its independent status, Guinea decided to strike out alone. Compared to the conservative policies of the other African states which adhered to the Associations established by the European Community, Guinea's policy was adventurous. The results of the Guinean adventure, however, were disappointing, as shown in Chapter 3.

The first Association's main success was that it led the newly independent African states to accept a subsequent period of Association. The Association was also successful in that the original European opponents of the idea, mainly Germany and the Netherlands, became reconciled to it. For a policy forced on the EEC by France, a policy which faced the upheavals of African independence, criticisms from the GATT, UNCTAD, Sekou Toure, Nkrumah, and others, the Association thrived remarkably. As one former senior Commission official noted, 'The development of the association has been much more favourable than the negotiators of the Treaty ever dared to hope.'[92]

Notes

1. Bull, Hedley, *The Anarchical Society*, London, Macmillan, 1977, discusses new states in the international system.
2. Van Bogaert, E., 'The Association Agreements of Yaounde and Lome', *Studia Diplomatica*, vol. 29, no. 1, 1979.
3. Quoted in Deschamps, Hubert, *Methodes et Doctrines Coloniales de la France*, Paris, Armand Colin, 1953, 'Preface'.
4. Quoted in Betts, R., *Assimilation and Association: French Colonial Theory*, New York, Columbia University Press, 1961, p. 122.
5. Stibbe, P., 'French-Speaking Tropical Africa', in Judd., P. (ed.), *African Independence*, New York, Dell, 1962, p. 272, received this impression.
6. 'Development Aid: Fresco of Community Action Tomorrow', *Bulletin of the European Communities*, Supplement 8/74, Brussels, Commission of the European Communities.
7. Preamble to the 1946 constitution in Deschamps, *op cit*.
8. French constitution of 1958 in Grimal, H., *Decolonisation*, trans. S. De Vos, London, Routledge and Kegan Paul, 1965.
9. 1946 Constitution of France *ibid*.
10. *ibid*.
11. Young, Crawford, 'The End of the Belgian Congo', in Smith, T. (ed.), *op cit*, p. 194. Also, Young, Crawford, *Politics in the Congo*, Princeton, Princeton University Press, 1965.
12. Grimal, *op cit*, p. 372.
13. Chaffard, Georges, *Les Carnets Secrets de la Decolonisation*, Paris, Calmann-Levey, 1967, vol. 2, p. 167.
14. *ibid*, p. 189.
15. Deschamps, *op cit*, Preamble to the 1946 constitution.
16. Chaffard, *op cit*, p. 189.
17. For an extensive account see Chaffard, *op cit*.
18. de Gaulle in Smith, T. (ed.), *op cit*, p. 159.
19. Stibbe, *op cit*.
20. Grimal, *op cit*, Ch.4.
21. de Gaulle in Smith, T. (ed.), *op cit*, p. 160.
22. For this argument see H.H. the Aga Khan, 'The Great Gamble in Africa', *The Commonwealth Journal*, July–August 1962.
23. Stibbe, *op cit*.
24. Berg, Eliot, 'The Economic Basis of Political Choice in French West Africa', *American Political Science Review*, June 1960, also concluded that the determinants of political choice were not solely economic. For the French Community see also, Luchaire, F., 'La Republique Francaise et la Communaute', *Revue Administrative*, vol. 12(71), 1959.
25. Matthews, J.D., *The Association System of the European Community*, New York, Praeger, 1977.
26. 'EEC Declaration of Intent', EEC Council of Ministers, Brussels, 1963.
27. *Convention of Association between the European Economic Community and the African and Malagasy States Associated with that Community*, London, HMSO, 1965, Article 58.

28. See Declarations attached to the *Treaty Establishing the European Economic Community*, Rome, 25 March 1957; London, HMSO, 1962. (Treaty of Rome).
29. 'Development Aid: Fresco of Community Action Tomorrow', Brussels EEC Commission, *Bulletin of the European Communities*, Supplement 8/74, p. 10, ('The Fresco').
30. See *Treaty of Rome*, especially Part IV.
31. *Treaty of Rome*, Article 131.
32. Twitchett, Carol Cosgrove, *Europe and Africa: From Association to Partnership*, Westmead, Saxon House, 1979, Ch.1. Also, Robertson, A.H., *The Council of Europe*, 2nd edn, London, Stevens and Sons, 1961, pp. 124–6.
33. *The Strasbourg Plan*, Strasbourg, Council of Europe, 1952.
34. *Manual of the Council of Europe*, London, Stevens and Sons, 1970. For more details of the Berlin West Africa Conference and the practice of colonialism in the two World Wars, see Lister, M., *The Lome Convention between the European Community and the African, Caribbean and Pacific States: L'Entente Discrete*, University of York, D.Phil, 1985.
35. Robertson, *op cit*, pp. 124–5.
36. Twitchett, *op cit*, p. 7.
37. *ibid*, Ch.1.
38. Curzon, G. and V., 'Neo-colonialism and the European Economic Community', *Yearbook of World Affairs*, 1971.
39. van der Lee, J.J., 'Association between the European Economic Community and African States', *African Affairs*, July 1967. Also, Mazrui, A., 'African Attitudes to the European Common Market', in Krause, L. (ed.), *The Common Market: Progress and Controversy*, New Jersey, Praeger, 1964.
40. Okigbo, P.N.C., *Africa and the Common Market*, London, Longmans, 1967, Ch.2.
41. Twitchett, *op cit*, p. 8.
42. See H.J. de Koster, former Netherlands Secretary of State for Foreign Affairs, in *Revue du Marche Commun*, May 1969.
43. Dodoo and Kuster, 'The Road to Lome', in Alting von Geusau (ed.), *op cit*.
44. Wall, David, *The European Community's Lome Convention*, London, Trade Policy Research Centre, 1976, p. 2.
45. Ndongko, W.A., 'The Economic Origins of Association of Some African States with the EEC', *African Studies Review*, September 1973.
46. *ibid*.
47. *ibid*.
48. Barnes, William G., *Europe and the Developing World: Association Under Part IV of the Treaty of Rome*, London, Chatham House, February 1967.
49. *ibid*. Although the GATT Working Party was not convinced that association meant freer world trade.
50. Twitchett, *op cit*, p. 14.
51. *Treaty of Rome*, 'Implementing Convention Relating to the Association of Overseas Countries and Territories', Annex A.
52. Zischka, Anton, *Europe Complement d'Afrique*, Paris, Laffont, 1952, p. 253.
53. Twitchett, *op cit*, p. 10, emphasizes French moral responsibility.
54. *Treaty of Rome*, 'Implementing Convention', *op cit*.
55. *ibid*, Annex B.
56. *Treaty of Rome*, Part IV, Article 136.
57. Barnes, *op cit*.
58. Swann, Dennis, *The Economics of the Common Market*, 2nd edn, Harmondsworth, Penguin, 1972, p. 178–9. NB Concessions for traditional suppliers of

bananas had already been made under the Treaty of Rome, although it has been suggested that this was due to the power of the United Fruit Company rather than to EEC concern for developing countries.
59. Barnes, *op cit*, p. 13.
60. Soper, Tom, 'A Note on European Trade with Africa', *African Affairs*, April 1968.
61. Ouattara, Alassane D., 'Trade Effects of the Association of African Countries with the European Economic Community', *Staff Papers*, International Monetary Fund, 1973.
62. Twitchett, *op cit*, p. 66.
63. Barnes, *op cit*.
64. Lemaignen, Robert, *L'Europe au Berceau*, Paris, Plon, 1964, p. 155.
65. Ouattara, *op cit*.
66. *ibid*.
67. Lawrence, R., 'Primary Products, Preferences, and Economic Welfare: the EEC and Africa', in Robson, P. (ed.), *International Economic Integration*, Harmondsworth, Penguin, 1972.
68. *European Development Aid*, Brussels, EEC Commission, (undated).
69. Ouattara, *op cit*.
70. *ibid*.
71. *ibid*.
72. *The First Stage of the Common Market, op cit*.
73. *ibid*.
74. Twitchett, *op cit*, p. 52.
75. *European Development Aid, op cit*, p. 30.
76. Twitchett, *op cit*, p. 40.
77. Lemaignen, *op cit*, Ch.4.
78. Twitchett, *op cit*, p. 43.
79. *European Development Fund 1958–1968*, Brussels, EEC Commission.
80. Twitchett, *op cit*, p. 40.
81. Lemaignen, *op cit*, p. 136.
82. *European Development Fund 1958–1968, op cit*, p. 1.
83. Swann, *op cit*, Ch.8.
84. *European Development Aid, op cit*, p. 30.
85. *The First Stage of the Common Market, op cit*.
86. Lemaignen, *op cit*, Ch.4.
87. *ibid*.
88. *ibid*.
89. *European Development Fund 1958–1968, op cit*, p. 2.
90. de Gaulle, Charles, 'Memoirs of Hope', in Smith, T. (ed.), *The End of the European Empire*, Lexington, D.C., Heath, 1975.
91. Sekou Toure, A., 'The Republic of Guinea', *International Affairs*, April 1960.
92. van der Lee, J.J., 'Association between the European Economic Community and African States', *African Affairs*, July 1967.

2 Association under the Yaounde Conventions

Although the two Yaounde Conventions of Association have often been considered as economic relationships, the economic results of their trade and aid provisions were modest.* The Yaounde Conventions are better understood as a political entente arising from the Treaty of Rome Association. More important than the debates which arose over reverse preferences or trade diversion was the fact that the newly independent Associates sought and obtained a special relationship with the European Community. The Community also continued its special interest in the developing countries of Africa.

The Yaounde Conventions, the first signed in 1963 and the second in 1969, were a force for stability in what otherwise might have been a more unsettled post-colonial period. As the Treaty of Rome had done, the Yaounde Conventions created a system of Association. The exact nature of the Association was never defined by the Conventions, just as it was never precisely defined under the Treaty of Rome. There were changes in the form of the Association under the Yaounde Conventions, recognizing that the EEC was now negotiating with eighteen sovereign states and not with their colonial powers. New joint institutions were established, but decision-making power still rested mainly with the EEC. The overseas countries and territories which had not gained independence could not sign the Yaounde Convention or participate in the joint institutions. However, they received

* The name 'Yaounde' was given to the Conventions because of the place in which the agreements were signed, Yaounde, Cameroon.

much the same treatment from the EEC as the Yaounde signatories through the agreements established by the EEC Council of Ministers under Part IV of the Rome Treaty which continued to apply to them during the Yaounde (and later Lome) Conventions.

The decade of the Yaounde Conventions (in force 1964–75) is considered here largely as a whole because the two Conventions were very similar. Yaounde II was, and was perceived to be, an extension of Yaounde I. It was not until the 1975 Lome Convention that there was an apparent departure from the Yaounde arrangements.*

Yaounde I negotiations

The Yaounde negotiations were protracted and of a complexity not easily fitted into theories of negotiation.[1] The results of the four sets of negotiations — the intra-EEC, intra-African, EEC–African and UK–EEC negotiations — are summarized below.

There had been differences of opinion within the European Community over the Treaty of Rome Association, and there were still differences over renewing the Association. France continued to be the strongest proponent of the Association and hoped for a permanent arrangement. Belgium and the EEC Commission were also strongly in favour of a new Association. Germany and the Netherlands, however, initially opposed it. They wanted the African Associates to be economically independent of the Community. They viewed the Association as a transitional arrangement to be terminated as soon as possible.[2]

In the course of the intra-EEC negotiations, Germany and the Netherlands gave up their objections to the new Association. France agreed to the reduction of tariffs on tropical products imported into the Community from non-Associates which had been desired by Germany and the Netherlands (and the USA).[3] Although the negotiations among the Six were contentious, they did reach a common position. They had the benefit of much experience in negotiating with each other, the desire not to let disagreements rupture their Community, and sophisticated institutions and technical services to back up their negotiations.

The African and Malagasy states did not have benefit of experience, established institutions and services for their negotiations. The eighteen newly independent African and Malagasy states — Burundi, Cameroon, the Central African Republic, Chad, Congo (Leopoldville), Congo (Brazzaville), Dahomey, Gabon, Upper Volta, Ivory Coast, Madagascar, Mali, Mauritania, Niger, Rwanda, Senegal, Somalia and Togo — were

---

* It is argued later that this departure was more apparent than real.

not the same group as the Treaty of Rome Associates. They were fewer in number and located in a smaller area of sub-Saharan Africa and Madagascar, no longer including territories from the Caribbean to the Antarctic.

Thus, although the Africans lacked experience and established channels for negotiations, they had the benefits of a similar geographic location, similar level of economic development and a common language (French). They also made great efforts to establish a common front in their negotiations with the EEC. As the foreign minister of Madagascar at the time noted, despite the Africans' lack of institutions, their political will was the most important factor in developing a common policy.[4]

For the Yaounde negotiations, the Africans created a Council of Coordination at ministerial level, a Committee of Coordination at Ambassadorial level, and a secretariat. As well as establishing their own institutions, the Associates pressed for joint institutions under the Yaounde Convention.[5] These new joint institutions gave a semblance of parity in the relationship, if not much actual equality.

At the signing of the Yaounde agreement in 1963, the Associates were officially constituted as the Etats Africains et Malgache Associes (Association of African and Malagasy States or AAMS). Within the AAMS institutions, there was a great deal of dialogue among the Associates as they worked out common positions.[6] Negotiating and signing the Yaounde Convention thus faciliated the development of institutions for cooperation among the Associates.

Like the Europeans, the Africans approached the new Association with varying degrees of enthusiasm. Togo was more favourable toward it than Senegal or Mali; however, in general the Africans did want a new Association (as the Commission was at pains to point out) and they gradually reached a common understanding of what the new Convention ought to entail. Nevertheless, they were unable to achieve many of their common objectives.

The African Associates lacked experience in negotiating with the Community. In the negotiations the Associates emphasized principles such as equality, whereas the Europeans argued about specific measures. As Professor I.W. Zartman observed, the AAMS were short of alternatives to the European proposals, short of negotiating experience and the technical expertise needed to wrest substantial concessions from the EEC.[7]

Nevertheless, it was not the case that the Africans' main bargaining tool was their appeal to the Europeans' sense of 'richesse oblige'. In his reduction of EurAfrican relations to 'strong versus weak', Professor Zartman argued that: 'the Africans' greatest strength was their weakness. Their underdevelopment gave them the substance for appeals to the Six'.⁸ But it was not primarily the AAMS' poverty which appealed to Europe. India and Asia were also poor. It was the EurAfrican philosophy which saw a natural symbiosis between the two continents, as well as the long history of alliance between Europe and Africa, which lay behind Europe's interest in preserving the Association.

A long series of negotiations between the Africans and the EEC culminated in the signing of the Yaounde Convention in July 1963. As early as 1960 the EEC Council of Ministers had agreed to continue Association for the newly independent African states which wished it. Throughout 1961 the EEC prepared for the new Association.

In the negotiations the Africans were offered a 'take it or leave it' package by the Europeans.⁹ The eighteen underdeveloped Associates had little bargaining power. As in all of the subsequent EEC–African negotiations up to the present, there was little doubt that the Africans would finally accept the EEC package.* The EEC's success in obtaining a final text in harmony with its own position was expressed by the Development Commissioner at the time, M. Lemaignen: 'Directorate General VIII can consider with serenity the text finally adopted, which takes up almost all its initial proposals.'¹⁰

The European Commission was satisfied with its ability to control the terms of the Yaounde Convention, but it nevertheless tried to justify its position. To the Associates and others critical of its hard line, it argued that the EEC had such great difficulty in agreeing a position among its members that it was difficult to make concessions to the Associates. However, it was not internal disagreements which prevented the EEC from accepting proposals such as co-management of the EDF by the Associates.

The EEC offered the AAMS a Convention compatible with their new legal equality. But it was a Convention designed mainly by the EEC which reserved to the Community most of the crucial decisions over aid and trade. Another sign of the Africans' relative weakness was demonstrated by the negotiations for the entry of the United Kingdom into the EEC.

As early as 1958 the EEC considered how Commonwealth members might be associated with the Community and the problem of imperial (later Commonwealth) preferences.¹¹ The negotiations between the UK and the EEC in the early 1960s about the question of British entry into the Community became involved with the Yaounde negotiations and the issue of whether the Commonwealth countries could become affiliated to the EEC. When Prime Minister Macmillan announced in 1961 that the British government was opening negotiations with the Community about British membership, he promised to consult the

---

* Although there were at times indications that individual countries might, like Guinea, take a different line.

Commonwealth countries about the negotiations.[12] But by May 1962 the minister in charge of the negotiations, Edward Heath, stated that Commonwealth Africa would not be consulted about possible association with the EEC.[13]

This lack of promised consultation, and the fact that Britain was negotiating with the EEC over the future of Commonwealth Africa without involving the African governments in the process, led to acrimonious feelings. The Commonwealth Africans had been expected to accept the offer of Association the British government negotiated for them because of its prospects for trade preferences and aid.[14] But only Sierra Leone finally decided to accept the offer of Association. The rejection of Association resulted partly from the British failure to consult the Commonwealth African states and partly from the neocolonial reputation which the Association had acquired.

For reasons external to the Association, the UK entry negotiations were terminated on 29 January 1963 by President de Gaulle. At this time the Yaounde Convention had been initialled, but not yet signed. The pressures within the Community caused by the failure of the British negotiations unfavourably affected the Yaounde Convention. The final signing of the Convention was delayed until 20 July 1963, and its entry into force was delayed until 1 June 1964. How better could the other EEC members show their disapproval of the French action than by obstructing the Association so favoured by France?

The AAMS were unhappy that the other Community countries used the Association as a political weapon against France. Although interim measures for disbursing aid and maintaining trade preferences were set up for the period between the expiry of the Treaty of Rome Association (Implementing Convention) and the entry into force of the Yaounde Convention, the eighteen months' delay was inconvenient for the AAMS.

Objectives of the Yaounde Association

The new Convention's objectives were much more elaborate than those of the Treaty of Rome Association. The objectives were in the form of general aspirations designed to satisfy three areas of concern about the Convention. They were phrased to appeal to the sensibilities of the newly independent AAMS, to counter the criticisms circulating about the relationship and to demonstrate that the basis of the Convention was in accordance with the international political norms of the day. In essence, the expressed objectives of the Convention were four: to continue the EurAfrican relationship, to cooperate equally within the relationship, to foster economic development and to promote economic cooperation among the Associates.

The Yaounde Convention did not specifically state that it continued the Treaty of Rome Association, but it was clear that this was the case. The Preamble commenced with the declaration that the signatories were, 'reaffirming accordingly their will to maintain their association'.[15]

Following this affirmation of continuity, the signatories resolved to 'cooperate on a basis of complete equality'. This goal reflected the AAMS' new sovereignty, their desire for equality, and a declaration to the world that the Convention was not a type of neo-colonial domination but a free alliance.

In the words of next objective of the Preamble, the parties were: 'resolved to continue their joint efforts for the economic, social, and cultural progress of their countries'. This differed significantly from the aspirations to development contained in the Treaty of Rome in two ways. The intention in the Yaounde Convention was no longer just 'to promote the economic and social development'[16] of the Associates, it was to foster economic progress in all of the signatories. This objective of mutual progress was a precursor of later theories of interdependence, and it was also in accordance with the EurAfrican idea that the two continents could best progress by sharing and exchanging their resources.

The second change mentioned above was the new aspiration to 'cultural progress' in the signatories. This objective suggested a wider interpretation of the Yaounde relationship than an economic one. It was again in accordance with the EurAfrican view of Europe and Africa engaging in interchanges in all possible fields.

Next the Preamble referred more specifically to the problems of the Associates: 'being concerned to promote diversification of the economy and industrialization of the Associated States', and recognized the problems of producing and exporting one or a few commodities and the lack of industrial development of the AAMS. But, as will be shown, it did not succeed in alleviating these problems.

Finally, the Preamble tried to answer the charges that Yaounde was divisive. The parties to the Convention declared: 'being mindful of the importance of extending inter-African cooperation and trade'. Although the Association was sensitive to the charges of dividing Africa into EEC-favoured and non-favoured states, this was an undeniable feature of the Yaounde Associations.

Of the four objectives mentioned in the Preamble, the Convention was notably successful in attaining only one of them: the continuation of the Association. In terms of AAMS–EEC equality, economic development and inter-African cooperation, the Convention's results were more limited.

Major provisions of Yaounde: Stability with change

Although the Yaounde Association was fundamentally a continuation of the previous Association, it did contain some changes. These resulted mainly from the new independent status of the Associates. Independence meant that the eighteen African and Malagasy states and the six European members of the EEC were formally equal. This permitted the AAMS to have direct relations with the EEC, no longer being obliged to present their wishes (where possible) through the metropole. The European Commission could also contact the Associates directly, without referring to a colonial power. The AAMS were thus able to negotiate with the EEC over the Convention and to choose whether to sign and ratify it. They were also empowered by the text to withdraw from the Convention after giving six months' notice.

By according the AAMS a special Association, the EEC was open to charges that it was creating unnecessary divisions within Africa and within the developing world. In response to these criticisms, Articles 8 and 9 of the Yaounde Convention permitted the AAMS to establish customs unions or free trade areas among themselves or with third countries where these were not incompatible with the principles of the Convention. In terms of the trade relations among the Associates, Yaounde was less rigorous in its requirements than the Treaty of Rome Association had been. The Treaty of Rome obliged the Associates to grant each other as well as the EEC the same preferential trade terms they granted to the metropolitan power. But the Yaounde Convention did not require the Associates to grant preferential treatment to each other. Instead of creating one large free trade area as the Treaty of Rome had done, the Yaounde Convention created eighteen free trade areas, one between each Associate and the EEC. But because trade among the Africans was minimal, this change had little effect.

The Yaounde Convention did have some success in fostering intra-African cooperation. The West African Customs Union (UDEAO) and the Central African Customs Union (UDEAC) have been seen as 'sub-regional spin-offs' from the AAMS.[17]

In addition to the institutions of the AAMS and EEC, the Convention created joint institutions. These institutions were favoured by the AAMS as symbols of their equality with the EEC, but they also followed the colonial tradition of joint institutions as in the French Union and French Community.

The Yaounde Convention's institutions were: the Council of the Association, assisted by the Committee of Association; the Parliamentary Conference; and the Arbitration Court. The Council of Association consisted of the EEC Council of Ministers and Commission as one part, and one member of the government of each Associate as the other.

Decisions were taken by agreement between the two sides, with each side left to determine its own internal decision-making. Meetings were to occur once a year, or as necessary, with the chairmanship rotating between the EEC and AAMS. The Council was empowered to take binding decisions in accordance with the Convention's text, and was to be consulted on matters such as the admission of new members.

The Committee of Association was composed of one representative of each of the Six and one Commission representative, and one representative from each Associate. The Council could define the work of the Committee and delegate such responsibilities to the Committee as it chose. The Council was formally in charge of the Association, but the Committee formed the 'operational core of the relationship'.[18] A secretariat, made up of equal numbers of EEC and AAMS nationals, provided support services for the Council and Committee.

The Parliamentary Conference of the Association met once a year. Composed of equal numbers of European and AAMS parliamentarians, it received an annual report from the Association Council. The Parliamentary Conference could pass resolutions, but it had no real powers. The Court of Arbitration could be called in to make a binding decision if the Yaounde signatories failed to settle their disputes.

Overall, the Yaounde institutions were parallel to those of the European Community. Both systems featured high-level Councils, a lower-level committee to handle ordinary business and delegated tasks (the Association Committee and EEC Commission), a relatively powerless parliament, and a court. Both organizations had a secretariat, although in the EEC's case it served the Council of Ministers, while in the Yaounde system it served both the Council and the Committee of Association.

In relation to their powers, the Yaounde institutions were overelaborate. The powers delegated to them in the Yaounde Convention were quite limited. The major provisions of the Convention on trade and aid were already settled by the text, and other powers such as approving projects for financing were reserved to the European Commission (in practice guided by the Committee of the European Development Fund).

Article 29 of the Yaounde Convention provided that the Association Council should 'lay down the general pattern for financial and technical cooperation within the framework of the Association', but in practice its influence was limited. The Association Council did shift more emphasis on productive rather than infrastructure projects. But even the European Commission observed

> Since the joint institutions were set up, the Association Council has never discussed in sufficient depth the general guidance of financial and technical co-operation.[19]

41

In summary, the changes in the Association under the Yaounde Convention were considerable: independence and sovereign equality for the Associates, the geographical concentration on Africa, the new joint and AAMS institutions, and the encouragement for new members to join. Nevertheless, the new Association was a direct descendant of Part IV Association; many of the changes in the relationship were formal, such as the equality of the parties, or incremental, such as the new aid and trade provisions.

Incremental development occurred in the European Development Fund. Like the term 'Associate', the name 'European Development Fund' was retained. The Yaounde Association's Fund was known as EDF II, showing its relation to the Treaty of Rome Fund, EDF I. Like EDF I, EDF II contributed to the dependencies of the Six. EDF II also contributed to the new AAMS. Thus, the EEC's treatment of the independent AAMS and the colonial dependencies was similar: both were Associated with the Community and both relied on the same source of financial aid.

Aid provisions

The Yaounde Convention disposed of more aid for a broader set of purposes than the Treaty of Rome Association. EDF I aid was directed to social and economic infrastructure projects, but EDF II aid could in addition be used for surveys, training personnel, aid to production and diversification, aid to price stabilization schemes, and aid to private projects. This extension of the uses of aid was generally welcomed, but another aspect of EDF II was more controversial.

All 581.25 million units of account of EDF I were in the form of grants, but the 730 million u.a. of aid under Yaounde included 110 million units as loans (provided by the EDF and the European Investment Bank).[20] Thus, EDF II funds were 21 per cent larger than EDF I funds in total, but the grant component rose from 581.25 million u.a. to 620 million u.a., or only about 7 per cent.

The EEC claimed that it increased aid to the Associates by 38 per cent in Yaounde, but this claim was based on factors such as the smaller number of Yaounde Associates. Pearson and Schmidt calculated that EDF I aid had been worth 564 million units of account (1 u.a. = 1 U.S. dollar) whereas EDF II was worth between 454 and 564 million u.a. in real terms. This disappointing real value derived from the fact that the recipients had to pay interest on the loan component of the aid.[21]

The EEC's aid policy under Yaounde was conservative; it marginally increased grants and created a loan facility. During the period of

EDF II, the Associates finally faced the loss of high French support prices (surprix) for their agricultural exports. Although these prices had been meant to be abolished by the Treaty of Rome, this was actually accomplished under Yaounde. France reckoned that 400 million u.a. were needed to offset this loss for the Associates, but only 230 million u.a. through EDF II were allocated for this.[22] Thus, part of EDF II was designed to compensate for the loss of French agricultural subsidies, thereby reducing the increase in the Associates' resources from the Yaounde Convention. As EDF II aid could only be spent on EEC-approved projects which required lengthy and complicated procedures before the disbursement of funds, the value of EDF II aid to the recipients was consequently reduced.*[23]

Trade provisions

In its trade provisions, the Yaounde Convention was also a continuation of the Treaty of Rome Association. Many of the same measures applied to trade under both Associations. Title I of the Yaounde Convention specified the major provisions. The EEC was progressively to eliminate customs duties against the Associates while establishing a common external tariff against imports from third countries. All AAMS goods, except those covered by a common policy such as the Common Agricultural Policy (CAP), were to enter the Community duty-free. Quantitative restrictions on imports from the AAMS were also to be abolished, except those which were also applied by the EEC member states to each other.

The Associates were to give equal treatment to products originating in all member states of the EEC. Customs duties on EEC exports were to be abolished progressively, except those necessary for revenue, development or industrialization. Tariffs on EEC goods were not to be higher than those charged to the most favoured third country and quantitative restrictions on EEC goods were to be abolished. Restrictions of imports on grounds of public order, morals, health, and so on, were permitted to both sides.

The EEC was obligated to take into consideration AAMS interests when setting up its Common Agricultural Policy. The Convention's 'escape clause' allowed the EEC and AAMS states to protect their economies and financial stability by consulting the Association Council and then taking such steps as were necessary, for instance, temporarily restricting imports.

---

* Although when the EEC's financial and technical expertise was applied to such projects, for instance through programming missions paid for by the Commission, it constituted an addition to the actual funds disbursed and reduced this loss in value.

The Yaounde system of reverse preferences, of the AAMS giving special treatment to EEC goods as well as receiving special treatment for their exports, was often criticized. It was ungenerous for the EEC to seek privileged access to AAMS markets. However, the AAMS supported the reverse preferences as a symbol of their equality with the EEC. Because of their desire for equality, the AAMS originally wanted to contribute to the EDF, making them responsible members of the aid relationship, not just aid recipients. Giving trade preferences to the EEC, the Associates felt, showed that they shared the responsibilities as well as the benefits of the Association.

In practice, the composition of AAMS trade meant that the benefits of Association were limited. AAMS exports, which were mainly primary products, continued to enter the EEC free of duties and quotas as they had under Part IV Association. However, the AAMS margin of preference provided by the duties charged to non-Associates for competing products was significantly reduced (see Table 2.1). The Community found it difficult, in the face of other international obligations, to honour its commitment that its treatment of AAMS products 'shall be more favourable than the general treatment applied to like products originating in third countries'.[24]

Table 2.1 Rates of common customs tariff (for non-Associated non-member countries) (percentages)

Principal products	Rome Treaty	Modified rates after Yaounde I	Modified rates after Yaounde II (suspension)
Coffee	16%	9.6%	7%
Cocoa	9%	5.5%	4%
Fresh pineapple	12%	9%	
Cloves	20%	15%	
Dried coconut	5%	4%	
Nutmeg	20%	15%	
Pepper	20%	17%	
Vanilla	15%	11.5%	
Tea*	18%	10.8%	
Palm oil	9%	9%	6%

* Total suspension since 1964, linked with an identical measure taken by the United Kingdom.

Source: *European Development Aid*, Brussels, EEC, (undated), p. 21.

Before considering the results of the Yaounde trade regime as a whole, Yaounde II and its provisions will be examined.

Yaounde II

The second Yaounde Convention, signed in 1969, is usually described as an extension of Yaounde I. It was divided into the same five titles as its predecessor: trade; financial and technical cooperation; right of establishment, services, payments and capital; institutions; and general and final provisions. The objectives expressed in the Preamble of the new Convention, despite some minor changes in wording and the inclusion of a reference to enabling the Associates 'to strengthen their economic independence and stability', remained fundamentally those of Yaounde I.[25] The institutions of the Association and many of its specific provisions were likewise unchanged.

The Economist criticized the inertia of Yaounde II: 'The lack of drive or inspiration that so often marks the Six's internal affairs has now spread to the Association too.'[26] For a newcomer to the Associations, the Africans' failure to make substantial changes in the Convention and the lack of enthusiasm demonstrated by the Belgians, Germans and Dutch appeared as discouraging signs of a moribund relationship.

However, from a longer perspective the extension of the Association in Yaounde II was less disappointing; it represented a continuation of the same policy which brought forth Yaounde I. That is, Yaounde II was a conservative aid and trade package which included incremental changes and changes reflecting the new international political situation (particularly the greater emphasis on African regional cooperation and the UNCTAD demands for a generalized system of preferences). Because the balance of power within the relationship remained in favour of the EEC, the text of the Convention again contained primarily what the EEC wanted and was again offered to the Associates on a 'take it or leave it' basis. In particular, the crucial question of how much aid was to be allocated to the EDF was not open to negotiation.

The Association was still a continuation of the special relationship between France and its former dependencies.[27] It still linked the Associates in an alliance with Europe and the West, not with the socialist or developing world. President Diori of Niger, the AAMS spokesman, explained that Association with Europe was 'an engagement of a political nature, based on a feeling of particular solidarity extending beyond the framework of simple arrangements of an economic or commercial nature'.[28]

Yaounde II negotiations

The negotiations for Yaounde II were slow and difficult, but not as difficult as the Yaounde I negotiations. The EEC suffered from inertia in its negotiations, but the political complications of the 1963 Convention were missing. Without the problems of decolonization and British entry into the Community, the Convention was no longer a 'political football'.[29]

Negotiations for the new Convention began in December 1969 but were not completed by the expiration of Yaounde I on 31 May 1969. Interim arrangements were made to allow duty-free access of Associates' goods into the EEC and to disburse aid (using funds from EDF III). The Africans insisted that Yaounde II must expire on 31 January 1975, no matter how long it took before the Convention came into force. They hoped in this way to speed the ratification of the Convention and cut down the time during which the allotted EDF funds were paid out. Yaounde II came into force on 1 January 1970, a gap of seven months from the last Convention. This was an improvement over the eighteen-month gap between the Treaty of Rome Association and Yaounde I.

Compared to the hopefulness which accompanied the conclusion of Yaounde I, the conclusion of Yaounde II was anticlimactic. The leaders of the AAMS and EEC delegations agreed that the early atmosphere of the negotiations had been 'bad'.[30] The tension arose primarily because the Africans were unable to achieve their main proposals and had to be satisfied with a new Convention very little different from the old. The AAMS asked for a total of 1500 million dollars in aid, citing their needs caused by demographic expansion, slow growing GNPs, and deteriorating terms of trade.[31] The EEC offered them 1,000 million dollars for the AAMS and Associated dependencies.

The Africans proposed a support fund for commodities to operate outside the EDF. They also wanted more aid for industrialization, a fund for industrial enterprise, and grants for emergencies.[32] The Six rejected the idea of a separate commodity support fund and industrial development fund and decided that all aid should be within the figure set for the EDF. However, within the EDF, the EEC established a reserve fund of 65 million dollars to compensate producers for losses caused by drops in world commodity prices or disasters such as famines or floods.[33] This reserve fund did not give the AAMS the extra resources they wanted, but it was a progressive development and a precursor of the STABEX system of the Lome Convention.

In addition to their frustration at not being able to get Community agreement to their proposals, the AAMS accused the EEC of not paying all 'the necessary attention' to the negotiations.[34] Both the

EEC and AAMS wanted to continue their Association, but to the Europeans the Association had become less significant. Even France was noticeably less forceful in its support of and participation in the negotiations.

The reason for the EEC's reduced enthusiasm was not just 'inertia' or 'general malaise'.[35] Two other factors were also important. First, renewing the Yaounde Convention after five years seemed less pressing to the EEC than negotiating with the newly independent AAMS had been in the early 1960s. Second, the diminished importance to the Community of the Association lay in the EEC's proliferation of agreements with developing countries.

The changing context of the Association

After Yaounde I came into force in 1964, the EEC had to divide its attention between two groups of Associates — the remaining Part IV Associates and the independent AAMS. In the later years of the operation of the Yaounde Convention, the EEC's relations with developing countries became more complex. As special agreements with third countries proliferated, the Association became less crucial. In the *Tenth General Report on the Activities of the Community* (April 1966—March 1967) as in all previous annual reports, a whole chapter was devoted to the Association of the AAMS and OCT (dependent overseas countries and territories).[36] However, the next year the *Second General Report on the Activities of the Communities* (1968) demoted the AAMS and OCT Associations to one section in a chapter which dealt with, *inter alia*, the Mediterranean, other ldcs, and countries comparable to the AAMS.[37] Clearly, the EEC's interests had expanded beyond the Yaounde framework.

Most significant among the new arrangements were the Lagos and Arusha Conventions concluded in accordance with the EEC's 1963 offer of other forms of association for countries economically comparable to the AAMS. The agreement with Nigeria represented the first time a Commonwealth African country sought affiliation with the EEC. The agreement was also important because of the economic and political weight of Nigeria, potentially the natural leader of Africa. The Nigerian agreement did not include technical or financial aid, but gave duty-free quotas for some Nigerian exports.[38]

The Nigerians wanted to avoid political links with the EEC, including remaining apart from the Yaounde institutions. By having a separate agreement, they also hoped to escape charges of neo-colonialism levelled at the Association. The Lagos Convention was concluded under Article 238 of the Rome Treaty, the same legal basis for the association of European countries such as Greece. Although not based on Part IV of the Rome Treaty, it was there that the inspiration for the agreement lay.

The Lagos agreement was signed in 1966, but the Nigerian political crisis prevented its ratification. The Lagos Convention might otherwise have been a model for other agreements. By 1975 Nigeria, pleased by the changes in the text, and wishing to join other Commonwealth countries, signed the Lome Convention.

The Arusha Convention was also negotiated under Article 238 of the Treaty of Rome. It established an association between the EEC and Tanzania, Uganda, and Kenya in the context of their Treaty for East African Cooperation (which created the East African Community). The first Arusha Convention of 1968 expired before it was ratified; the second Convention was negotiated at the same time as Yaounde II, contributing to the lack of EEC attention about which the AAMS complained. Arusha II was signed in 1969 and expired concurrently with Yaounde II. It created joint institutions and included trade preferences, rights of establishment and services, payments and capital movements, but was without aid provisions.[39] Like the Lagos agreement, it was superseded by the Lome Convention. When Arusha II expired its members joined the Lome Convention.

During the operation of Yaounde I, the EEC took on wide commitments to developing countries. The Food Aid Convention came into force in 1968, and the EEC contributed over 1 million tonnes of food in that year.[40] As well as a global commitment to food aid, the EEC undertook in 1968 at UNCTAD II to reduce tariffs to all ldcs on a non-reciprocal basis. This led to a reduction of some tariffs in Yaounde II and later to the generalized system of preferences introduced in 1971.

As well as signing Yaounde II in 1969, the EEC also concluded agreements with Morocco and Tunisia. This proliferation of agreements and commitments meant that the Association, originally the sole focus of the Community's development policy, became just one part of that policy, albeit a central one.

Yaounde II aid

In certain respects the new Convention compared favourably to previous Associations. Total aid to the Associates under Yaounde II rose to 918 million US dollars, an increase of almost 26 per cent over Yaounde I's 730 million dollars. This was a larger increase than Yaounde I's 21 per cent increase over the Treaty of Rome Association, but the increase in the grant component of Yaounde II's aid was more dramatic. The grant component rose by over 20 per cent in Yaounde II, from 620 million US dollars under Yaounde I to 748 million in the new Convention. (See Table 2.2.) In Yaounde I, the grant component of aid had risen only 7 per cent over Part IV Association. By Association standards, the provision of aid in Yaounde II was generous.

Table 2.2 EDF aid: Yaounde I and II

in units of account		Associated states		Overseas countries and territories and overseas departments		Total	
Period	Yaounde	I	II	I	II	I	II
EDF grants		620	748	60	62	680	810
special loans		46	80	4	10	50	90
Total		666	828	64	72	730	900
European Investment Bank normal loans		64	90	6	10	70	100
Total		730	918	70	82	800	1000

Source: *European Development Aid*, Brussels, EEC, (undated), p. 32.

The method by which the EEC divided its aid among the Associates was open to question. EDF I aid was allocated into amounts for the colonies of France, Holland, Belgium and Italy. In the Yaounde Conventions the EEC used a less straightforward method. While trying to match aid distribution to project applications from the AAMS, the EEC also tried to relate aid flows to undisclosed target allocations. The European Commission's development directorate made an indicative aid allocation for each Associate based on economic indicators, past aid receipts and aid absorbtive capacity. Then, if aid receipts during the Convention differed substantially from the aid targets for a particular Associate, aid was either increased or slowed down to approach the target level. In order to prevent the Associates or others from criticizing the indicative allocations, they were kept secret. This system had several drawbacks. It depended upon the subjective decisions of EEC officials, and it left the EEC open to charges that political bias or patronage were at work in the allocation of aid (as was often the case). The effect of the system was that the distribution of EDF aid was more in keeping with political than strictly development criteria.

The OCT, the remaining dependencies, and the French departments — both of which had stronger political ties with Europe than the AAMS — received significantly more per capita aid than the AAMS.[41] Among the AAMS the richer states, measured by per capita GNP, received more aid per capita than the poorer ones. Gabon, for instance, with a 1970 per capita GNP of 630 dollars received per capita aid of 50.73 u.a. under EDF II whereas Burundi with a per capita GNP of 60 dollars received per capita aid of only 6.34 u.a. (See Table 2.3.) Although David Jones considered that this was 'unjustifiable on any rational criteria', his judgement overlooked important political and structural considerations.[42]

Table 2.3 Aid and GNP of selected EEC Associates

	POPULATION mid 1970 (millions)	GNP per head (dollars) 1970	Net oda per head 1969—71 annual average disbursements (dollars)(includes EDF)	EDF/EIB commitments per head, u.a.	
				2nd EDF 1.6.64— 31.12.72	3rd EDF 1.1.71— 1.73
AAMS					
Burundi	3.54	60	5.01	6.34	4.47
Cameroon	5.84	180	9.05	12.18	5.23
Dahomey	2.71	90	7.06	9.62	7.53
Gabon	0.49	630	41.96	50.73	36.08
I.Coast	4.94	310	11.23	17.97	6.56
Madagascar	7.31	130	7.22	11.39	4.45
Mali	5.02	70	5.05	6.84	6.14
Rwanda	3.60	60	5.86	6.67	6.05
Senegal	3.87	230	13.29	17.58	8.74
Zaire	18.80	90	4.90	4.69	2.37
Weighted average AAMS	—	123	7.67	10.12	5.76
Weighted average OCT	—	874	147.56	29.66	11.90
Weighted average, AAMS, OCT and overseas depts	—	145	11.79	10.72	5.95

Source: Jones, D., *Europe's Chosen Few*, p. 32, see note 19.

Giving aid more generously to dependencies and favourably disposed ldcs was not irrational; it was a self-interested policy on the part of Europe. Giving more aid to dependencies and richer Associates was meant to reward and stabilize relations with those countries. It should be noted that not only EEC aid followed this pattern. In 1979, for example, total bilateral development aid was 17 billion dollars, 11 billion of which went to the middle-income developing countries. Countries of political importance such as Israel received a disproportionate share.[43]

Giving more aid to the richer ldcs could also be justified in terms of a conservative development philosophy. That is, if the EEC gave more aid to develop the richer Associates, these had more potential to become good customers for EEC goods than the poorer countries. Investing in productive projects in richer countries would boost EEC exports more than investing in poorer countries' infrastructure or social services. As well as benefiting the EEC, giving aid to richer, more productive states would create more global wealth than aiding poorer, less efficient ones.[44]

Although economic arguments such as these can be adduced to justify the EEC's aid allocations, the EEC itself did not express them. Instead, responding to criticisms that it gave too much aid to the richer countries, the Community established special measures for the least developed in the Lome Convention.

The EEC's desire to involve the developing countries in selecting and carrying out projects financed by the EDF called for administrative and technical skills from the AAMS. The richer countries tended to have more efficient administrations which could identify possible projects and prepare the detailed proposals needed for EEC financing. The richer AAMS could also devote more time and staff to lobbying the EEC for funds. The EEC's system of making indicative allocations based, *inter alia*, on past aid receipts, meant that the richer countries — which had received more aid in the past — continued to be disproportionately aided.

EEC aid had many limitations. It was tied to purchases from Europe. It had political overtones and lengthy application and disbursement procedures. The aid was directed to individual projects rather than to a fully integrated development programme, although the EEC tried where possible to fit its projects into national development programmes. Despite the limitations of Community aid, the first three Associations, 1958–75, allocated over 2.3 billion dollars to the OCT and AAMS, and they regarded EDF aid as attractive.

Yaounde II trade

The trade provisions of Yaounde II were only minimally changed from Yaounde I. The Associates asked for their preferences over other suppliers to be maintained and for all their products, including temperate agricultural products, to be admitted duty-free into the EEC. They also wanted the EEC to create a marketing organization for tropical products, to abolish excise taxes on the consumption of tropical products, to control shipping rates, and to establish guarantees for private European investment in Africa. None of these proposals was accepted.[45]

In the field of trade, the EEC was bound by its undertakings to the 1968 UNCTAD conference. The EEC and all its member states had agreed to institute a generalized system of preferences (GSP) for all less-developed countries without seeking reciprocal preferences in return.[46] In accordance with this, the EEC reduced its tariffs on coffee, cocoa and palm oil from all sources. The Associates were unhappy with this reduction in their preferences over other ldcs, but they were unable to prevent it.[47]

Changes in favour of the Africans in the new Convention were minor. The EEC allowed the AAMS more freedom to enter regional groupings and specified more clearly what customs or trade arrangements would conflict with the Convention. African companies were allowed a margin of preference of up to 15 per cent on contracts tendered for EDF financed projects of under 500,000 dollars. AAMS companies won over 20 per cent of contracts financed by the EEC during Yaounde I and II (but not 20 per cent by value).

The EEC's conservatism was evidenced in the trade provisions of Yaounde II. The Community maintained the basic structure of AAMS preferences without venturing into new areas such as marketing organizations for tropical products. Whereas aid was increased in the Convention, the trade preferences of the Associates were eroded.

A survey of the data available for the Yaounde Conventions reveals that many of the trends of the earlier period of Association continued. That is, the positive effects of the preferences were limited. AAMS exports to the EEC grew at a disappointing pace compared to the growth in other sectors of EEC trade. Nevertheless, AAMS exports to the EEC did grow in absolute terms. EEC imports from the AAMS increased from 915 million u.a. in 1958 to 3,327 million in 1974, that is, by 3.6 times. The 8.4 per cent annual growth rate of EEC imports from the AAMS from 1958 to 1974 was respectable, but did not equal the growth rate of 12.5 per cent per annum of EEC imports from ldcs as a group (Table 2.4).

From 1958 to 1973, AAMS exports to the EEC grew more slowly

Table 2.4 EEC trade with major developing areas (millions of units of account)

	1958	1973	%Change	%Annual Growth	1974	%Change	%Annual Growth
Imports from:							
AAMS	915	2,217	+142	6.1	3,327	+264	8.4
Non-associated Africa	979	4,785	+389	11.2	10,086	+930	15.7
Central and South America	1,584	4,426	+179	7.1	5,365	+239	7.9
Middle East	1,805	8,078	+348	10.5	20,143	+1,016	16.3
Far East	782	3,022	+286	9.4	4,037	+416	10.8
Other	762	1,277	—	—	1,883	—	—
Total	6,827	23,805	+249	8.7	44,841	+557	12.5
Exports to:							
AAMS	714	1,669	+134	5.8	2,178	+205	7.2
Non-associated Africa	1,517	3,634	+140	6.0	5,843	+285	8.8
Central and South America	1,531	3,802	+148	6.3	6,155	+302	9.1
Middle East	695	3,268	+370	10.9	5,629	+710	14.0
Far East	1,082	2,727	+152	6.4	3,815	+253	8.2
Other	636	1,811	—	—	2,450	—	—
Total	6,175	16,911	+174	7.0	26,070	+322	9.4

Source: Matthews, J., *The Association System of the European Community*, p. 45, see note 39.

than for any other group of developing countries. Up to 1974, AAMS exports to the EEC increased at a slower rate than those of non-Associated Africa, the Middle and Far East, and Central and South America. The AAMS dropped from fourth major ldc exporter to the EEC in 1958 to fifth place in 1973 and 1974. As a percentage of developing countries' exports to the EEC, the AAMS' share fell from 13.4 per cent in 1958 to 7.4 per cent in 1974.[48]

Part of the reason for the AAMS' poor export performance can be attributed to the fact that the French market had long been open to the Associates' products. The margin of preference the AAMS had enjoyed in the French market under colonialism was reduced by the EEC. This resulted in a growth rate of only 2.8 per cent per annum for AAMS exports to France for the period 1958 to 1969.

The AAMS were dependent upon the export of non-oil primary

products. For 1967 to 1969, the most important AAMS exports were copper at 21.8 per cent of total export earnings, timber at 13.8 per cent, coffee at 10 per cent and cocoa at 8.5 per cent.[49] The Associated states received preferences on only about one-third of their exports, not including minerals or timber. Tariff reductions in Yaounde II reduced their margin of preference on several tropical goods. From 1959 to 1968, the AAMS significantly improved their position as suppliers to the EEC only for cocoa and groundnut oil.[50]

During the Yaounde period one trend shifted in favour of the AAMS. Whereas for the first Association EEC exports to Associates grew faster than imports from the Associates, this was reversed under the Yaounde regime. From 1958 to 1974, EEC imports from the AAMS grew by 8.4 per cent, but EEC exports to the AAMS grew more slowly, by 7.2 per cent per annum.[51] Thus, Association no longer benefited the exports of the EEC more than those of the AAMS, as was the case in the Treaty of Rome Association.

The reverse preferences granted to the EEC by the Associated states helped EEC exports to the Associates.[52] But despite the preferences given to EEC goods by many Associates, EEC exports to non-Associated developing countries grew faster than exports to the AAMS.* Table 2.4 shows that EEC exports to all developing countries, 1958—73, grew by 7 per cent per annum, while exports to the AAMS grew by just 5.8 per cent per annum.

More encouraging was the growth of intra-AAMS trade. Although the Yaounde Conventions did not create a free trade area among the AAMS, intra-AAMS trade did grow. The AAMS share of AAMS imports rose from a mere 1.1 per cent in 1960 to 5.6 per cent by 1969.[53]

The fears of other developing countries that the Associates' preferential access to EEC markets would give them an unfair advantage proved groundless. The reasons for this were complex. It was due to the weakness of the AAMS' economies, their failure to expand production and marketing of products which received EEC preferences and to diversify their economies to avoid depending on exporting a few commodities. Long protected by French subsidies, many of the AAMS were inefficient producers who found it difficult to compete on the world market. Many primary commodities suffered from low price elasticity of demand, the tendency for demand to rise little even if prices fell, making it difficult for the AAMS to export more primary products to Europe.

The AAMS' poor trade performance was also partly due to the insignificance of the EEC preferences. The preferences covered only

---

* Congo (Kinshasa), Rwanda, Burundi, Somalia and Togo did not discriminate between EEC and non-EEC imports.

one-third of AAMS exports and were reduced in value by the tariff-cutting in Yaounde II and the introduction of the generalized system of preferences for all developing countries in 1971. Another reason for the AAMS' disappointing trade performance was that from Yaounde I the operation of the 'rules of origin' prevented them from incorporating imported components into AAMS products and then re-exporting them to the EEC.[54]

The preferences (and reverse preferences) of the Yaounde system were of some benefit to the parties concerned. However, they were not sufficient to offset the weakness of the trade performance of the AAMS.

Conclusion

Yaounde I emerged in 1963 from the uncertainty of the end of colonialism in Africa as a sign of continuity in EurAfrican relations. The Convention faced criticisms that it was neo-colonial and divisive of Africa, but it benefited from its ability to be presented as a new policy. As a newly negotiated agreement, Yaounde I did not explicitly embrace its past; instead it espoused the ideals of equality and development. Yaounde I was a successful continuation and development of the policy of association between Europe and Africa. It succeeded despite a political environment even more uncertain than that which faced the much-vaunted Lome Convention in 1975.

The principal accomplishment of Yaounde I was that it preserved the EurAfrican entente. This entente was renewed in 1969 by the second Yaounde Convention. Yaounde II did not face the upheavals of African independence. It followed its predecessor closely and in some respects, for example, amounts of aid, even compared favourably to it. However, the negotiations for Yaounde II were rendered difficult by the fact that the AAMS could not get the EEC to agree to their proposals for change or to negotiate over the aid package.

The EEC — and even the Association's architect, France — were by 1969 less interested in the Association because of the proliferation of other agreements with developing countries. The trade results of the successive periods of Association, in the period 1958 to 1974, were disappointing, showing the limited economic potential of the Association formula.

It was to the disappointment with the stagnation of the Yaounde Association, to the criticisms of its divisiveness and neo-colonialism, and to the disillusionment of the developing countries with an international system unable to work in their interests, that the Lome Convention was offered by the European Community as an answer.

But, as the next two chapters demonstrate, the Lome Convention was not a departure from the long-standing EurAfrican alliance. It was only a further elaboration of the policy of association.

Notes

1. See, for instance, Druckman, Daniel (ed.), *Negotiations: Social-Psychological Perspectives*, Beverley Hills, Sage, 1977.
2. Dodoo, C. and Kuster, R., 'The Road to Lome', in Alting von Geusau, F.A.M. (ed.), *The Lome Convention and a New International Economic Order*, Leyden, Sijthoff, 1977.
3. Barnes, W., *Europe and the Developing World: Association under Part IV of the Treaty of Rome*, London, Chatham House, 1967.
4. Rabemanjara, J., 'L'Organization des Dix-Huit, Leur Coordination, Leurs Rapports avec les Autre Pays Africains', *Revue du Marche Commun*, May 1969.
5. Twitchett, Carol C., *Europe and Africa: From Association to Partnership*, Westmead, Saxon House, 1978, pp. 109–10.
6. Rabemanjara, *op cit*.
7. Zartman, I.W., *The Politics of Trade Negotiations Between Africa and the European Community*, Princeton, Princeton University Press, 1971, Ch.2.
8. *ibid*, p. 64.
9. Gruhn, I.V., 'Inching Towards Interdependence', *International Organization*, vol. 30, no. 2, 1976.
10. Lemaignen, Robert, *L'Europe au Berceau*, Paris, Plon, 1964, p. 160.
11. *First General Report on the Activities of the Community*, Brussels, EEC, 1958.
12. Camps, Miriam, *Britain and the European Community*, London, Oxford University Press, 1964, p. 357.
13. Twitchett, *op cit*, p. 145.
14. Nye, J., *Pan-Africanism and East African Integration*, London, Oxford University Press, 1966, Ch.7.
15. *Convention of Association between the European Economic Community and the African and Malagasy States Associated with that Community* (64/346/EEC), Brussels, EEC, 1964. 'Preamble' (Yaounde I Convention).
16. *Treaty Establishing the European Economic Community*, 25 March 1957; London, HMSO, 1962, Article 131 (Treaty of Rome).
17. Rabemanjara, *op cit*.
18. Twitchett, *op cit*, p. 110. This same general working pattern was maintained in the Lome Convention.
19. Jones, David, *Europe's Chosen Few: Policy and Practice of the EEC Aid Programme*, London, Overseas Development Institute, 1973, p. 98, note 3.
20. *European Development Aid*, Brussels, EEC, D.G.X., (undated).
21. Pearson, S. and Schmidt, W., 'Alms for AAMS: A Larger Flow?', *Journal of Common Market Studies*, vol. 3, no. 1, 1964.
22. *ibid*.
23. Jones, *op cit*, p. 40.
24. *Convention of Association between the European Economic Community and the African and Malagasy States Associated with that Community and Annexed Documents*, 1969, Brussels, EEC, (Yaounde II). Protocol No. 1, Article 1.

25. *ibid*, 'Preamble'.
26. 'Six into Eighteen Won't Go', *The Economist*, 5 July 1969.
27. Cosgrove, C. and Twitchett, K., 'The Second Yaounde Convention in Perspective', *International Relations*, May 1970.
28. *West Africa*, 1969, vol. 23, p. 691.
29. *ibid*, p. 605.
30. *European Community*, September 1969.
31. *The Economist, op cit.*
32. *West Africa*, vol. 23, *op cit*, pp. 24, 359, 605.
33. *European Community, op cit.*
34. *West Africa*, vol. 23, *op cit*, p. 691.
35. General malaise was noted by *The Economist, op cit*; that of inertia by *West Africa, op cit*, vol. 23.
36. *Tenth General Report on the Activities of the Community* (1966–7), Brussels, EEC.
37. *Second General Report on the Activities of the Community* (1968), Brussels, EEC.
38. Matthews, J., *Association System of the European Community*, New York, Praeger, 1977.
39. *Agreement Establishing an Association Between the European Economic Community and the United Republic of Tanzania, the Republic of Uganda, and the Republic of Kenya and Annexed Documents*, Brussels, EEC, 1969, (second Arusha Convention).
40. *Food Aid*, Brussels, EEC, 594/x/77 EN.
41. However, the relatively large amounts of aid spent on the OCT – specifically the French and Dutch Caribbean dependencies – were of little economic benefit to them. See Andic, F., 'The Development Impact of the EEC on the French and Dutch Caribbean', *Journal of Common Market Studies*, vol. 8, no. 1, 1969.
42. Jones, *op cit*, p. 53.
43. *Financial Times*, 20 July 1981, p. 11.
44. See, for example, Bauer, Peter, *Dissent on Development*, London, Weidenfeld and Nicolson, 1976.
45. *West Africa*, vol. 23, *op cit*, pp. 24 and 691.
46. *Second General Report on the Activities of the Community, op cit.*
47. *West Africa*, vol. 23, *op cit*, p. 691.
48. Matthews, *op cit*, p. 46.
49. *European Development Aid, op cit.*
50. Kreinin, Mordechai, 'European Integration and the Developing Countries', in Balassa, Bela (ed.), *European Economic Integration*, Oxford, North-Holland, 1975.
51. *European Development Aid, op cit.*
52. Reverse preferences may also have helped EEC exporters (mainly French) to charge higher than world market prices to the AAMS. See, Kreinin, Mordechai, 'European Integration and the Developing Countries', in Balassa, *op cit*. Kreinin also suggested that the AAMS received above market prices for some products in the EEC.
53. Kreinin, *op cit*, p. 348.
54. *Second General Report on the Activities of the Communities, op cit.*

3 Lome: The new Association

Introduction

The Lome Convention, signed in 1975, was inaugurated in a haze of goodwill and broad generalizations. Commentators on both sides — European and ACP — were at pains to emphasize its revolutionary character. However, in many respects the new Convention resembled the previous Associations and many of the apparent changes were semantic rather than concrete.

Despite the Lome Convention's widespread image of being a break with the past, the Preamble of the Convention was very similar to that of Yaounde II. Both Preambles referred to the parties' complete equality, their desire for cooperation with each other, their recognition of the importance of industrialization, intra-Associate trade and cooperation.

In order to emphasize its newness, the 1963 Yaounde Convention made no reference to its predecessor, the Treaty of Rome Association. Similarly, the Lome Convention stressed its novelty by not mentioning any previous Associations.

Lome emphasized 'safe-guarding the interests of the African, Caribbean and Pacific (ACP) States, whose economies depended to a considerable extent on the exportation of commodities'.[1] This was a reference to the new STABEX system for supporting export receipts. Whereas Yaounde I's objective of diversifying the Associates' economies held open the prospect of unlimited development, the Lome objective of stabilizing export earnings was comparatively conservative.

Under the Lome Convention no longer did the parties seek 'the economic, social and cultural progress of their countries', as in Yaounde II; the goal became 'the economic development and social progress of the ACP States'. This showed a change from seeking mutual benefits to benefits specifically for the ACP states. The new Lome phrasing resembled the ideas of the Treaty of Rome Association. Article 131 of the Rome Treaty stated the Association's objective 'to promote the economic and social development of the countries and territories'. It is doubtful whether the guiding principles of the Community varied from altruism under the Treaty of Rome, to a desire for mutual benefits under the Yaounde system, back to a more altruistic interest in ACP development under Lome. However, these changing principles did reflect development strategies. Parallel to these changing objectives, changing measures were taken: reciprocal preferences between the Associates and the EEC under the Treaty of Rome and Yaounde systems were replaced by non-reciprocal preferences under Lome.

The most innovative and the oft-quoted statement in the Lome Preamble was:

> Resolved to establish a new model for relations between developed and developing States, compatible with the aspirations of the international community towards a more just and more balanced economic order.[2]

This statement gave many commentators the impression of a radical change; but neither the Preamble nor the provisions of the Lome Convention justified this view. Some assessments of Lome's newness are given below:

> ... an agreement which, I say it with some pride, is unique in the world and in history.
>
> EEC Commissioner Claude Cheysson

> Lome has seen the birth of a new economic order.
>
> *Togo-Dialogue*[3]

The assertion that the Lome Convention was of a new and different kind suited both sides. It was, in fact, more convenient than accurate. It was a way of escaping the previous bad reputation of the Associations and distancing Lome from the colonial past.

The African, Caribbean and Pacific states felt more comfortable with a 'new relationship'; it enhanced their dignity to enter freely into treaties without colonial connotations. The provisions for stabilizing export earnings (STABEX) appeared to satisfy the ACP states' desire for a new international economic order. The Europeans also gained a great deal of goodwill in the third world from the Convention. Even the US took seriously the EEC's claim to have a new model for North–South relations.

Nevertheless, not everyone was convinced that a new age had dawned with the Lome Convention. The Guyanese foreign minister, S.S. Ramphal, warned that it was impossible to believe that the Convention fulfilled all the ideals of cooperation it proclaimed.[4]

Like previous Associations, this one was based upon a European proposal: the offer to Associate former British colonies with the enlarged EEC. The impetus for Lome came not from the ACP's desire for a new economic order, but from the British accession to the European Community. In this way, the Lome Convention was neo-colonial because its structure and membership were still based on colonial relations. However, although neo-colonialism is usually considered as a wholly objectionable phenomenon, it was the ties of neo-colonialism which enabled the 46 ACP countries to create a degree of collective solidarity.

The new Convention performed the same general functions as its predecessors. It maintained privileged political and economic relationships between Europe and Africa by giving aid and trade preferences to the developing countries, while expecting certain privileges in return.

Although the Convention eliminated the reciprocal preferences accorded to EEC goods, the Europeans got most favoured nation treatment for their exports, and rights of establishment for their companies in ACP countries.* In terms of aid, the EEC Commission claimed:

> No previous negotiations have ever shown so patently that the labels of 'aid donors' and 'aid recipients' are things of the past.[5]

In fact, the donors remained donors and the recipients remained as such despite new terminology and aid schemes.

According to the European Commission, both the ACP and EEC wanted 'to stake out a new world economic order, a new pattern of relations between the industrialized and developing countries'.[6] The ACP in general did look forward to new benefits from Lome, and to a new economic order which would ensure their prosperity. The EEC, however, was not interested in major changes; it wanted ACP development and secure access to African raw materials. The Europeans were not interested in changing the international economic order to their detriment or offering the full amount of aid, US $8000 million, the ACP wanted. The EEC's objectives were fundamentally the same as

---

* Rights of establishment were reciprocal under Title V of Lome.

those followed since Yaounde I: to keep good political and economic relations with the Associates; and to maintain European prosperity while aiding the developing countries.

It may be wondered why, if the Lome Convention was similar to its predecessors, the impression of radical change was so prevalent. On one hand, as mentioned earlier, the image of Lome as revolutionary produced political benefits for both sides. In addition, the Lome Convention differed so much in scale from the previous Associations that it was thought to be different in kind. Instead of the 19 Yaounde* II Associates, at the signing of Lome I there were 46 ACP states: the 19 AAMS, 21 African, Pacific and Caribbean Commonwealth states, and six other sub-Saharan African states.** Thus, the magnitude of the changes in Lome made them seem more fundamental than they were.

The Lome negotiations coincided with the flood-tide of the new international economic order. In the wake of the success of the OPEC states in altering their relations with the developed world, other ldcs were anxious to effect a comparable change. The Lome Convention seemed, with its new membership, its ideals, and provisions such as the stabilization of exports earnings scheme (STABEX), to be an instrument for accomplishing a new international economic order (NIEO). But although the Lome Convention borrowed the rhetoric of the NIEO, it continued the association policy of the Treaty of Rome.

British entry into the European Community

Before its eventual success, Britain had twice previously tried to join the EEC.[7] Final negotiations for British entry into the EEC opened in 1970 and culminated in the Treaty of Accession known as the Treaty of Brussels, signed in 1972.

It has been argued that the British situation regarding the dependencies and Commonwealth at the time of accession and the French position with respect to its dependencies at the time of the signing of the Treaty of Rome were analogous.[8] Both countries viewed special arrangements for dependent territories (or former colonies) as essential.

---

* The original 18 Associates and Mauritius.
** The 46 ACP states comprised: the Bahamas, Barbados, Botswana, Burundi, Cameroon, Central African Republic, Chad, Congo, Dahomey, Equatorial Guinea, Ethiopia, Fiji, Gabon, Gambia, Ghana, Guinea, Guinea-Bissau, Grenada, Guyana, Ivory Coast, Jamaica, Kenya, Lesotho, Liberia, Madagascar, Malawi, Mali, Mauritania, Mauritius, Niger, Nigeria, Rwanda, Senegal, Sierra Leone, Somalia, Sudan, Swaziland, Tanzania, Togo, Tonga, Trinidad and Tobago, Uganda, Upper Volta, Western Samoa, Zaire, and Zambia.

However, there were notable differences in the two cases. These differences lay in the political leverage of the acceding country, and in the role the Association was to play in their respective policies.

When France made special terms for its dependencies a precondition for entering the Community, it was addressing the Community from a standpoint of considerable power: without France the European Economic Community was unviable. France's political leverage can be observed in its success in creating the Association despite the reluctance of some of its EEC partners.

By contrast, when Britain sought admission, the EEC was already established. The Community could exist perfectly well without the UK; thus, Britain had less bargaining power than France had possessed. Along with EEC states such as the Netherlands and Germany, the UK would have preferred a development policy to include Commonwealth Asia.[9] But in order to join the Community and obtain privileges for its colonies and former colonies, Britain had to accept the existing, French-designed Association. Britain played an active role in the Lome Convention; nevertheless, many features such as the Consultative Assembly were not to British liking and Britain retained its preference for a global development policy.[10]

In addition to its lesser bargaining strength vis à vis the EEC, the UK's development policy was substantially different from France's, and Lome had a different role in it. The French Community created after the 1957 referendum never fully came to life; instead the European Community's Association played in large part the role originally intended for the French Community. What could be called the British version of the French Community — the Commonwealth — proved more durable. It had escaped the epithet of neo-colonialism which plagued the French Community and EEC Association. Membership in the Commonwealth was seen as an adjunct of sovereignty, not a threat to it. Ali Mazrui compared Commonwealth membership to a seat in the UN.[11] Even the most radical of African anti-colonial states, Ghana, did not reject the Commonwealth. The centre-piece of British post-colonial policy was the Commonwealth, not the Association, and it remained so even after Britain joined Lome.*

Considering the importance of Association to France, it may be asked why France accepted British participation and influence in it. There were several reasons for this. The French were not averse to extending the Association to former British dependencies provided that their relations with francophone Africa were not damaged. They also looked forward to having their relations with British Africa strengthened and more funds for development provided by the British.[12]

---

* Although the Commonwealth was moribund in the early 1970s, it acquired new life after 1975 with the advent of Secretary-General Ramphal and his emphasis on development.

For the UK, the Association *per se* was not a major attraction of the Community. The British Government's White Paper of 1971 on the entry into the EEC referred only in passing to the Association, characterizing it as a potential new trade partner. In contrast, the White Paper sought to answer qualms about the effects of Britain's entry into the EEC by portraying the Commonwealth and Britain as drifting apart both politically and economically, although the UK was working to safeguard Commonwealth interests.

The Treaty of Brussels which united the UK and the EEC was a technical document without the idealistic language of the Associations. Its preamble referred only indirectly to third countries and not at all to the Commonwealth. The treaty provided that the dependencies of new member states (UK, Ireland, Denmark and Norway) could be Associated by a decision of the EEC Council of Ministers. The new member states were not bound by Yaounde II or Arusha II. Imports from the Commonwealth to the UK could continue, but these could not be re-exported to the Community. A new Association or Associations would be constituted in 1975 and Commonwealth preferences would then be abolished.[13] In addition to the generalized system of preferences the Commonwealth countries would benefit from in 1974, the EEC declared itself 'Inspired by the will to extend and strengthen the trade relations with the developing independent Commonwealth countries in Asia' (Ceylon, India, Malaysia, Pakistan and Singapore).[14]

Provisions for the 'Associables' — the independent Commonwealth countries of Africa, the Caribbean and Pacific — were more extensive. The EEC reiterated what amounted to the same options offered in 1963: participation in Yaounde II's successor, association under Article 238 of the Rome Treaty (more limited), or trade agreements.[15] Protocol 22 of the Treaty of Brussels declared:

> The Community's relations with the Associated African and Malagasy States ensure for those States a range of advantages and are based on structures which give the Association its distinctive character in the fields of trade relations, financial and technical cooperation and joint institutions.
>
> The Community's objective in its policy of association shall remain the safe-guarding of what has been achieved.

Thus the Community made it clear that it was not seeking a radical revision of the Yaounde Convention by extending the Association. Instead, the EEC wanted to safeguard the fundamental principles of Yaounde. It wished to conserve its relations with the AAMS and maintain the Association's major provisions for trade, aid and institutions.

The basis of what was to become the Lome Convention was set out in the Treaty of Brussels. Who was to negotiate with whom — the enlarged EEC and its invited Associates and Associables (See Table 3.1) — and for what — trade and aid concessions which did not alter the 'distinctive character' of the Association — was already determined in the Treaty of Brussels. Since the fundamentals of the Lome Convention were determined in a wholly EEC treaty, the ACP states' ability to effect substantial changes in the Association was extremely limited.

Table 3.1 List of Associable countries mentioned in the Treaty of Brussels*

Barbados	Kenya	Tanzania
Botswana	Lesotho	Tonga
Fiji	Malawi	Trinidad and Tobago
The Gambia	Mauritius	Uganda
Ghana	Nigeria	Western Samoa
Guyana	Sierra Leone	Zambia
Jamaica	Swaziland	

* All of which joined the Lome Convention.

Source: Treaty of Brussels, Annex VI.

The AAMS view

The Treaty of Brussels' Protocol 22, which invited the Commonwealth Associables to participate 'side by side' with the existing Associates, expressed the fundamental wish of the AAMS to safeguard the Association. In particular, the AAMS wanted to maintain their trade preferences. However, despite the fact that the EEC had undertaken to protect the AAMS' interests, these countries were not unequivocally in favour of the expansion.

The AAMS feared that an expanded Association might dilute their benefits. Aid might be spread more thinly. In addition, the influx of anglophone states might alter the character of the Association and the influence of large and powerful anglophone states such as Kenya and Nigeria might submerge their own views.[16] This overwhelming of the francophone states did not occur. The francophone states continued to play an important role in Lome. Nevertheless, many of the AAMS would have preferred to keep the Association as it was. The President of Niger remarked in 1973, 'For me, the ideal would be to continue a policy for the nineteen, that is to say, an improved Yaounde.'[17]

In some respects the Yaounde Conventions had advantages over the later Lome Conventions. Although the Yaounde Conventions suffered from being seen by outsiders as neo-colonial, there was a significant amount of satisfaction on both the European and African sides about the relationship. The Lome system, in contrast, was more troubled. Three characteristics differentiated Lome from its predecessors and created a more uncertain and acrimonious relationship. First, the rising expectations of the developing countries of what the Lome relationship ought to provide — a new international economic system, guaranteed prosperity, and so on — led to greater demands from the ACP. Second, EEC relations with the Commonwealth were never as intimate as those with the AAMS and new problems such as those over sugar arose between them and the EEC. In the third place, the smallness of the previous Associations meant that they were more easily administered and contained fewer conflicts.

Despite the advantages inherent in the Yaounde system or perceived in it by the AAMS, when faced with the EEC's desire to expand the Association, the AAMS accepted this. Within three months of the signing of the Treaty of Brussels, the Associates' ministers agreed to the expansion of the Association. Their main concerns were: to obtain satisfactory preferences for commodity exports to the EEC, to maintain the value of aid from the Community, and to preserve the role of the joint institutions.[18] The EEC–AAMS Parliamentary Conference which met in March 1973 expressed its satisfaction with the Treaty of Brussels. Notably, the parliamentarians confirmed their 'attachment to the policy of association'. The conference commended the European Development Fund and the institutions of the Association; it opposed any change from the EEC–AAMS 'partnership' to a simple aid contract. The AAMS wished to work within the Association while waiting for similar structures on a worldwide scale.[19]

The AAMS' acceptance of the expanded Association demonstrated that Community and the Associates had good communication; the Community did understand the Associates' qualms and worked to allay them. Also, it showed that the extension of the Association was in keeping with the AAMS's wider political objectives.

The AAMS had a strong interest in their special political and economic relations with Europe, but they also had other goals. As well as their desire to preserve the benefits of Association, the AAMS identified with the interests of the 'third world' group. In addition to their global affiliation to the less-developed countries, the AAMS felt a community of ideals and interests with the rest of Africa. Thus, the AAMS were interested not just in their benefits as the Associates of the EEC, they also wanted to show solidarity as pan-Africanists and members of the third world, and to work for common benefits in these other contexts. It was to these latter aspirations that the expansion of the Association appealed. And if — as the EEC assured them — their special relations and economic benefits would be maintained in a wider Association while their African and third world solidarity were enhanced, then the AAMS had no objections to the expansion. In fact, they could see political advantages within the Association and in respect of the international system. As *West Africa* described it:

> The 19 states broadly welcomed the extension of associate status to Commonwealth states. The association would gain in political weight and would give a boost to the campaign for world commodity agreements, and failing these, regional agreements.[20]

Although the original Associates, in the name of greater global and regional cooperation among developing countries, agreed to an extended Association, there were still problems in realizing it. The Commonwealth Associables were less easily persuaded to accept Association and the two groups experienced problems of coordination. The Commonwealth Secretariat (acting for the Associables) and the Association Secretariat were described as playing 'hide and seek' in Brussels during 1972.[21] The francophone countries mistrusted the Commonwealth Secretariat and worried that its considerable resources and expertise might give the Commonwealth countries an advantage over them.[22] At one point the African Associables decided to utilize the East African Community's secretariat instead of the Commonwealth's. But by 1974, a single secretariat for all non-European parties was established (which later became the ACP Secretariat).[23]

The Commonwealth: Unprepared

After the abortive 1961 British attempt to join the EEC, many Commonwealth countries retained a dislike of the Association. Despite the fact that it had long been generally accepted that the UK would eventually enter the European Community, the Commonwealth had no clear policy to meet this contingency.[24] On one hand, the structure of Commonwealth institutions made the taking of a political decision by developing country members difficult; on the other hand there was a reluctance to face an unpleasant transition before it was necessary. According to a former Nigerian ambassador:

> the Commonwealth countries did not think seriously of their relationship with Europe until Britain signed the Act of Accession to the Treaty of Rome in 1972.[25]

By failing to have a policy on British entry to the EEC and the changes this would make in their status, the Commonwealth countries lost an opportunity to exert a concerted influence over Britain in the negotiations. Whereas close EEC—AAMS communication meant that the EEC tried to safeguard what the AAMS saw as their vital interests, the interests of the Commonwealth were not articulated.

It took over a year after the signing of the Treaty of Brussels for the Commonwealth to adopt the idea of an expanded Association. The Commonwealth Africans' doubts about the Association can be divided into the political and the economic, the former being more serious and widespread.

To turn to the political objections first, countries outside the Association generally conceived of it as a continuation of French colonial policy. To the Nigerian ambassador, Olu Sanu, Yaounde was 'an expression of the political desire of the African signatory states to be associated with Europe' and was thus objectionable.[26] Furthermore, the Commonwealth Associables were apprehensive about Yaounde's political institutions and the linkage between them and aid.[27] Some countries worried about the divisive effects if certain countries chose trade agreements while others joined the Association. The independent Caribbean Associables feared that Association could separate them from the remaining Caribbean dependencies.*

Another fear was that joining the Association would harm the Commonwealth. A stronger, enlarged EEC Association would bind Africa with aid, trade and institutional links to the European Community. This might supersede the Commonwealth, which was based on special ties to Britain.[28]

As well as the hesitations which resulted from perceiving the Association as an alignment with a neo-colonial system, some countries hesitated over East—West issues. The EEC was part of the West; it was designed to 'reinforce the coherence of the free world'.[29] Joining the EEC's Association (which included recognizing West Berlin as part of West Germany) might, some Africans felt, impede trade and aid from Eastern Europe.[30]

From an economic point of view, some Commonwealth states were reluctant to exchange their Commonwealth preferences from Britain for lower EEC preferences in a wider market, although these offered potentially greater returns. The Standard Bank reckoned that the effect of tariff changes on Commonwealth states who became associated in some form with the EEC would be marginally favourable. But if they stayed out of such preferential arrangements, the effect of losing British preferences would be marginally negative.[31]

---

* Communication between the ACP states and the dependent Associates was virtually non-existent under Lome.

The Asian Commonwealth stood to suffer most from losing UK preferences. However, the EEC was unwilling to offer Association to the Asian Commonwealth. Changing trade patterns and the potential effects of the generalized system of preferences for all developing countries made it hard to quantify potential losses.[32] But the Commonwealth had no policy of its own to oppose the EEC's plan, and it is doubtful whether the African Associables would have wished to include the Asians. Asian countries with independent foreign policies, such as India, might also have regarded joining the Association as incompatible with their political aims.

As well as doubts about the value of EEC preferences, some Associables worried about the long-term economic effects of Association. They questioned whether the Community's trade preferences and aid would lock them into dependency on the export of primary products. They worried that the short-run benefits of EEC aid would remove the impetus to gain the long-term benefits of industrialization.[33]

But despite the Commonwealth Africans' qualms, they finally accepted the expanded Association. Three principal reasons for this can be adduced: the lack of other well-articulated policy options, the desire to obtain the trade and aid benefits offered, and the desire for pan-African solidarity. The lack of other policy proposals by the Africans was noted above. The British negotiated three options for the Commonwealth Associables: (1) Association; (2) a weaker association; or (3) trade agreements. These were the basis of African thinking. The Nigerians, for example, wavered between (1) and (3) but did not propose anything different.[34]

Although there was doubt about the value of the Association's trade and aid concessions, most of the Associables wanted to avail themselves of these. The example of Guinea, which rejected Europe's help and then faced severe economic consequences, made the model of saying 'no' unattractive.

The desire for African unity was the overwhelming factor which led the Associates to select option (1), the enlarged Association. While option (1) involved the institutions the Associables disliked, it alone offered the prospect of African unity along with greater prospects for aid and trade preferences. Both the AAMS and Associables were pleased that Liberia, Ethiopia, Sudan, Guinea Bissau, Equatorial Guinea and Guinea joined the new Convention. This enhanced the pan-African appeal of the Convention and gave it a less colonial image. Except Guinea, these states had no colonial links with the EEC. Thus, the new Convention united virtually all black Africa — not just the ex-colonies of the EEC — with Europe.

Nigeria's leadership helped to galvanize African opinion. Once Nigeria decided that African solidarity was best served by an expanded

Association, it used its considerable political and economic influence and its role as chairman of the Organization of African Unity (OAU), to press its case.[35]

Intra-ACP negotiations

At the same time that African, and then ACP, solidarity was forged in the Lome negotiations, other regional third world groupings were created. The Caribbean Common Market (CARICOM) agreement was signed in 1973 and negotiations for the Economic Community of West African States (ECOWAS — less of a success than CARICOM) proceeded concurrently with the Lome negotiations. During the early and mid-1970s the ideal of third world collective self-reliance was conducive to African, ACP and wider cooperation.

At the meeting of African Commonwealth trade ministers in February 1973, the ministers decided to negotiate jointly with the EEC, without preconditions.* Guinea, Sudan, Ethiopia and Liberia were also showing interest in the Association; but it was not yet clear whether the anglophone and francophone Africans could form a common front.[36]

The common African front was achieved in May 1973 at a meeting in Abidjan of African trade ministers. This meeting, sponsored by the United Nations Economic Commission for Africa (UNECA), the African Development Bank (ADB) and OAU, agreed principles for the negotiations with the EEC. These included: non-reciprocity of trade concessions to the ACP, the extension to developing countries of rights of establishment accorded to Europe by Yaounde, the guarantee of stable and remunerative prices for African exports, and that agreements between Europe and Africa should not harm intra-African cooperation.

The Abidjan meeting allowed the Africans to do what the Europeans had done almost a century earlier at the Berlin West African Conference. The former colonies and the other African states involved considered the future of Africa's relations with Europe. The meeting produced amendments to the Community's Association rather than a new African policy; nevertheless it was a:

> major breakthrough in inter-African economic relations ... the first time that francophone and anglophone Africa sat down to discuss their relations with Europe.[37]

An OAU summit meeting in Ethiopia later in May 1973 adopted the

---

* Although there were in theory no preconditions, in practice the negotiations were based on the three options offered by the EEC.

69

Abidjan principles. A subsequent OAU meeting of trade ministers in July prepared for the negotiations and recommended that all OAU member states attend the first meeting with the EEC later in July. The Somali minister heralded the solidarity created at the meeting among Africans, stating that there were no longer anglophones and francophones: 'We are Africaphone'.[38]

Negotiations with the European Community about the enlarged Association opened on 25 July 1973, with one spokesman for the Africans, one for the Caribbean and one for the Pacific. But by October 1973, the new ACP spoke through one representative.[39] The remarkable solidarity achieved by the countries of Africa was replicated on the ACP level.

Despite the importance of unity as a goal to the ACP, complete unanimity was not attained. Professor Frey-Wouters considered that the African, Caribbean and Pacific countries became 'the homogeneous group called the ACP'.[40] But even at the time of the negotiations, the ACP countries had different views and interests. Sugar, for instance, was of major concern to the Caribbean and Pacific, but not to most African countries. The Caribbeans' active involvement in the negotiations was sometimes resented by other ACP states, and by the Europeans. Thus, although the ACP maintained a common front in the negotiations, their differences never disappeared.

Guinea and the EEC: A case of policy reversal

One of the most interesting, and surprising, aspects of ACP unity was the decision of the Republic of Guinea to participate in the Lome negotiations. Guinea was a determined opponent of the EEC's Association which reversed its policy and embraced Lome.

Since voting for immediate independence from France in 1958, Guinea stayed outside of the Association. Guinea's attitude was not just one of benign neglect: it was a complete rejection of the Association on political and economic grounds.

Guinea saw the Association as an unacceptable vestige of colonialism which would unduly promote European and especially French influence. Politically, Guinea wanted complete independence. In economic terms, Guinea considered that benefits from Association would be insignificant and that Guinea would do better to develop its considerable natural resources by itself. Guinea's President Sekou Toure explained his view in 1960:

> At present Europe is busy setting up the Common Market and is anxious to include Africa in it. We say no. We constitute at present too small a market. We must first increase our own free market. We have nothing against anyone,

but we prefer freely negotiated agreements, and we think it is more honest to say so . . . . If we voted 'no' the reason was precisely because we had developed a new outlook, that we had confidence in our own future.[41]

Sekou Toure's iconoclastic stand was seen in some quarters as a noble experiment in independence. Sekou Toure is often classified among African nationalist leaders such as Nkrumah for his uncompromising stance, guarding independent Guinea's fragile liberty from dangerous foreign entanglements. As one writer described the example of Guinea's policies:

> Was her all but unanimous vote against the French Community the megalomaniac deviation claimed by the more disappointed of the French, or has she been able to give the example which led to the collapse of the French Community by showing that even a poor underdeveloped African country can be truly free?[42]

To many observers, for almost twenty years it was Guinea which set the progressive model for relations between developed and developing states. The EurAfrican Associations — under the Treaty of Rome and the Yaounde Conventions — were perceived on virtually all sides as neo-colonial. In French-speaking Africa it was only Guinea which escaped the French sphere of influence, albeit at the price of bad relations with France.

But by 1975 it was the EurAfrican Association which claimed to be establishing a model for European—African relations. The philosophy of interdependence rather than complete non-alignment had become the favoured model — even for Guinea. What caused this reversal? According to the Guinean government there was no change: Guinea was continuing its policy of non-alignment.[43] But Guinea's change from a country which decisively rejected Association to one which participated in the Lome Conventions cannot be discounted. The principal cause of Guinea's acceptance of the Lome Convention was the failure — especially in economic terms — of the policy of non-involvement with Europe.

Guinea's rejection of Association under the Treaty of Rome derived mainly from its bad relations with France. President Sekou Toure and President de Gaulle's relations were acrimonious both personally and politically.[44] French aid was cut off after independence and, in a representative gesture, France alone failed to support Guinea's membership of the UN.

In addition to its stormy relations with France, Guinea had many disputes with its African neighbours. The Ivory Coast, for instance, was frequently accused of supporting anti-government elements.[45] Relations with Ghana were broken after the fall of Nkrumah in 1966, and not restored until the 1970s. Although in practice relations with neighbouring states were often strained, Sekou Toure maintained an idealistic fervour for pan-African unity. 'Unions' between Guinea and Ghana, then Mali were negotiated but never realized. When Sekou Toure spoke of the Africa which he conceived of as one country and one nation, he referred not to individual states, but to 'the Congolese part of the African continent'.[46] This desire for African solidarity was important for Guinea, as it was for Nigeria, in choosing to join an expanded Association.

After its rejection of the French Community, in the late 1950s and early 1960s Guinea looked to the Soviet Union for help. However, Guinea discovered that Soviet aid was not efficient or well-adapted to Guinea. In 1961, for example, the USSR delivered two snowploughs to this tropical country. Discontent with Soviet aid and policies led to the expulsion of the Soviet Ambassador in 1961, and since then Guinea received a steady supply of US aid. Guinea maintained good relations with socialist countries such as North Korea and Rumania, but it avoided depending solely on either the West or East for aid. It tried to keep one foot in each camp. According to President Sekou Toure in 1979, Guinea's constant policy was one of socialism internally and externally 'total independence and non-alignment'.[47]

As demonstrated by its willingness to criticize the Soviet Union, its acceptance of US aid, its unwillingness to grant the Soviets a naval base, and its subsequent 'opening' to Europe and beyond, Guinea pursued an independent foreign policy. The major change which led to the 'overture' of Guinea to Europe and its African neighbours began in the early 1970s. Guinea, potentially rich agriculturally, had become dependent on importing food. Well-endowed with bauxite and iron ore, only the latter was being successfully exploited (with help from the US and USSR). Heavy investment in the mining sector left little capital available for industrial development.

Guinea's per capita GNP of $90 in 1971 and $130 in 1975 meant that Guinea was (and remains) one of the world's least developed countries, despite its potential wealth.[48] The poor performance of Guinea's economy can be seen in comparison with the neighbouring countries of Senegal and Ivory Coast which followed liberal economic policies. By 1971 these countries had per capita GNPs of $250 and $330 respectively; and in 1979 the figures were Guinea $230, Senegal $420 and Ivory Coast $710.[49]

Although Guinea's economic performance was extremely disappointing, there were successes in other fields. Despite a turbulent political life laden with plots* — some more plausible than others — Guinea

---

* These ranged from the 'Teachers' Plot' of the early 1960s, attributed fantastically to East Germany, Moscow, the Vatican and the editor of the *Financial Times*, to the unsuccessful 1970 Portuguese-backed invasion of Conakry.

maintained its independence and a stable internal political system. The one-party system of the Guinean Democratic Party (PDG) led by Sekou Toure did not tolerate opponents and Guinea's record on human rights was poor.[50] Nevertheless, Sekou Toure's one-man rule (he was consistently elected President with 95 to 100 per cent of votes cast) preserved Guinea from the political convulsions experienced by states such as Ghana. In addition, the Popular and Revolutionary Republic of Guinea progressed in terms of literacy and education.[51]

Recognizing that Guinea's estrangement from Europe and neighbouring countries had contributed to an unsatisfactory economic situation of low productivity, high foreign debt and balance of payments difficulties, Sekou Toure began a series of rapprochements in the early 1970s. By 1972, relations with the Ivory Coast and Ghana had improved and by 1973 interest was shown in the Lome Convention.[52] In 1975 Guinea joined Lome and then the West African Community (ECOWAS).

Political changes in France such as the election of Giscard d'Estaing in 1974 and the resignation of de Gaulle's foreign policy advisor M. Foccart (whom Sekou Toure particularly disliked) facilitated reconciliation with France.[53] Relations with both Germany and France were restored in 1975. Guinea was interested in the Lome Convention even before it renewed diplomatic relations with France (broken since 1969). Thus the Lome Convention's separate identity and appeal to African solidarity made it attractive to Guinea even when relations with France were strained.

Guinea's improved relations with France — exemplified by President Giscard's visit to Conakry in 1978 and the return visit of Sekou Toure to France in 1982 — enabled Guinea to exercise its new policy of rapprochement by joining the Lome Convention. Without at least formal diplomatic relations with France, Guinea could not have become party to the Convention.

Guinea's new openness to international contacts extended beyond its traditional relations with Africa and Europe. In the 1970s President Sekou Toure's new-found Islamic fervour helped to secure aid from the Arabs. From 1973 to 1980 Guinea received more Arab aid than any other sub-Saharan African state.[54] Guinea's outward-looking policy continued with its accession to Lome II in 1979 and to the Mano River Union in 1980.

In summary, Guinea's accession to the Lome Convention was substantially motivated by the desire for economic benefits. Under Lome I (1976–80) Guinea received 64 million Ecu from the EDF and 9.7 million Ecu as emergency aid. Under Lome II Guinea was allocated 74 million Ecu, and it actively lobbied for support for its industrial development.[55] In addition to its financial benefits, the Convention's appeal to African solidarity was a characteristic extremely attractive to Guinea.

The changes which appeared to make the new Convention a break from the past made it easier for Guinea to join without seeming to reverse its long-standing rejection of Association. Thus, Guinea could join the new Convention and maintain that it was still following its policy of non-alignment.

President Ahmed Sekou Toure died in March 1984. The army regime which succeeded him almost immediately through a widely welcomed coup criticized his years of bloody internal repression, but praised his foreign policy.[56] The army regime continued his 'ouverture' towards the West, improving relations with governments and international organizations such as the World Bank.[57]

Many posthumous assessments of Sekou Toure applauded his uncompromising independence, even if its domestic results were poor. Sekou Toure's defiance of France and his refusal to accept a qualified independence, according to *West Africa*, earned him immortality.[58] The Nigerian Government praised the late president, saying that 'history will remember him as one who fought colonialism and liberated the spirit of the down-trodden and oppressed, not only in his own country, but everywhere'.[59]

The tragedy of Sekou Toure's regime, and of Guinea, was its failure to make the most of its economic potential and its failure to come to terms amicably with its internal critics and external relations. Sekou Toure's internal repression and external defiant independence were not completely separate: both reflected his intolerance towards adversaries. He rejected both internal criticism and external pressure.

The Guinean experiment was partially successful by showing that Guinea could exist as an autonomous state without French support. However, the political struggles and economic failure of the regime made the Guinean model one which other Africans did not copy.

By the end of his life in 1984, Sekou Toure was a tragic figure of classical proportions. His uncompromising love of Africa marked him as an heroic figure, but his hubris brought about the tragedy of underdevelopment and repression for Guinea, and after his death, the overthrow of his regime.

ACP—EEC negotiations

The ACP—EEC negotiations on the Lome Convention began in Brussels in July 1973. They continued intensively for 18 months, comprising 183 ACP—EEC negotiating sessions, 350 joint documents, and 453 ACP coordinating meetings.[60] The negotiators reached agreement shortly after the expiration of Yaounde II on 31 January 1975 (the date also set for the expiration of transitional measures for Commonwealth imports into the UK by the Treaty of Accession). However, even though Lome I was signed on 28 February 1975, it was not in force until April 1976, leaving a 15-month gap to be filled with transitional measures (the usual pattern of the Associations).

The most outstanding feature of the negotiations was the unity of the ACP. Nigeria's Federal Trade Commissioner Briggs remarked that the ACP were more united than the nine EEC countries.[61] ACP unity, reinforced by the assertiveness of the new Commonwealth members, allowed the ACP to extract some concessions. ACP unity, particularly when it encountered divisions among the EEC states, enabled the ACP to negotiate more forcefully and successfully than the Yaounde countries had done. In this sense, the Lome negotiations were the first 'real' negotiations between the EEC and the developing countries.[62]

The Community entered the negotiations knowing that the ACP could not force it to concede more than it wished. In the negotiations the EEC set the parameters. This process was described by the Chairman of the Council of Ministers at the time, Dr G. FitzGerald:

> I certainly think that they got a remarkable number of concessions from the Community during the negotiations; I think they have every reason to be satisfied with it. And on our side, I don't think anybody feels that we gave too much.[63]

Although the ACP benefited from their unity and determination, problems remained. They lacked the experience and technical expertise of the Community. The ACP could request agencies such as the Commonwealth Secretariat for technical assistance, but the ACP's own secretariat was not as well-developed or well-financed as the EEC institutions. Another difficulty was the introduction of non-francophone Associates. Unlike the EEC, the ACP sensibly decided to have just two working languages — English and French. But the introduction of English added to the ACP's burdens. In one high-level ACP–EEC meeting it was decided to dispense with interpreters, and considerable confusion resulted.[64]

By mid-1974 the negotiations were bogged down and reference to ministers was necessary. The ACP instigated the Kingston Conference of ministers in July 1974 — referred to by the EEC's Development Commissioner as 'the outstanding occasion of the negotiations'.[65] Despite the initial climate of confusion and the critical treatment by the Jamaican press, the Kingston Conference helped to resolve some of the negotiators' problems and gave impetus to the negotiating process. The major subjects under negotiation were trade, aid, industrial co-operation, and institutions.

Trade

Trade issues included reciprocal preferences, free entry for ACP goods into European markets, the stabilization of export earnings (STABEX), and the Sugar Protocol.

Reciprocal preferences   Reciprocal preferences were incorporated in the two Yaounde Conventions and the Arusha and Lagos agreements. To France and some African states, reciprocal trade obligations meant that Association was based on equality. Each side had both responsibilities and benefits. But from the point of view of the Commonwealth, reciprocal preferences were unjustified; the ACP should not give special treatment to goods from the developed countries of the Community.

At the Abidjan meeting of May 1973 the ACP agreed to seek non-reciprocal preferences in the new Convention. Some Europeans felt that GATT rules required reciprocal preferences.[66] The ACP argued that arrangements such as the generalized system of preferences which offered non-reciprocal preferences to all less-developed countries meant that non-reciprocal preferences were justifiable under GATT. At the Kingston meeting, the inclusion of non-reciprocal preferences in the Lome Convention was accepted.

A number of reasons why the Europeans' accepted the ACP case that reciprocal preferences meant they could not buy in the cheapest market, as they needed to, can be adduced. First, since the old reciprocal preferences had not been strictly applied — and in some case, for example, Togo and Zaire, had not been applied at all — their loss was not significant. European exports would still be granted most favoured nation status. EEC trade with the ACP was relatively small and any loss of preference would be unlikely to disrupt traditional trade patterns or reduce EEC export earnings unduly. In addition, the United States disliked reciprocal preferences between Europe and Africa, considering they harmed prospects for US exports.[67]

Free entry   Another trade issue was the access of ACP goods to the Community market. The ACP wanted free access to the EEC for all their products. They did not achieve this, but they got some concessions.

According to the European Commission's calculations, 99.2 per cent of ACP-originating imports would enter the EEC free of duty or other restrictions under Lome, and the rest, mostly products covered by the Common Agricultural Policy (CAP), would receive preferential treatment over third country goods.[68] Although the ACP wanted free entry for all agricultural products, the Community refused this for agricultural products covered by the CAP. The EEC also refused to eliminate non-tariff barriers such as quality and health regulations on the grounds that these were the prerogative of individual member states. The ACP obtained the concession of being treated as one unit for purposes of originating status (that is, processing could take place in more than one ACP state), and the percentage of value added needed for originating status for several product categories was dropped from 50 per cent to 25 per cent (although a large number of processes were excluded from conferring originating status).[69]

Stabilization of export earnings According to Commissioner Cheysson, the stabilization of export earnings system (STABEX) was something completely new.[70] Now that the preferences granted under the old Association had been eroded and shown to be ineffective in overcoming the Associates' economic problems and promoting their economic progress, in M. Cheysson's view it was STABEX which was to take over this role.[71]

But like the Lome Convention itself, STABEX was not completely new. The STABEX provisions which were designed to help the ACP stabilize their earnings from primary and semi-processed exports to the EEC were the result of long-standing international, especially British and French, concern with commodity prices. After World War Two the United Nations Food and Agriculture Organization (FAO) and the never-established International Trade Organization (ITO) favoured individual commodity agreements between producer and consumer states to stabilize prices. International agreements on commodities were made as long ago as the 1903 International Sugar Agreement; but it was after the Second World War that commodity agreements proliferated.[72] International commodity agreements for tin, coffee, wheat, cocoa, olive oil and sugar were established, but failed to stabilize prices or solve the problems of developing countries' fluctuating export earnings.

The first two Associations abolished the French preferences for the AAMS and replaced them with aid to production and diversification. But the Associates' economies needed more help and Article 20 of the Second Yaounde Convention established a reserve fund of up to 80 million u.a. to cope with exceptional difficulties such as a fall in commodity prices. Article 21 authorized aid to be given to the stabilization funds of the AAMS to help control commodity price fluctuations.

Both the Associates and the Community felt that the Yaounde II provisions were inadequate to stabilize commodity prices and export earnings. The funds were insufficient and the rules for disbursement were unclear.[73]

Protocol 22 of the Treaty of Brussels undertook to protect the interests of states 'whose economies depend to a considerable extent on the export of primary products, and particularly of sugar'. The system which the Community proposed to include in the new Convention to improve the provisions of Yaounde II and fulfil this commitment was set forward in the Memorandum of the Commission to the Council of April 1973 (Deniau Memorandum).[74]

The system proposed in the Deniau Memorandum formed the basis of STABEX in the Lome Convention. The stabilization of export earnings system was designed: not to interfere with market forces; not to create obstacles to international trade; and to be compatible with existing and future international commodity agreements. Thus, like the Yaounde II provisions, it was to be supplementary – compensating for the effects of market forces rather than restructuring the market. The principal features proposed by the Deniau Memorandum and incorporated into Lome were:

1. A system which would stabilize the export receipts of the Associates from exports to the European Community derived from certain primary products.
2. Credits given to stabilize export earnings would be repayable when receipts rose, except in the case of the least-developed countries.
3. Special provisions would be made for sugar.
4. Funds for the system would be separate from other funds.

Under the Deniau proposal, the transfer of funds to stabilize an ACP country's export earnings was to be largely automatic once the conditions for the transfer were met. In the Lome Convention, by contrast, the transfer of funds was discretionary. Once the appropriate conditions were met by an ACP country – experiencing a drop of at least 7.5 per cent (2.5 per cent for the least developed) in its export earnings from a covered commodity – the ACP state would request a transfer.[75] However, for several reasons, such as lack of funds or questionable ACP government economic policies, the transfer could be reduced or cancelled.

Another change in the Lome Convention from the Deniau proposals was the supervision of STABEX payments. The Deniau proposal called for strict controls over how STABEX funds were spent. But the ACP resisted this and under Lome, although the recipient was supposed to tell the Community how the funds were spent, in practical terms there was no control over their use.

The STABEX system of the Lome Convention borrowed heavily from the experience of Yaounde II. It learned from Yaounde II's shortcomings in that the rules for STABEX were set out more precisely. It also avoided Yaounde II's problem of funds for earnings stabilization which were callable when needed from the general funds of the EDF;

STABEX funds were a separate part of the EDF. This reduced uncertainty over the amounts available. STABEX also followed Yaounde II in being a reserve fund and being discretionary rather than automatic.

As well as the lessons of Yaounde, two other influences worked on STABEX. The first was the Compensatory Financing Facility (CFF) of the International Monetary Fund (IMF). The CFF, established in 1963 to stabilize the export earnings of developing countries, was the first such fund.[76] It disbursed monies based upon a total decline in export earnings for a country rather than a decline for specified commodities. Disbursements were in the form of repayable low-interest loans (rather than STABEX's interest-free loans and grants), and beneficiaries had to undertake measures to improve their financial situation. Thus, the terms of CFF loans were more comprehensive — covering more countries and earnings from all exports — and stricter than STABEX. (See Table 3.2.) The CFF disposed of much more money than did STABEX; in 1980 its disbursements were roughly ten times greater than STABEX's.[77]

Although some officials of the EEC's Directorate-General VIII denied that the CFF had any influence on the development of STABEX, this was unlikely. The two organizations, the European Community and the International Monetary Fund, kept close contacts: staff moved from one organization to the other, and regular working relations existed.[78] The two systems — STABEX and the CFF — had different conditions and different (but overlapping) beneficiaries, but in their objective of helping ldcs in temporary difficulties owing to commodity price and export earnings fluctuations without re-shaping international markets, they were the same. Although the European Commission recognized that STABEX and the CFF were similar, the Commission stressed the importance of STABEX as a model and a 'major innovation in international economic relations'.[79] Thus, EEC officials resisted acknowledging their debt to the IMF to underline the success and newness of STABEX and to avoid unflattering comparisons of scale. The systems are compared in Table 3.2.

The second influence on STABEX, the New International Economic Order (NIEO) proposals, appealed more to the ACP than the EEC. The Commission emphasized that STABEX was proposed in April 1973, six months before the oil crisis directed attention to the NIEO: 'So STABEX was not produced in reaction to the new international situation, but was an offer made by the Community quite independently of these developments on the world scene.'[80] Although calls for a New International Economic Order date back to the first UNCTAD session in 1964, nevertheless it was true that the proposals for STABEX preceded the oil crisis and resulting specific NIEO programme.[81]

Table 3.2 Main differences between CFF and STABEX

	CFF	STABEX
1. Coverage	Total merchandise exports to all destinations; possibility to include earnings from tourism and worker's remittances.	Limited list of specific commodities and some of their processed products, taken individually, exported to EEC.
	All members, in particular primary product exporting countries and developing countries.	ACP states.
2. Estimation of shortfall	Five-year moving geometric average centered on the shortfall year minus earnings in the shortfall year.	Four-year moving arithmetic average of the years preceding the year of application minus earnings in the shortfall year.
The shortfall year	'year' may be any 12 months' period.	'year' is calendar year.
3. Limitations	One quota limitation.	———
	———	Fixed annual instalments.
4. Conditions	The shortfall must be of a short-term character.	———
	The shortfall must be largely beyond the control of the member.	Clause referring to changes in the structure of total export earnings.
	The member must have a need to draw.	———
	The member must cooperate with the Fund.	———
	———	Two thresholds must be fulfilled.
5. Repayment	Drawings have to be repaid within a period not exceeding three to five years.	For least-developed countries, transfers take the form of grants; in the other cases, repayment is linked to economic recovery of the product which suffered from a shortfall.
6. Charges	Drawings bear interest.	Transfers given to other than least-developed ACP states bear no interest.

Source: Comprehensive Report, Annex III.B, see note 78.

The United Nations General Assembly Resolution 3202 (S-VI) for a 'Programme of Action on the Establishment of a New International Economic Order' was passed in May 1974, before the Kingston Conference of the Lome negotiations. Thus, the negotiations for the Lome Convention took place contemporaneously with the proposals for the NIEO.

The NIEO 'Programme of Action' for raw materials was:

1   To facilitate the aims and functioning of commodity producers' organizations.
2   To work for a link between the prices of exports from developing countries and the prices of their imports from developed countries.
3   To reverse the trend of stagnation or decline in the prices of several primary commodities exported by developing countries.
4   To expand the markets for natural products vis-a-vis synthetics.
5   To promote the processing of raw materials in the producer developing countries.

Of these objectives, (2), to index-link the prices of imports and exports of developing countries, was of particular interest to the ACP. However, the EEC was not prepared to undertake this. The other objectives were not catered for in the Lome Convention although the extension of STABEX to cover some semi-processed raw materials such as roasted coffee to some extent furthered objective (5).

The Lome Convention often used the language of the NIEO in a slightly modified way. The preamble to Lome called for 'a more just and more balanced economic order' and another EEC document for 'a fairer world economic order'.[82] But the Lome Convention did not specifically refer to the New International Economic Order endorsed by the UN, while it appeared to call for the same thing. Instead of creating a new economic order, Lome was an elaboration of the old order.

The Lome negotiations addressed the underlying concerns of the NIEO — the problems of developing economies — but dealt with them in a limited way, governed by the past experience of the Association. The NIEO's call for greater cooperation among developing countries at regional, sub-regional and inter-regional levels also influenced Lome.

In terms of STABEX, the ACP succeeded in getting the original eight products (including sugar) designated for coverage by the EEC extended to twelve product groups, including iron ore, whose insertion the Community long but unsuccessfully resisted.* However, the

---

* First proposed were: sugar, groundnuts, groundnut oil, cotton, cocoa, coffee, bananas and copper. Lome covered: products of groundnut, cocoa, coffee, cotton, coconut, palm, palm nut and kernel; raw hides and leather, wood products, bananas, tea, sisal and iron ore.

determination of the EEC to stick closely to its original offer on STABEX was fully manifested in its refusal for STABEX to operate without a fixed financial ceiling, and its refusal to increase the 375 million u.a. allocated for STABEX over the life of the Lome Convention. (This was a more than four-fold increase over the 80 million u.a. callable under Yaounde II, but was still inadequate in view of the magnitude of the problem.)

Sugar Title II of the Lome Convention, 'Export Earnings from Commodities', had two divisions — STABEX and sugar. Sugar was an issue of crucial importance to the UK and Commonwealth: without the EEC's agreement to make adequate arrangements for Commonwealth sugar producers, the UK might well not have joined the Community. The significance of sugar was apparent from the early interest the UK showed in the arrangements for Commonwealth sugar exporters after UK accession to the EEC, and in the UK's efforts to consult sugar-exporting countries. The 1971 White Paper, 'The United Kingdom and the European Communities', stressed the UK's concern to 'safeguard the interests of the developing countries concerned whose economies depend to a large extent on the export of primary products and in particular of sugar'. In June 1971, the UK consulted 13 Commonwealth sugar producers (Antigua, Barbados, Fiji, Guyana, Trinidad and Tobago, India,* Jamaica, Kenya, Mauritius, Swaziland, Uganda, St Kitts-Nevis-Anguilla, British Honduras). They agreed to the plan to offer them Association or a trade agreement after Britain joined the Community. According to the White Paper, 'The British Delegation assured other delegates that the Community's proposals constituted a specific and moral commitment.'

The terminology of the White Paper was repeated in Protocol 22 to the Brussels Treaty which again promised to protect the interests of sugar-dependent economies. The Deniau Memorandum too mentioned sugar as a commodity whose export earnings should be stabilized. However, it recognized that special arrangements might be needed for sugar owing to the Commonwealth Sugar Agreement, the requirements of the forthcoming Common Agricultural Policy, and the International Sugar Agreement.

In the end, sugar was not included in the export earnings stabilization system (STABEX). Instead, the Sugar Protocol to the Lome Convention provided for the Community:

> to purchase and import, at guaranteed prices, specific quantities of cane sugar, raw or white, which originate in the ACP States and which these States undertake to deliver to it.[83]

* India was given a quota for sugar exports to the EEC outside the Lome Sugar Protocol.

Thus, the sugar provisions took the form of a supply contract, with the EEC agreeing to buy and the ACP to sell specific quantities of sugar at prices 'negotiated annually, within the price range obtaining in the Community'.[84] Each ACP State had to deliver its sugar quota every year or risk the reduction of its quota. In this way the EEC was assured of stable supplies and the ACP were assured of a market.

The linking of the Community's internal sugar price to the price paid to the ACP was meant to facilitate what the Sugar Protocol called 'the common organization of the sugar market'. The Sugar Protocol fell short of organizing the European and ACP sugar markets on the same basis, but like the Commonwealth Sugar Agreement before it, it gave the ACP 'some of the benefits of the organization of markets which all industrial countries find essential'.[85]

According to one observer, Lome's Sugar Protocol was 'revolutionary'.[86] True, the linkage between the prices of EEC beet and ACP cane sugar was new, but many aspects of the Protocol derived from the Commonwealth Sugar Agreement (CSA) first concluded in 1951.

Like the CSA, the Lome Sugar Protocol was concluded for an indefinite period. The Sugar Protocol, in fact, was more iron-clad than the Lome Convention. In the event that the Convention ceased to function, the Sugar Protocol provided that institutions should be established to continue the sugar regime.[87] The 'indefinite period' for which the Sugar Protocol was to operate was interpreted by the ACP to mean 'forever'.[88] Thus, the 'specific and moral' commitment to Europe to the sugar-producing states was so fundamental to them that it was guaranteed even more firmly than the Lome Convention. As the Fijian Ambassador said after the Lome negotiations: 'Fiji's main concern is sugar.'[89]

Like the CSA, the Sugar Protocol guaranteed the producers a market and an attractive price. (The ACP sugar producers continually complained that the price they received did not cover the costs of production or counteract their deteriorating terms of trade, but the Community sugar price usually exceeded the volatile world price and the ACP were keen to maintain the Protocol.) The Sugar Protocol's guarantee of a sugar supply for Europe had also been a major concern of those who negotiated the CSA after the disruption of the world sugar market by World War Two.

The Commonwealth Sugar Agreement, in its indefinite duration and guaranteed purchase of sugar served as a model for the Lome Protocol, but two other influences on the sugar market were also important. The Common Agricultural Policy was at odds with the sugar provisions of the Lome Convention. *The Economist* reckoned that although before the accession of the UK to the EEC and the association of the Commonwealth sugar producers the Community already produced a million tons more sugar than it consumed per year, the EEC could hold down internal production and take over the 1.4 million metric tons imported under the CSA. 'It is, in fact, unlikely that either Britain or France or Belgium are going to be allowed to raise their production between now and 1975, as so many critics of the Brussels agreement have said', it argued.[90] In fact, the critics were correct and the Community's increasing sugar production took it from being a net importer in 1975 to exporting 1.2 million tonnes in 1976 and 5.3 million tonnes in 1981. This was a source of great concern to sugar producers internationally, including the ACP.[91]

In April 1976, ten sugar-exporting countries complained that the EEC's policies contravened GATT regulations. Previously the GATT had found that the EEC's sugar export subsidies 'constituted a continuing threat'[92] to the market. According to sugar-exporting developing countries, the EEC's sugar exports were flooding the world market, depressing the sugar price, and gravely damaging their interests. The Community itself recognized the problems its policies caused for the world sugar market in two ways. First, the Community and the member states were aiding development projects designed to increase sugar production 'at a time when the world market is suffering from a serious excess of structural capacity resulting in the persistent depression of prices'.[93] In addition, the EEC's over-production, leading to the export of large tonnages of sugar, depressed sugar prices on the world market.

The other influence on the sugar market — the International Sugar Agreement — was also at odds with the Community's agricultural policy. Although the EEC considered joining the International Sugar Agreement (ISA) — a prospect favoured by the ACP — it did not join the Agreement which entered into force in 1978. The European Commission recognized that Community policy on exporting sugar was at odds with the ISA's attempt to stabilize world sugar prices by setting export quotas for its members.[94] The Community criticized the ISA's inability to control fluctuating sugar prices; but, the Community's own sugar policies were the major cause of this. As one ISA official observed, 'the biggest single factor prejudicing the operation of the agreement at present is the non-participation of the EEC'.[95]

In the Lome negotiations, an agreement on sugar was a crucial condition of British entry into the EEC and a *sine qua non* of ACP agreement to the Lome Convention.[96] This ACP stress on the Sugar Protocol was due to the high level of dependence of many ACP countries on sugar (which contributed up to 80 per cent of export earnings in countries such as Mauritius, and was the major employer in some countries). In addition, these sugar-exporting countries had been protected by the Commonwealth Sugar Agreement, which provided a system so that:

> Commonwealth sugar has been substantially sheltered from fluctuations of the free market, crises of foreign exchange earnings and depression of values in terms of purchasing power for most primary produce; wages, labour conditions, housing and social services have been greatly improved. This can be said of no other tropical commodity.[97]

In insisting on the Sugar Protocol, the Associables asked for what the existing Associates of the Community also wanted from the new Convention: the safeguarding of what had already been achieved in relations with Europe. The Community, too, recognized the principle that Lome had to offer at least the same level of benefits as the arrangements it replaced. Thus, whereas the AAMS had never been able to get their sugar freely admitted to the Community, the EEC accepted that it had to give the ACP arrangements for sugar roughly comparable to those they enjoyed under the CSA (which was allowed to lapse in 1974).[98]

Sugar was the last outstanding issue of the Lome negotiations. At the time of the negotiations in 1975, the world sugar price was higher than the internal EEC price. The ACP wanted a price for their sugar near the world price; the EEC offered the same price its own sugar beet producers received. Politically, the EEC could not pay ACP growers more than its own farmers for sugar. The Community also expected the world price to fall (as it did — from 60 cents per pound in 1975 to under 10 cents in 1977), making the EEC price more remunerative. The sugar producers finally accepted the EEC price in exchange for long-term guaranteed market access.

It may be asked why sugar was not included in STABEX as originally proposed in the Deniau Memorandum, as a simpler solution. The high sugar price of 1975 — likely to fluctuate violently — and the high dependence of sugar exporters on sugar would have made stabilizing sugar export earnings very expensive for the EEC. A sugar arrangement which guaranteed the Community's sugar supply at a time of relative world shortage seemed attractive: including sugar in the STABEX system would not have guaranteed supplies. The past success and popularity of the Commonwealth Sugar Agreement made it an attractive model. STABEX was a yet unproven. Following the example of the CSA seemed a more reliable and probably less expensive course.

Aid

Many ACP countries paid lip-service to the principle of 'trade not aid', of being given a fair chance to sell their products to the Community rather than being given hand-outs. Ambassador Jackman of Barbados expressed this principle: 'Nowhere is the truism "trade, not aid" more apt in the relations between North and South than in the Lome

Convention.'⁹⁹ But, in terms of the Lome negotiations, 'aid, then trade' was more apt. The ACP were interested in preserving and if possible increasing financial aid from the EEC. According to a senior ACP secretariat official, in the Lome Convention the ACP wanted to take the EEC 'to the cleaners': that is, to get as much aid as possible along with other benefits.

Although the ACP suggested a figure of 8,000 million u.a. to be disbursed by Lome over its five years of life, the EEC did not negotiate on the basis of this demand. Instead, at the Kingston Conference the Nine proposed to treble the funds offered under Yaounde II in accordance with the trebling of the ACP population since Yaounde I. The final agreement, reached after long negotiations ending on 1 February 1975, was more generous than the 2,700 million u.a. this formula produced.¹⁰⁰ Lome disposed of 3,390 million u.a. for the ACP plus 160 million u.a. for the dependencies (OCT).

Considering the disappointing economic and trade performance of the Associates, the aid provisions of the Convention were of crucial importance. David Wall reckoned that the inability of the EEC to provide substantial trade preferences for the ACP 'meant that the only meaningful form of compensation that any convention could offer would have to take the form of aid'.¹⁰¹ The EEC itself recognized its ambivalence towards increasing trade with developing countries:

> As for the Community, it has offered to open its frontiers to the industrial products of certain developing countries; but where, with Community assistance, a country has started exporting, limits have been placed on its market access.¹⁰²

Thus, the restrictions on trade in Lome made the aid content more important. The ACP's inability to achieve more than half their financial target for EDF IV was disappointing.

Although Lome I funds were increased by 269 per cent over Yaounde II funds while the recipients' populations increased by 243 per cent, the high level of inflation during this period meant that in real terms per capita aid fell by over 40 per cent in value. (But in nominal terms per capita aid rose from 11.83 to 12.75 u.a.)¹⁰³ The Lome Convention then, rather than being a vast improvement on the terms of Yaounde II, had difficulty in making its trade concessions worthwhile and keeping the real value of its aid constant. However, the ACP recognized that it was difficult for Europe to allocate large sums of aid during a time of recession.

The ACP were primarily interested in the amount of aid available in Lome, but they were also concerned with aid administration. The ACP, particularly Nigeria, wanted greater participation in the administration of EDF aid.

The aid chapter of the Lome Convention was entitled 'Financial and Technical Cooperation' (as it was in Yaounde II) to stress its collaborative nature. Emphasis was placed not on 'donors' and 'recipients' but on 'partners'. The European Commission was proud of its aid administration:

> The Lome Convention is several steps ahead of the usual methods of aid management. In some cases, responsibility falls solely on the recipient country and in others it is shared, but no other form of aid today involves such a degree of co-management.[104]

In fact, the Lome provisions fell far short of ACP aspirations to co-management of the aid programme. Nigeria's offer to become an aid donor rather than recipient and its request to participate in the administration of the European Development Fund were rejected by the EEC.[105] Whereas under the Lome Convention the ACP States were to cooperate closely in 'the aid programming, the submission and appraisal of projects, the preparation of financing decisions, execution of projects and final evaluation of the results' (Article 50), the final decision on projects rested with the EEC.

The ACP States were, in collaboration with the appropriate Community departments, to present financing proposals to the decision-making body, nominally the European Commission. But in practice the Commission deferred to the judgement of the EDF Committee. This committee was chaired by the Commission and composed of representatives of the member states of the EEC who voted on projects presented (votes were weighted in accordance with their contributions to the EDF). The project could be — if not approved — re-submitted, withdrawn or modified. Thus, although the ACP could select projects in keeping with their development priorities, the final decision rested with the member states of the Community.

A number of problems would have arisen from ACP participation in the EDF Committee. Dodoo and Kuster observed that the main concern of the EEC countries which had paid for the EDF was to keep control of how the funds were used.[106] If Nigeria had become an aid donor, this would have largely overcome this objection, but further difficulties existed.

Although the EDF Committee was supposed to evaluate projects on their financial and technical merits, political considerations did enter the discussions. A particular ACP country's attitude to the EEC, political pressures from outside as in the case of the Grenada airport project, representations from the EEC delegate or the ACP government, and the country's general economic performance could be considered in deciding whether or not to finance a project. Behind the closed doors of the EDF Committee, there was often a tendency for the former colonial power to lobby for the acceptance of projects for its former dependencies. It would have been difficult to include an ACP representative in such sensitive discussions.

Furthermore, if all 46 ACP states were represented, this would delay discussions. If only some ACP states were represented, this would be unequal representation compared to the European members. In addition, the concept of ACP solidarity would make it very difficult for any ACP country to oppose a project in another ACP country — no matter what its reservations about the project's viability.

The introduction of co-management of the EDF would have limited the discussion of a project's political ramifications to those issues acceptable to the ACP. Harsh technical criticism of projects would have been muted as the representatives of the EEC countries tried to avoid alienating a project's ACP originators. It would no longer have been possible to conceal which European countries had opposed a particular ACP project, thus leading to possible ill-feeling or retaliation.

Nevertheless, if it were possible to overcome substantial problems such as these, significant benefits for the Lome relationship would be gained. Achieving co-management of the EDF would be a breakthrough in aid financing, giving the ACP real participation in their own development. The EDF's version of 'co-management' did not allow more recipient decision-making than some Scandinavian bilateral programmes.[107] Achieving real co-management with the ACP of the European Development Fund would give substance to the EEC's claims of partnership. Thus, although the obstacles to co-management of the European Community's aid seemed insuperable, the benefits of creating a co-management system which would be a model for others to emulate would make the effort worthwhile.

In addition, co-management might improve the slow disbursement of EDF monies for projects — one of the most frequent and serious criticisms of the EDF. For example, in September 1979, six months before the expiration of Lome I, only 27 per cent of EDF IV had been disbursed.[108] EDF I was closed in 1980, 16 years after it was superseded by EDF II. Projects were being funded by the first three EDFs as well as the fourth during the operation of Lome I (see Table 3.3). Involving the countries waiting for their projects to be financed in aid management could markedly speed disbursement.

In the Lome Convention the EEC developed a loose system of consultation, not co-management. The Convention obliged the Community to consult the ACP in a variety of circumstances, for example whenever the Commission rejected a project (Article 54). Consultations were also prescribed, if an ACP state requested, for: any matter concerning the Sugar Protocol, any trade matter affecting their interests,

Table 3.3 Utilization of the first three EDFs (cumulative position 31.12.80) (millions of units of account)

Resources and utilization	1st EDF 1959–64	2nd EDF 1964–70	3rd EDF 1970–75	Total
A. Available resources:				
Initial Allocations	581.2	730.0	905.0	
Transfer of balances from EDF I	−12.2	12.2	–	
from EDF II	–	−8.1	–	
Miscellaneous non-allocated revenue		0.1		0.1
Total resources (a) available	569.0	734.2	913.1	2216.3
B. Utilization of funds:				
Global commitments (financing decisions)	569.0	733.2	900.3	2202.5
Final commitments (contracts concluded)	569.0	728.9	821.1	2119.0
Payments (b)				
C. Not yet paid at 31.12.1980 (a − b)	0.0	5.3	92.0	97.3
Not yet paid at 31.12.1979	1.0	8.0	111.0	120.0

Source: *Official Journal of the European Communities*, C244, 13.12.81.

any preferential agreement concluded by the EEC (Article 11). However, the term 'consultation' has been interpreted differently by the EEC and the ACP who were often not satisfied (under Lome I or II) that they were consulted rather than presented with *faits accomplis*. What constituted a 'consultation' — whether a letter, telephone call or series of meetings — was not specified in the Convention, allowing the EEC quite a lot of latitude in its obligation 'to inform and consult' the ACP.

Industrial cooperation

The EEC was somewhat more successful in achieving co-management of industrial cooperation. A programme for EEC–ACP industrial cooperation was set out in Title III of the Lome Convention. Part of the programme was the establishment of a Centre for Industrial Development (CID). The CID was supervised by a joint ACP—EEC committee and staffed by ACP and EEC officials. The Committee on Industrial Cooperation which supervised the CID was a sub-committee of the Joint Committee of Ambassadors and was composed of 17 ACP and 11 EEC members. The CID's director was assisted by an Advisory Council of 14 members, 8 appointed by the EEC and 6 by the ACP.

The director was appointed by the EEC and the deputy director by the ACP members of the Committee on Industrial Cooperation. 'This', observed a senior ACP official, 'reflects the EEC's concept of parity.'[109]*

The limited experiment in co-management in the CID was not followed elsewhere in the Lome Convention. Partly this reflected the unwieldy nature of the system established to run the CID. The Committee on Industrial Cooperation which supervised the centre had an overtly political composition and tended, to the discomfiture of the staff, to interfere with management decisions. (The political supervisors of the ACP secretariat were also over-involved in routine matters.) In addition, there was considerable distrust among the EEC member states of co-management. It was the relatively small importance of the CID, and of industrial cooperation, in the Lome Convention which made possible a degree of joint management.

The inclusion of a chapter on industrial cooperation in the Lome Convention was a step forward. The Focke Report considered that the objectives of industrial cooperation 'were one of the outstanding features of the Convention'.[110] Industrial cooperation was not based on the EEC's Deniau Memorandum, but stemmed from an ACP paper presented at the 1974 Kingston Conference.[111] Thus, industrial cooperation was important because it was an ACP initiative which seemed to have been embraced by the EEC.

Industrial development for the ldcs was a principal concern of the New International Economic Order. Although development specialists have been divided over the relative importance of industry and agriculture, developing countries generally accorded industrial development a higher priority. The importance of industrialization was reflected in the UNIDO (United Nations Industrial Development Organization) Lima Conference of March 1975 which set 25 per cent as a target for the ldcs' share of world industrial production by the year 2000. In the Lome Convention, it appeared that the EEC was establishing a model for North—South cooperation in this field. The chairman of the ACP Council of Ministers during the Lome negotiations, Babacar Ba, cited STABEX and industrial cooperation as the two most important provisions of the Convention.[112]

---

* The posts of director and deputy director were later rotated between EEC and ACP appointees.

Despite the hopes with which they were introduced, by the end of the Lome Convention it was almost universally acknowledged that the industrial cooperation provisions were a failure. The provisions were ambitious but vague. The name 'industrial cooperation' implied a broad area of EEC–ACP interaction, but it was only a small-scale programme with few results.

The industrial cooperation title of the Lome Convention called for the EEC and ACP to proceed hand in hand to accomplish the industrial development of the ACP, but it failed to provide a clear programme for this. According to Article 26 of the Convention, 'The Community and the ACP States, acknowledging the pressing need for the industrial development of the latter, agree to take all measures necessary to bring about effective industrial co-operation.' Specifically, the objectives were:

1 To promote the development and diversification of industry in the ACP states.
2 To promote EEC–ACP industrial and trade links.
3 To increase links between ACP industry and other sectors of the economy, notably agriculture.
4 To promote the transfer of technology to the ACP states.
5 To promote the marketing of the industrial products of the ACP states in order to increase their share of international trade in those products.
6 To encourage the participation of ACP nationals in the industrial development of their countries.
7 To encourage EEC firms to participate in the industrial development of the ACP states.

This wide range of objectives was to be met in two ways: through EDF and European Investment Bank-funded projects and through the newly established Centre for Industrial Development, a small organization with no investment funds of its own. Industrial development projects were therefore funded from EDF and EIB resources.

Under Lome I nearly 17 per cent of EDF IV was disbursed for industrial projects by the end of 1979 (about 168 million Ecu). (See Table 3.4.) However, this average industrial aid of 3.7 million Ecu for each of the 46 ACP countries was not sufficient to remedy their industrial underdevelopment. Twenty-four of the ACP were listed by the EEC as least developed. The majority of the 46 ACP countries were located in sub-Saharan Africa, the least industrially developed of all developing areas. (See Table 3.5.)

EEC aid alone was not enough to stimulate ACP industrial development. Furthermore, instead of undertaking 'all measures necessary' for industrial cooperation with the ACP, the EEC's protectionist policies

Table 3.4 Net sectoral disbursements of EDF IV (at the end of 1979)

	%
Transport and communications	14.0
Rural production	13.8
Education and training	3.5
Industrialization	16.9
Health and water supply	3.3
Misc.	18.8
STABEX	29.8
Total	100%

Source: House of Lords Select Committee Report, see note 10.

Table 3.5 Share of manufactures in exports 1978 (per cent)

Countries	sub-Saharan Africa	other ldc
Low income	5	14
Middle income	5	24

Source: Persaud, B., 'Industrial Cooperation in the Lome Convention', see note 117.

closed its markets to ACP manufactures. Although Title I of the Lome Convention promised that 'Products originating in the ACP States shall be imported into the Community free of customs duties and charges having equivalent effect', EEC non-tariff barriers such as quotas and health regulations hindered ACP exports. The 'rules of origin' requirement that manufactures had to have 25 per cent, 40 per cent or even 50 per cent of their value added (depending on the product) in the ACP also hampered ACP industrial development.

When a manufacture exported by the ACP increased its market share, as textiles did from 1975 to 1979, the EEC reacted with protectionist measures. In 1979, it imposed a quota on ACP textile exports.[113]

EEC concern to prevent free access to its market by low-priced manufactures was a constant theme of its relations with the developing world. Arnold Smith, Commonwealth Secretary-General until 1975, wrote that a French minister explained to him that the Asian Commonwealth countries were not to be offered Association with the EEC to prevent a flood of cheap imports. In other words, considered the Secretary-General, 'those countries that could take real advantage of the free entry into the EEC market that association involved were to be excluded from it'.[114]

Although she was unable to obtain comprehensive data for the ACP countries' manufactured exports, Carol Twitchett in a 1978 study of trade for the ACP Secretariat concluded:

> Industrial exports − defined as processed, semi-finished or manufactured products − remained marginal. Individual ACP States such as Ivory Coast, Kenya and Trinidad and Tobago successfully increased the share of their industrial exports going to the EEC, but their experience was not typical for the ACP as a group.[115]

From 1976, the first year of Lome I's operation, to the end of 1978, the ACP's share of manufactured goods in their exports to the EEC rose by only 0.6 per cent to 4.6 per cent. Thus, Lome's treatment of ACP industrial exports did little to alter ACP industrial backwardness.

In addition to the Community's half-hearted interest in ACP industrial development and the difficult economic circumstances of the middle and late 1970s, some of the ACP governments' own policies contributed to their poor economic growth. The European Commission was often frustrated by ACP governments' lack of ability to create an effective industrial development strategy. The Commission cited as reasons for the failure of development aid to produce significant results:

> administrative difficulties and the priority given to the Machinery of State, to the towns, to large-scale projects and to the elites trained in the North. Prisoners of the short-term, rare are the Governments which have succeeded in defining a policy and sticking to it.[116]

In the Lome negotiations it was proposed to insert an investment guarantee scheme for European companies to encourage them to invest in ACP projects. However, the ACP opposed this plan, fearing that it would restrict their ability to pursue their industrial policies and thereby undermine their sovereignty.[117] The ACP states' unwillingness to accept an investment guarantee scheme contributed to the declining rate of European investment in the ACP, particularly in minerals. Furthermore, the readiness of the EEC to close its markets once ACP industrial exports became competitive discouraged foreign investment in ACP industries.

In 1978, EEC Commissioner Cheysson acknowledged industrial cooperation in the Lome Convention was 'hollow', but maintained that just having a declaration of intent on industrial cooperation was significant:

> We have inscribed a principle in the Lome Convention, such that the European countries undertook to support the efforts for industrialization of their partners: a very beautiful declaration! When it had been made, we, in any case I, underlined that it was a hollow declaration; we didn't know what it meant. Because no one ever, in the history of the world, engaged in a systematic effort to support the industrialization of a partner whose economic, social and political structures are totally different. No one has ever done it but the declaration is there.[118]

In the wake of considerable criticism of the functioning of industrial cooperation in Lome, notably in the Focke Report and the 1980 Report on the ACP–EEC Council of Ministers, the European Commission retreated from even Claude Cheysson's qualified optimism. In 1980 the EEC Director General Klaus Meyer wrote that the Convention contained ambitious objectives for industrial cooperation, but the underdevelopment of the ACP states made the provisions 'more of a long-term target programme'.[119]

Industrial cooperation in the Convention remained at the declaratory level. Instead of encouraging potentially viable ACP industries such as textiles, the Community protected its markets against them. It used quotas on processed goods such as rum and refined sugar and applied restrictive rules of origin to protect European producers. By inserting an industrial cooperation chapter in the Lome Convention, the Community appeared sympathetic to ACP aspirations. But it failed to provide means or structures to achieve the objectives of the chapter. As the ACP ministers noted at the end of Lome I, 'the Community has not established a precise and meaningful policy on industrial cooperation with developing countries such as the ACP States'.[120]

The reasons for the failure of ACP–EEC industrial cooperation fall into four main categories:

1. Lack of political will for cooperation, and protectionism on the part of the Community
2. Insufficiency of funds and instruments provided by the Lome Convention
3. Lack of coherent ACP industrial development strategies
4. As the EEC was fond of emphasizing, the problems and magnitude of the undertaking.

Centre for Industrial Development

The Centre for Industrial Development (CID), established under Article

36 of the Convention, was the only Lome institution specifically devoted to industrial cooperation. Yet the area of operations of the Centre, like its budget, was restricted. The Centre's role was to gather and disseminate industrial information; to carry out studies on industrial development opportunities in ACP states; to organize meetings between EEC and ACP firms, personnel, and financial institutions; and to identify opportunities for industrial training and research.

The CID commenced operations in January 1977 after a considerable delay. It was allocated a budget of 6.2 million Ecu for the following three years, or under 1 per cent of Lome's industrial cooperation funds, which was insufficient for any large-scale undertaking. With a full-time staff of 39, the CID was more comparable to a management consultancy firm than an international organization capable of promoting industrialization.

The 1980 Annual Report of the Centre for Industrial Development considered that its activities were 'modest':

> By the end of 1980, the Centre had made a total of 490 substantive interventions in furtherance of the industrial development of ACP States. These have resulted in 6 new enterprises which are now in production, another 5 enterprises under physical implementation, whilst 8 others have reached the stage of commitment by all parties to invest. With respect to existing industries, the Centre provided study assistance for the rehabilitation or expansion of 14 enterprises, and this resulted in the reactivation or expansion of 4 industries.[121]

The Centre also established a computerized 'Lome Industrial Development Information System' (LIDIS) to store and retrieve industrial information.

Problems of the Centre for Industrial Development included difficulties of communication with the European Development Fund and European Investment Bank, and over-supervision by the Committee on Industrial Cooperation. The Centre also felt limited by its lack of funds to invest in the projects it investigated. The resources of the CID were of most value to countries with the administrative and industrial infrastructure to make use of them. Thus, the industrial development role of the Centre was beneficial primarily to the richer ACP countries. Nevertheless, it was generally felt by the ACP that the CID could play a useful if limited role in industrial development.

The EEC believed that it would be too expensive to give the CID its own investment funds, and any viable projects it found could be financed through the EIB or EDF. Therefore, although the CID was established to further the industrial development of the ACP, the responsibility for funding their industrial development remained with the Community-managed EDF and EIB.

The institutions of the Lome Convention

Continuity and conservatism governed the Lome institutions. The Yaounde joint institutions — the Association Council, Association Committee, Parliamentary Conference and Court of Arbitration — were transposed into the Lome context to become the Council of Ministers, Committee of Ambassadors and Consultative Assembly. Only the Yaounde Court was replaced by informal disputes procedures in Lome because it had never been used.

With its Council of Ministers, Committee of Ambassadors and Assembly, the Lome Convention inherited a set of institutions more appropriate to a government than to an aid and trade agreement. Complaints about the effectiveness of the institutions and particularly the cost of the Consultative Assembly were made, but the Commission was proud of the joint institutions. Despite the fact that the institutions were little changed from Yaounde, the Commission's summary of the Lome provisions maintained:

> the institutional framework is appropriate and solid; here too there are new features. These institutions are on a joint basis, and they are formed in accordance with convention requirements and the importance the contracting parties attach to their cooperation.[122]

Although some EEC and ACP officials acknowledged shortcomings in the Convention's institutions, most academic observers of Lome devoted little attention to these. One American study merely echoed the Commission's view that the institutional framework of Lome was 'appropriate and solid'.[123]

ACP frustration in being unable to exact greater aid and trade concessions from the Lome institutions stemmed not mainly from European domination of the institutions, but from the fact that these institutions had limited powers under the Convention. As the institutions were composed on the basis of parity and required either the agreement of both the ACP and EEC (in the case of the Council of Ministers) or a majority (in the Consultative Assembly), the EEC could not carry out actions unilaterally. Equally, ACP initiatives required EEC agreement. This institutional structure, as well as the limited role of the institutions under the Convention, meant that the institutions were not a force for change in the relationship.

During the Lome negotiations, the Commonwealth Associables opposed the creation of a Parliamentary Assembly as in Yaounde I and II. The Commonwealth had no such body and it was felt to indicate undue political involvement with the EEC. A small change was effected whereby the Lome Consultative Assembly was 'composed on a basis of parity of members of the Assembly on the side of Community, and of the representatives designated by the ACP States on the other' (Article 80). Thus, the ACP States could send parliamentarians or any other persons to the Assembly.

This change served the interests of ACP states without parliaments. It preserved the institutional format of Yaounde, but allowed greater freedom to ACP governments in choosing their representatives. It also meant that there was less chance of the Assembly taking on a 'super-parliamentary' role.

A number of reasons for the continuity of the Lome institutional system, despite minor changes, can be adduced. The joint institutions were a source of pride to the Community as a sign of equal partnership with the ACP. The institutional pattern, tested under Yaounde I and II, had proved reliable. The continuity in institutions also pleased the AAMS states, who wanted to preserve their relations with the EEC under Lome.

The Lome institutions were largely parallel to those of the Community. The EEC equipped its Associates and then 'partners' with a modified version of its own structure. However, it may be wondered whether such a structure was appropriate to the Lome relationship. Given that the 46 ACP countries were unlikely to evolve into an ACP Economic Community, the institutions were inappropriate. The institutions of Lome reflected the legacy of the past and the influence of the EEC.

The contract

The most important Lome institution was the Convention itself. The importance of the Lome contract was not much analysed by academics, but it was occasionally expressed by former development Commissioner Cheysson. The Lome contract, signed by the EEC member states and Commission and by the ACP states, was the constitution of the EEC–ACP relationship.

A formal contract was in effect since the first Yaounde Convention of 1963. Prior to this, the Treaty of Rome between the EEC member states on behalf of themselves and their dependencies formed the basis of the Association (the Treaty of Rome continued to be the source of authority for EEC relations with the member states' remaining dependencies). The French Association and Community were also based on contracts.

The Lome contract was thought by the EEC to display: (1) equality between the EEC and ACP; (2) stability in the relationship; and, closely linked to stability, (3) political neutrality. Equality was said to derive from the fact that the Convention was freely negotiated and signed by equal, sovereign states.

Nevertheless, the idea of an international contract was derived from European rather than African sources. In the long history of contracts between Europeans and indigenous peoples, the Lome Convention was one of the more equal. However, although the contractual arrangement had its benefits, it was based on a European concept of contractual law rather than African customary law.[124] Thus, the 'constitution' of Lome, like the rest of its institutions, followed a European model.

The stability of the Lome contract, the fact that the EEC's obligations under the Convention could not be disrupted by political events, was emphasized by Commissioner Cheysson in 1981:

> The obligations of Europe toward the Caribbean, obligations consecrated, I insist, by an international treaty so that whatever political regimes are in place, there is an element of stability for the region.[125]

Thus, the Caribbean and other signatories could count on Lome aid despite any changes in regime. One measure of the success of the contract in assuring stability was the fact that although the Convention provided means for withdrawal, no state withdrew.

Despite the colonial associations of the Lome contract, it did help create a durable relationship. It is doubtful that the Commonwealth Associables in 1975 (although the Commonwealth was based on informal understandings) would have accepted anything less explicit than the Lome contract.

The political neutrality of the Lome Convention was said to rest in the fact that, through contractual obligation, the Convention removed decisions from the sphere of politics into the sphere of law. Commissioner Cheysson described the lack of political compulsion upon the ACP:

> On the other hand, once the treaty has been concluded, the other partner makes of it what he wishes: even if he is in difficulty with one or other of the European states, that doesn't entail the rupture of the contract. Thus, Ehtiopia broke off diplomatic relations with Germany without affecting its relations with Europe.[126]

However, in practice the administration of the contract was less neutral than this theory suggests. Distributing or withholding aid and admitting new members to the Convention, for instance, were sometimes politically motivated. Nevertheless, having a contract which dealt primarily with economic and trade matters reduced the appearance of politics. Referring to the obligations of the contract enabled the EEC better to resist political pressures, for example pressure from the US to halt aid to Grenada's airport. But the contract allowed politics on a more discreet level to continue.

The Council of Ministers

The Lome Council of Ministers was virtually identical in form and function to the Yaounde Association Council. Like the Association Council, the Lome Council of Ministers was composed on one side by ministers of the EEC states and members of the EEC Commission, and on the other by ministers of the ACP States. Again, like the Association Council, the presidency of the Council of Ministers rotated between the EEC and ACP and meetings were held once a year with extraordinary meetings when necessary.

The Lome Council of Ministers, with the power to take binding decisions, was based on the EEC's Council of Ministers. Like the EEC Council, the Lome Council was to take decisions not by majority vote, but by 'mutual agreement between the Community on one hand and the ACP states on the other' (Article 74). Thus, as mentioned earlier, this decision-making procedure meant that the Council could not take actions opposed by one side or the other.

In one area the express powers of the Council were increased. Article 74 of the Lome Convention allowed for discussions in the Council on technical and economic matters of mutual interest not directly related to the implementation of the Convention. Just as since 1969 the EEC Council of Ministers broadened its horizons with political cooperation — an informal arrangement for the Council of Ministers to discuss political matters of interest outside of the framework of the Treaty of Rome — the Lome Ministers likewise extended their functions. The Lome Council of March 1978, in its official communique, noted:

> the provisions adopted will enable the Council, by strengthening the role of the Committee of Ambassadors, to concentrate on fundamental political issues or questions which present special difficulties.[127]

Owing to its infrequency of meeting, the demands on the ministers' time which did not allow them to become expert in the workings of the Convention, and the difficulties of its internal decision-making, the Council was content to allow the Committee of Ambassadors to play a leading role in running the Convention and it usually adopted the recommendations the Ambassadors made.[128]

Committee of Ambassadors

Although the Committee of Ambassadors has been called a 'little-known institution', it was the most active and powerful of the joint bodies.[129] The Council of Ministers was the highest organ of the

Convention, but the ACP—EEC Ambassadors Committee, which met twice a year, was more in contact with the implementation of the Convention. Sub-committee and working party meetings took place virtually weekly.

The Committee of Ambassadors was modelled on the EEC's Committee of Permanent Representatives. The Committee of Permanent Representatives (COREPER) assisted the EEC Council of Ministers and was composed of the permanent representatives of the member states to the Community. Likewise, the Lome Committee of Ambassadors assisted the Council of Ministers of the Convention. However, the Committee of Ambassadors was criticized for having excessive influence in the Council of Ministers. The ACP Secretariat and the CID objected to the excessive interference of the ambassadors in their affairs. In the Joint Consultative Assembly, to which ACP governments could send either parliamentarians or representatives, ambassadors sometimes took on the role of representatives and were felt unduly to influence debates and decisions.

Critics of the Committee of Ambassadors suggested that ACP ambassadors accredited to the EEC had too little to do and therefore devoted themselves with excessive zeal to the Lome institutions. Although some ACP ambassadors were over-involved in the Convention, others — some of whom were accredited to a large number of governments — had little time to devote to the Convention. Some sub-committees of the ambassadors, such as the one supposed to oversee the joint publication of the ACP—EEC magazine *The Courier*, were virtually dormant.

The economic constraints which prevented ACP governments from posting ambassadors in individual European countries, and prevented them from sending parliamentarians to Consultative Assembly meetings, could not be easily solved. However, the Council of Ministers could have taken a more active role in the Convention and the ambassadors could have allowed more independence to the institutions they supervised. In the European Community, the Commission, Council and Parliament were independent institutions and this added to their strength. By contrast, the joint and ACP institutions were less independent and less respected than their EEC counterparts.

Consultative Assembly

The composition and powers of the Consultative Assembly of the Lome Convention were disposed of in one article of the Convention. The Assembly, composed on a basis of parity between EEC parliamentarians and ACP representatives, with roughly 200 members, met once a year and received an annual report from the Council of

Ministers. It could make resolutions but there were no provisions for these to be heeded by any other body.

Compared to the European Parliament, the Consultative Assembly was a poor relation. It lacked the prestige and legitimacy of being elected, and it had no powers such as the European Parliament had to reject budgets or dismiss officials. It is generally expected that the European Parliament will gain greater powers within the EEC; no comparable expectation exists for the Consultative Assembly. One EEC official concerned with the Assembly reckoned that there was 'no hope' of it ever achieving greater power. Power in the Lome Convention seemed certain to remain with the member governments rather than a supranational parliament. Since the Consultative Assembly had no legislative or administrative power, it might be asked what its purpose was. The Community's response to this was that the Assembly allowed EEC and ACP representatives to get to know each other and their problems. New ideas and resolutions could be generated. The Assembly also created a joint committee which energetically produced informative reports.

Support for the Assembly came largely from the French and francophone ACP. A senior British diplomat described the institution simply as a 'farce'. Some ACP officials too had doubts about the Assembly. One described it as an institution 'where the Europeans think they are training us in democracy'.

The size and complexity of the Consultative Assembly were ill-suited to its minimal powers. As a training ground for democracy, the Assembly was unsuccessful. Its role in producing reports and transmitting information could have been performed by a less elaborate body.

ECOSOC

A small, informal elaboration of the institutions took place under Lome I. Under the auspices of the Consultative Assembly, four meetings were organized between representatives of the economic and social groups of the EEC and ACP. Since 1977 such meetings had occurred regularly with the intention of 'establishing a dialogue between the various economic and social circles'.[130]

In the EEC system, the Economic and Social Committee (ECOSOC) was composed of representatives from different social sectors, such as unions and management. It gave its opinions to the Commission and Council on various matters, but its decisions had no binding authority. ECOSOC, based on a French tradition, was often criticized for having too little influence.

The small-scale consultations between ECOSOC, members of the

Lome Consultative Assembly and ACP social and economic groups were useful in making the Lome Convention better known. The establishment of the 'joint ECOSOC' showed that the Lome institutions could evolve in a modest way. However, such developments mirrored the Community, instead of coming from an independent spirit of innovation.

The European Development Fund

Although at one time establishing the European Development Fund as an entity with legal personality was mooted, this never occurred. Despite its impressive title, president and staff of experts, the EDF was not independent of the EEC's Development Directorate, DG-VIII. As one veteran Commission official described it: 'The European Development Fund is just a bank account of DG-VIII.' The EDF was managed by the European Commission rather than the officials who were nominally its own.

The first president of the EDF, Jacques Ferrandi, wanted to create an independent identity for the Fund and therefore clashed often with Development Commissioner Cheysson. M. Ferrandi eventually resigned and was replaced by a less forceful official.

Financial decisions of the Fund were made by the EDF Committee (composed of representatives of the EEC member states, usually civil servants), which was chaired by the Fund's president. Making the Fund independent of DG-VIII, or reducing the Commission's influence over it, might have reduced the influence of the EEC governments who were paying for the projects — something they would deem undesirable.

The ACP–EEC Council of Ministers Report for 1976–80 claimed: 'No one today doubts the advantages of the ACP–EEC ministerial dialogue or the satisfying balance which marks relations between the ACP–EEC institutions.'[131] However, it was clear that no satisfying balance, no efficient relation of structure to function existed.

Re-organizing the Lome institutions would have been a major undertaking, but it would also have been a source of strength in the ACP–EEC relationship. Desirable changes included improving the performance of the Council of Ministers, reducing the influence of the Ambassadors, enhancing the independence of the CID, and streamlining the Consultative Assembly. The Lome institutions more accurately reflected the structure of the European Community than the needs of the EurAfrican relationship and revealed the Convention as a 'prestige project' rather than a development-oriented one. They also demonstrated a lack of innovation at the heart of the Convention.

The new language

As mentioned in the introduction to this chapter, the Lome Convention introduced new terminology. Some old terminology was retired and some of the language of the New International Economic Order was borrowed. The new terminology was designed to satisfy ACP desires for a non-colonial Convention and for a greater role within it. Without the new language and the new image it helped create, it is doubtful whether the Commonwealth countries would have accepted the Convention.

Nevertheless, even the new-fashioned language of Lome was not completely new: much of it could be found in the Yaounde Convention and other international relationships. The new or newly emphasized terms — partnership, cooperation, equality — gave greater status to the ACP. The use of new language eliminated some of the colonial overtones of the EEC–ACP relationship, for example in the case of 'Association', and made it possible to present the Lome Convention as innovative or even revolutionary. The new language enhanced the position of the ACP in the Convention and the position of the Convention (now 'a model for relations between developed and developing States') in the eyes of the international community.

The new terminology in the Lome Convention, while improving the image of the EEC–ACP relationship, did not create a new policy. It increased expectations and increased disappointment when the Lome Convention, and later Lome II, failed to live up to words like 'partnership' and 'equality'. The Convention, with its new language, was more successful in creating expectations than fulfilling them.

The EEC enhanced the status of the ACP by changing the name of the treaty. The second Yaounde Convention was called a 'Convention of Association between the European Economic Community and the African and Malagasy States associated with that Community'. In the Lome Convention the ACP were given top billing in the 'ACP–EEC Convention of Lome'. The Lome Council of Ministers was likewise usually referred to by the EEC as the ACP–EEC Council of Ministers. The magazine published by the Community about the Convention was transformed from the *Courier de l'Association* (*Association News* in English) to the *ACP–EEC Courier*.

The Commonwealth Associables disliked both the names 'Association' and 'Yaounde Convention'. The name 'Yaounde' derived from the signing of the Convention in Yaounde, the capital of Cameroon, a former French colony. By moving the location of the signing to Lome, Togo, the EEC hoped to appeal to the non-francophone states. Although the name of the agreement was changed, both Conventions followed the custom of being named after the city in which they were signed.

'Association' was more difficult to replace. It was a cherished French theory of colonialism and, in the French Association, a predecessor of the Treaty of Rome Association. In addition, it had been widely used by the EEC in its external relations since 1957. As early as 1973, the Associable countries considered alternatives to the term 'Association'. The EEC's April 1973 Deniau Memorandum referred to the future 'Association' and 'Associates', but also mentioned the term 'partners', which replaced them.[132] However, the document's use of old terminology was seen by some Commonwealth states as a deficiency.[133]

Although the Commonwealth Associables disliked the term 'Association', the old Associates were not eager to change it.[134] The OAU's Secretary General proposed in mid-1973 that 'Association' should be replaced, but not until after a contentious meeting in Dakar in 1974 did the ACP agree to abandon it. The ACP were more successful in changing their name from Association to partnership than the Commonwealth was in escaping the name 'British Commonwealth', but 'Association' did sometimes still appear in connection with the Lome Convention, even in EEC publications.[135]

The term 'partnership' was adopted enthusiastically by some observers. Carol Twitchett, for instance, wrote: 'The EEC–ACP partnership represents a symbol of hope in a divided world.'[136] However, critics of the Lome Convention referred to the concept of partnership expressed by a British governor of Rhodesia in the 1950s. He considered partnership as the relationship between horse and rider.[137]

The vocabulary of political science contains many expressions for relations of inequality: colonialism, neo-colonialism, imperialism, dependency, etc. Terms which express equality are fewer, and these, like partnership, are subject to differing interpretations. 'Alliance', for example, suggests a political dimension ostensibly lacking in Lome. 'Friendship' is often employed in (unequal) treaties concluded by the Soviet Union. The term 'partnership' was used by US Vice-President Rockefeller in 1969 to indicate a change in the relations between the US and Latin America. No longer was there to be US dominance in the Alliance for Progress, but partnership.[138]

Lome, six years later, adopted 'partnership' to give a similar impression. The Commonwealth, too, has used the language of partnership.[139] Thus, partnership became an accepted part of the political vocabulary to indicate an equal, co-operative relationship between developed and developing countries. However, it is neither as a relationship of complete equality nor as the partnership of horse and rider that the Lome Convention can best be interpreted. The ACP did not have complete equality with the EEC, despite the declarations of Yaounde and Lome. But they did have more options, for example, to lobby the EEC or withdraw from the Convention, than did the proverbial horse. The

Lome Convention was a complex political phenomenon which owed its existence to the past and to Europe's commitment to having a sphere of influence in Africa. Although politically unacceptable in the mid-1970s, 'association', with its implications of continuity and inequality was more descriptive of Lome than 'partnership'.*

Legitimacy

From his comparative studies of political systems, Seymour Lipset concluded that stability in democratic systems depended on the 'believed-in title to rule' of their political elite. This legitimacy, he noted:

> has been most secure where the society could admit the lower strata to full citizenship and to the rights of participation in the economic and political systems, and could at the same time allow the traditionally privileged strata to keep their high status while yielding their power.[140]

Caution must be used in comparing inter-state and domestic politics, but clearly in the Lome Convention the reverse of the process described above occurred. That is, instead of yielding power in the Lome relationship, the EEC yielded its high status. The EEC admitted the ACP to 'complete equality' without admitting them to co-management of major institutions such as the EDF or to equal participation in the formulation of the Convention. This practice contributed to the legitimacy and longevity of the EurAfrican association, but if the ACP acquired more power through solidarity and economic or political leverage, Europe would have found it hard to satisfy them with concessions of status alone.

The legitimacy of the Lome Convention was both ascribed and instrumental. It rested on the inherent qualities of the relationship such as its historical legitimacy, its existence as a relationship 'en famille', its friendly cooperation and partnership. The Convention's legitimacy was also, particularly to the Commonwealth ACP and non-francophone European states, instrumental, that is, based on the concrete benefits it could deliver.

The new language of the Lome Convention was directed at the ascribed legitimacy of the relationship. New terminology could not alter the aid or trade statistics, but it added to the legitimacy of the Convention by enhancing its ascribed characteristics.

---

* Although 'Association' was more appropriate than 'partnership', it is argued in Chapter 7 that, taking into account developments since the first Association, the policy can be termed 'welfare neo-colonialism'.

Notes

1. 'The ACP–EEC Convention of Lome', (Preamble), *The Courier*, Brussels, EEC, March 1975, no. 31.
2. *ibid*.
3. *The Courier*, Brussels, EEC, March 1975, no. 31, pp. 12, 18, 19.
4. *European Community*, London, EEC, April 1975. Quotations from Ramphal, S. and Whiteman, K., pp. 8–9.
5. *Bulletin of the European Communities*, Brussels, EEC, no. 1, 1975, p. 6.
6. *ibid*.
7. *British Membership of the European Community*, London, HMSO, 1973; also, Broad, R. and Jarrett, R., *Community Europe Today*, London, Oswald Wolff, 1972.
8. Wall, David, *The European Community's Lome Convention*, London, Trade Policy Research Centre, 1975, p. 5.
9. Dodoo, C. and Kuster, R., 'The Road to Lome', in Alting von Geusau, F. (ed.), *The Lome Convention and a New International Economic Order*, Leyden, Sijthoff, 1977.
10. House of Lords, Select Committee on the European Communities, *Development Aid Policy*, London, HMSO, 1981.
11. Mazrui, Ali, *The Anglo-African Commonwealth*, Oxford, Pergamon, 1967, p. 74.
12. *West Africa*, 2 July 1973.
13. 'Treaty concerning the Accession of the Kingdom of Denmark, Ireland, the Kingdom of Norway and the United Kingdom of Great Britain and Northern Ireland to the European Economic Community and European Atomic Energy Community, Brussels, 22nd January, 1972', London, HMSO, Articles 109–115.
14. *ibid*, Protocol 23.
15. *ibid*, 'Joint Declaration of Intent on the Development of Trade Relations'.
16. Dodoo and Kuster, *op cit*, p. 29.
17. Frey-Wouters, Ellen, *The European Community and the Third World*, New York, Praeger, 1980, p. 28.
18. *West Africa*, 21 April 1972.
19. *Moniteur Africain*, Dakar, 3 May 1973.
20. *West Africa*, 21 April 1972, p. 1216.
21. *West Africa*, 5 March 1973, p. 298.
22. A view expressed by informed sources.
23. *West Africa*, 14 January 1974.
24. Mazrui, *op cit*, Ch. 4.
25. Olu Sanu, E., *The Lome Convention and the New International Economic Order*, Lagos, Nigerian Institute of International Affairs, 1977, pp. 8–9.
26. Olu Sanu, *op cit*, p. 5.
27. Pinder, John, 'The Community and the Developing Countries', *Journal of Common Market Studies*, 1973, no. 1.
28. Mazrui, *op cit*, Ch. 4.
29. *First General Report on the Activities of the Communities*, Brussels, EEC, 1958, p. 110.
30. Mazrui, *op cit*, Ch. 4.
31. Economic Department of the Standard Bank, 'Commonwealth Africa and the Enlarged European Community', *African Affairs*, October 1972.
32. Ghai, D.P., *Asian Commonwealth Countries and the EEC*, London, Commonwealth Secretariat, Commonwealth Economic Papers, no. 2, 1973.

33. Mazrui, *op cit*, Ch. 4.
34. Olu Sanu, *op cit*.
35. *ibid*, p. 14.
36. *Moniteur Africain*, Dakar, 22 March 1973.
37. Olu Sanu, *op cit*, p. 12.
38. *West Africa*, 23 July 1973, p. 993.
39. Dodoo and Kuster, *op cit*.
40. Frey-Wouters, *op cit*, p. 32.
41. Sekou Toure, Ahmed, 'The Republic of Guinea' (translated), *International Affairs*, April 1960, p. 171.
42. A Correspondent, 'Guinea After Five Years', *The World Today*, March 1964, p. 113.
43. 'La point economique sur la Guinée au debut de 1980', *Europe Outremer*, Paris, September 1979.
44. Chaffard, G., *Les Carnets Secrets de la Decolonisation*, Paris, Calmann-Levey, 1967, Partie II, p. 1, de Gaulle referred to 'Ce Sekou Toure, quel orgueilleux'.
45. Cowan, L., 'Guinea', in Carter, G. (ed.), *African One Party States*, Ithaca, New York, Cornell University Press, 1962.
46. A Correspondent, *op cit*, p. 119.
47. 'La point economique sur la Guinée au debut de 1980', *op cit*, p. 23.
48. *ACP States Yearbook*, (1980–81) Brussels, Editions Delta, 1981, and *The Convention of Lome: Analytical Sheets*, Brussels, Eurodelta, 1975.
49. *The Courier*, Special Issue, November 1979, no. 58.
50. *Amnesty International Report 1981*, London, Amnesty International Publications.
51. 'La point economique sur la Guinée au debut de 1980', *op cit*.
52. *West Africa*, 21 and 28 April 1972.
53. *Africa Confidential*, 19 August 1981.
54. 'La point economique sur la Guinée au debut de 1980', *op cit*.
55. *West Africa*, 22 March 1982.
56. *West Africa*, 9 April 1984, p. 756.
57. *West Africa*, 16 July 1984, p. 1442.
58. *West Africa*, 2 April 1984, p. 703.
59. *West Africa*, 9 April 1984, p. 787.
60. *The Courier*, March 1975, no. 31, p. 3.
61. *West Africa*, 17 June 1974, p. 741.
62. Green, R.H., 'The Child of Lome: Messiah, Monster or Mouse', in Long, F. (ed.), *The Political Economy of EEC–ACP Relations*, London, Pergamon, 1980.
63. *The Courier*, no. 31, *op cit*, p. 7.
64. *Marches tropicaux*, 9 August 1974.
65. *The Courier*, no. 31, *op cit*, p. 12.
66. *ibid*, p. 2.
67. Dodoo and Kuster, *op cit*, p. 40.
68. *The Courier*, no. 31, *op cit*, p. 23.
69. Wall, D., *op cit*.
70. Cheysson, Claude, 'Europe and the Third World After Lome', *The World Today*, June 1975.
71. *West Africa*, 4 February 1974.
72. Brown, W.A., *The United States and the Restoration of World Trade*, Brookings, Faber, 1950.
73. 'Memorandum of the Commission to the Council', April 1973, (Deniau Memorandum), Brussels, EEC, COM (73/500/fin).

74. *ibid.*
75. *Lome Convention*, Title II, Article 19, paragraph 2.
76. Persaud, B., 'Export Earnings Stabilization in the ACP–EEC Convention of Lome', in Long, F. (ed.), *op cit.*
77. *Africa's Economic Crisis*, Briefing Paper, London, Overseas Development Institute, September 1982.
78. *Comprehensive Report on Stabex 1975–9*, Brussels, EEC document (Sec81-1104), 1981, p. 76.
79. *ibid*, p. 74.
80. *ibid*, p. 8.
81. *UNCTAD Monthly Bulletin*, August–September 1982.
82. *Comprehensive Report on Stabex 1975–9*, *op cit*, p. 74.
83. *Lome Convention*, 'Sugar Protocol', Article 1.
84. *ibid*, Article 5.
85. Southgate, John, 'The Origin and Present Significance of the Commonwealth Sugar Agreement', *Commonwealth Sugar Exporters Annual Review*, 1972, p. 12.
86. Twitchett, C., *A Framework for Development: The EEC and the ACP*, London, Allen and Unwin, 1981, p. 44.
87. *Lome Convention*, 'Sugar Protocol', *op cit*, Article 8, paragraph 2.
88. Jackman, Oliver, 'The Sugar Protocol', *The Courier*, September–October 1982, p. 57.
89. Rabukawaga, J., quoted in *The Courier*, no. 31, *op cit*, p. 11.
90. *The Economist Newspaper*, (Knight, Andrew (ed.)), *Britain Into Europe*, London, 1971, (pamphlet), p. 21.
91. Hannah, A., 'The Functions of the International Sugar Organization', *The Courier*, September–October 1982.
92. 'EEC Faces New Sugar Protest', *Financial Times*, 6 April 1982.
93. 'Lack of Proper Coordination between the Policies of the Community and the Member States – the Case of Sugar', Brussels, EEC, COM (78)623 final, p. 2.
94. *ibid*, Annex III.
95. Hannah, A., *op cit*, p. 68.
96. Dodoo and Kuster, *op cit*, p. 17.
97. Southgate, *op cit*, p. 10.
98. Te Pass, A., 'From the Commonwealth Sugar Agreement to the Lome Sugar Protocol', *The Courier*, September–October 1975, no. 75.
99. Jackman, *op cit*, p. 59.
100. *Marches tropicaux*, 9 August 1974.
101. Wall, *op cit*, p. 7.
102. 'The Community's Development Policy to Date', *The Courier*, November–December 1982, no. 76, p. 66.
103. Dodoo and Kuster, *op cit*, p. 53.
104. *The Courier*, November–December 1982, no. 76, pp. 45–74.
105. Olu Sanu, *op cit.*
106. Dodoo and Kuster, *op cit.*
107. Hewitt, A., *The European Development Fund and its Function in the EEC's Development Aid Policy*, London, Overseas Development Institute, Working Paper no. 11, 1982.
108. Stevens, C. (ed.), *The EEC and the Third World: A Survey 1*, London, Hodder and Stoughton, 1981, p. 41.
109. Interview at the CID, Brussels.

110. Focke, Katarina, *From Lome 1 towards Lome 2*, text of the report and resolution adopted on 26 September 1980 by the ACP—EEC Consultative Assembly, 'Industrial Cooperation', (Focke Report).
111. Dodoo and Kuster, *op cit*.
112. *The Courier*, no. 31, *op cit*, p. 7.
113. Twitchett, C., *ACP Foreign Trade*, Brussels, ACP Group, 1978, p. 108.
114. Smith, Arnold, *Stitches in Time: the Commonwealth in World Politics*, London, Andre Deutsch, 1981, p. 185.
115. Twitchett, Carol, with Eston, Ann and Cable, Vincent, *ACP Foreign Trade*, Brussels, ACP Group, 1979, p. 103.
116. *Memorandum on the Community's Development Policy* (Pisani Memorandum), Brussels, EEC, 1982, COM 82 640 final, p. 19.
117. Persaud, B., 'Industrial Cooperation in the Lome Convention', in *The Recognition of the Lome Convention*, London, Catholic Institute for International Relations, 1978.
118. Cheysson, Claude, quoted in Hoyos, G., 'De Lome I a Lome II', *Afrique no. 1*, (Brussels), April, May, June 1981, p. 55.
119. *The Courier*, May—June 1980, no. 61, p. 11.
120. *Report of the ACP—EEC Council of Ministers 1976—1980*, Brussels, EEC, July 1980, p. 113.
121. *Annual Report of the Centre for Industrial Development*, Brussels, 1980, p. 3.
122. *The Courier*, no. 31, *op cit*, p. 37.
123. Frey-Wouters, *op cit*, p. 76.
124. Bozeman, A., *Conflict in Africa*, Princeton, Princeton University Press, 1976, Ch. 18.
125. *Le Monde*, 13 March 1983, p. 4.
126. *Jeune Afrique*, 6 August 1980, p. 54.
127. *The Courier*, May—June 1978, no. 49, pp. 8—10.
128. See also Jones, D., *Europe's Chosen Few*, London, Overseas Development Institute, 1973, for a critique of the Council.
129. *The Courier*, May—June 1978, no. 49.
130. *The Courier*, January—February 1980, no. 59, p. 36.
131. *Report of the ACP—EEC Council of Ministers 1976—80*, *op cit*, p. 166.
132. Deniau Memorandum, *op cit*, p. 32.
133. *West Africa*, 2 July 1973.
134. *West Africa*, 23 July 1973.
135. See *Europe 82*, December 1982, London, EEC, p. 9; also, *Commonwealth*, June 1983.
136. Twitchett, C., *Europe and Africa: From Association to Partnership*, Westmead, Saxon House, 1978, p. xv.
137. Achebe, Chinua, 'Viewpoint', *Times Literary Supplement*, 1 February 1980.
138. 'The Rockefeller Report on the Americas', New York, *New York Times*, 1969.
139. *Commonwealth Currents*, April 1982, (The Queen's Commonwealth Day Speech).
140. Lipset, S.M., *The First New Nation*, London, Heinemann, 1963, p. 290.

4 The results of the Lome Convention

As shown in Chapter 3, the Lome Convention excited many hopes about changing the structure of international economic relations. However, it was not equipped to make major changes in this area. The Lome Convention was a conservative agreement aimed at maintaining the preferences previously enjoyed by the AAMS and by the Commonwealth Associates. It bolstered the old, instead of creating a new, economic order.

Although Lome was disappointing in its trade results and in many of the development projects it financed, it was not completely unsuccessful. The Lome Convention failed to fulfil its objective of achieving complete equality between its European and developing participants and its objective of establishing a new model for North–South relations, but it did accomplish its primary, if unwritten objective: the continuation of the EurAfrican association.

Trade results

The trade preferences the EEC gave to the ACP were small: over three-quarters of ACP exports (which were mostly raw materials) would have entered the EEC duty-free even without Lome preferences.[1] Furthermore, more than 90 per cent of ACP industrial exports would have entered the EEC duty-free under GSP arrangements. Only seven of the twenty-five most important ACP exports received any preferences over other ldc suppliers.[2]

The Lome Convention's 'principle of free access to the Community market for products exported by the ACP States', except for products covered by the CAP or sensitive items such as textiles, did not establish a major protected market for the ACP. Rather, it allowed this group of largely poor and economically weak countries to compete with other developing countries for their share of the EEC market.

ACP export performance

Although many of the ACP and other observers of the Lome Convention were profoundly disappointed by the failure of the Convention to change traditional ACP–EEC trade patterns, the trade results of the Lome Convention were marginally positive. Despite the fall in the ACP share of extra-EEC imports from 1973 to 1979, during the period of operation of the Lome trade provisions — from 1976 to 1979 — the ACP share of extra-EEC imports rose by 0.2 per cent. Again, although from 1973 to 1979 the ACP's share of EEC imports compared with the shares of all developing countries fell, during the operation of the Lome Convention it rose by 2.6 per cent (Table 4.1).

ACP exports to the EEC increased by 41 per cent from 1976 to 1979, but this increase cannot be solely attributed to the new Lome trade provisions. Some effects of the new trade provisions were not fully experienced by 1979. Nevertheless, the aggregate results of the Lome trade regime were rather more encouraging than those for the previous Associations. Whereas the Yaounde Associates' exports to the EEC from 1959 to 1973 grew more slowly than those of other developing countries, from 1976 to 1979 under Lome the ACP increased their exports to the EEC faster than developing countries generally (41 per cent compared to 26 per cent).

This apparently improved export performance, however, largely reflected the strength of some Commonwealth ACP states and the increased price of crude oil. Two countries, Nigeria and Ivory Coast, accounted for 40 per cent of ACP exports. Twelve countries accounted for over three-quarters of ACP exports while 32 countries each accounted for less than 1 per cent of ACP exports (see Table 4.2).

In terms of products, ACP exports were heavily dependent on the export of a few commodities. Crude oil alone accounted for more than 25 per cent of all ACP exports. The first two ACP commodities exported to the EEC by value — oil and coffee — comprised 39.72 per cent of ACP exports; under the previous Associations the first two commodities in order of importance were copper and timber which accounted for 35.6 per cent of exports.[3] Thus, dependence on the export of a few commodities continued and even increased under Lome.

Table 4.1 Development of ACP–EEC trade (compared with the development of trade between the EEC and third countries and the EEC and developed countries) (1,000 million units of account)

	1973	1974	1975	1976	1977	1978	1979
Imports into EEC from developing countries	84.3	130.8	125.5	159.4	171.4	178.3	218.2
	31.9	61.4	55.0	70.0	75.2	71.2	88.2
= OPEC	15.3	38.9	33.4	41.8	42.3	38.2	51.9
= ACP	6.2	10.5	8.7	10.5	12.5	11.9	14.8
ACP annual growth	+28%	+70%	−17%	+20%	+19%	−5%	+24.4%
ACP share in extra-EEC imports	7.4%	8%	6.7%	6.6%	7.3%	6.7%	6.8%
ACP imports compared to imports from other ldcs	24.1%	20.6%	18.8%	17.6%	19.9%	20.1%	20.2%
EXPORTS from EEC to ldcs	80.7	114.2	121.2	141.3	164.1	173.8	194.2
	22.9	35.2	44.1	50.9	61.8	66.5	69.7
= OPEC	6.6	11.4	18.4	24.1	29.7	31.1	30.3
= ACP	4.4	6.1	8.1	9.8	12.5	12.7	11.8
ACP annual growth	+10%	+37%	+33%	+22%	+27%	+2%	+7.1%
ACP share in extra-EEC exports	5.5%	5.3%	6.7%	7%	7.6%	7.3%	6.1%
Trade balance — in ACP states' favour + in EEC's favour	−1.7	−4.4	−0.6	−0.6	0.0	+0.8	−3.0

Source: Report of the ACP–EEC Council of Ministers, 1976–1980, p. 27, see note 3.

One way in which ACP countries benefited from the Lome regime was in diversifying their exports among the EEC countries, thus somewhat reducing their dependence on one traditional market. Table 4.3 shows a decline in the percentage of ACP exports going to the UK, France, Denmark and Ireland from 1975 to 1979, with increases in the percentages to Belgium and Luxembourg, Germany, Italy and the Netherlands. Nevertheless, some ACP countries remained unhealthily dependent on one export market, for example, Niger sent 85 per cent of its exports to France and 91 per cent of those of Botswana went to the UK.[4]

Table 4.2 EEC imports from the ACP states: classification in descending order of average volume for 1976–8 (ten largest exporters)

	Total by country	% of country in total ACP imports	Cumulative percentage
1. Nigeria	3,356	28.9	
2. Ivory Coast	1,283	11.1	40.0
3. Zaire	1,032	8.9	48.9
4. Cameroon	492	4.2	53.1
5. Gabon	417	3.6	56.7
6. Ghana	403	3.5	60.2
7. Kenya	398	3.4	63.6
8. Zambia	390	3.3	66.9
9. Liberia	363	3.1	70.1
10. Senegal	297	2.6	72.7

Source: Report of the ACP–EEC Council of Ministers, 1976–80, p. 32, see note 4.

Table 4.3 EEC states' shares of ACP exports to the Community (per cent)

| | Exports | | |
	1970	1975	1979
Belgium-Luxembourg	10.4	6.8	10.0
Denmark	0.7	1.4	1.0
France	19.6	24.4	23.5
Germany	13.3	14.7	23.8
Ireland	0.2	0.3	0.1
Italy	10.6	8.0	9.7
Netherlands	12.8	16.1	16.4
UK	32.4	28.3	15.0
Hirschman* index of concentration	44.7	44.5	42.5

*Larger numbers indicate greater concentration

Source: Moss, J. and Ravenhill, J., 'Trade between the ACP and EEC during Lome I', in Stevens, C. (ed.), *EEC and the Third World: A Survey 3*, London, Hodder and Stoughton, 1983, p. 140.

Products receiving special treatment

Except for sugar, which constituted 3.39 per cent of ACP exports, the other products subject to special arrangements under Lome accounted for less than 1 per cent of ACP trade.[5] But these exports, such as sugar in the case of the Caribbean and beef in the case of Botswana, played an important role in some ACP economies.

Sugar The operation of the Sugar Protocol was not entirely satisfactory to the ACP. They complained about the annually set sugar price being offered to them on a take it or leave it basis rather than being genuinely negotiated. The ACP felt that the price did not take into account their increased production and delivery costs, and although the sugar price increased yearly in money terms, it did not increase in real terms. Nevertheless, throughout the period of Lome I the EEC sugar price remained above the world price for the commodity.

Sugar quotas and sugar deliveries reached a high in the 1976–7 year and then fell in 1977–8 and 1978–9.[6] The sugar quota did not increase yearly but depended on the level of ACP take-up of quotas. The ACP and EEC disagreed over the reduction or reallocation of quotas for states which failed to deliver their allocated quota to the EEC market. After Congo, Suriname, Uganda, and Kenya failed to deliver their full quotas in 1975–6, the EEC wanted to reduce their future quotas. However, after strong representations by the ACP the EEC restored full quotas for those countries 'as a unilateral political gesture' not to be taken as a precedent.[7]

Suriname was allowed to accede to the Sugar Protocol in 1976, but in 1979 the Commission refused Zambia's application, citing the difficult prevailing market conditions.

Bananas The ACP share of EEC banana imports fell in quantity terms by 1 per cent from 1976 to 1978, but their share by value of imports remained constant. In absolute terms both the quantity and value of ACP banana exports to the EEC during this period increased.

The ACP alluded to the duty-free banana quotas allotted to other producers (notably Latin American ones) in explaining their failure to capture more of the EEC market.[8] The EEC referred to the inadequacy of ACP supply and marketing infrastructure, and the poorer quality of ACP compared to Latin American bananas. During Lome I the ACP banana producers attempted to establish a banana exporters organization to improve quality and marketing, but this failed.

Rum The ACP rum quota was increased from 1975–6 to 1979–80 by roughly 4 per cent. During this period the ACP take-up rate of the quota increased from 68 per cent in 1975–6 to 87 per cent in 1978–9. From 1975–6 to 1978–9 the ACP increased their exports of rum to the EEC by approximately 46 per cent; nevertheless the ACP were disappointed by this performance.[9] Although the ACP failure to fulfil the rum quota might imply that the quotas were more than adequate, if not generous, the ACP pointed out underlying structural obstacles in their rum trade with the Community. They complained about the method of allocating rum quotas among EEC states, challenged EEC statistics, objected to the EEC's import certificate system and to the varying definitions of rum in the member states.

Beef and veal Determined ACP bargaining, particularly on the part of Botswana, won significant concessions from the EEC over beef and veal. Beef and veal accounted for only 0.30 per cent of ACP exports to the EEC and were exported by three countries – Botswana, Madagascar and Swaziland – classified as least developed, island or landlocked by the EEC.

The ACP negotiated additional quotas for beef and veal exports and reduced levies on their basic quotas. The ACP under Lome I were thus able to increase their market share from 2.2 per cent of EEC beef and veal imports in 1974 to a high of 17.5 per cent by value in 1977, falling back to 13.6 per cent in 1978.[10]

Other issues The ACP and EEC disagreed over the sale of surplus Community agricultural products. The EEC offered to sell some surplus products to the ACP, but its terms were not acceptable to them. In the end a working party of the Committee of Ambassadors was established to consider the matter further.

One area in which the ACP did obtain concessions from the Community was in exporting tomatoes. The ACP argued that tomatoes from the Maghreb enjoyed better access to the Community than ACP tomatoes from Senegal. The Commission accepted the ACP case and allowed a quota of tomatoes to enter from Senegal (off-season) at reduced tariffs.

Implementation of the trade provisions: textiles

The ACP were highly critical of the implementation of the trade provisions of the Convention. During the Lome Convention on several occasions, 'the ACP States pointed out to the Community that the action taken by the Community was unilateral and against the letter and spirit of the Convention'.[11] In particular, the ACP felt they had been insufficiently consulted and their views not taken into consideration over proposed GSP measures and proposed agreements with third countries.

The EEC never invoked the safeguard clause, Article 10 of the Lome Convention which allowed the Community to take 'necessary safeguard measures' if any of its members' economies were seriously disturbed; it was able to refer to this clause in obtaining 'voluntary' export restraint from the ACP. ACP textiles accounted for only 1.8 per cent of EEC textile imports and the ACP, in fact, had a deficit in their textile trade with the EEC. Nevertheless the EEC insisted on setting quotas for ACP textile exports. In the case of Mauritius, the EEC insisted that certain textile exports to the EEC had to be reduced by 50 per cent.[12]

EEC trade balance with the ACP

During the 1976 to 1978 period of operation of the Lome Convention, ACP exports to the EEC increased by 46 per cent, whereas EEC exports to the ACP increased by roughly 18 per cent (Table 4.1). As Table 4.4 shows, the balance of trade in 1975, 1976 and 1979 was in favour of the ACP, and in 1977 and 1978 was in favour of the EEC.

Table 4.4   EEC–ACP trade balance (millions of units of account)

Year	Balance
1975	− 593
1976	− 588
1977	+ 43
1978	+ 800
1979	− 3019

+ in favour EEC; − in favour ACP

Source: *Focke Report*, p. 12, see note 13.

Thus, in terms of the balance of trade, the ACP fared reasonably well under Lome I, increasing their exports to the EEC faster than the EEC increased its exports to them. However, there was cause for concern in the structure or composition of ACP–EEC trade. Whereas ACP exports were primarily of raw materials, EEC exports were composed mainly of manufactured goods (roughly 80 per cent by value). The structure of ACP–EEC trade in this respect had not changed much since colonial times.[13] The ACP were drawers of oil and hewers of coffee and cocoa for the EEC.

Trade promotion

Chapter 2 of Title I 'Trade Co-operation' in the Lome Convention produced negligible results. Under EDF IV 16.5 million Ecu or 1.4 per cent of the total was spent on trade promotion activities. Nearly half of this sum was spent on trade fairs and exhibitions whose effectiveness was dubious. The EEC promoted products like handicrafts rather than goods like textiles which could more effectively have competed on the European market. Only a limited number of the ACP States participated in trade promotion activities and the Commission noted that only the ACP States with the most developed infrastructure for exports could, in any case, benefit from these activities.[14] In an attempt to answer criticisms of the unsatisfactory performance of trade promotion under Lome I, greater funds were committed to it under Lome II.

Summary

The trade provisions of the Lome Convention contributed to maintaining and increasing the volume of trade between the ACP and EEC without altering the structure of the trade. The preferences given to the ACP over other third world exporters were small because most ACP exports were primary products which would in any case enter the EEC market at low or zero tariff rates. The Lome trade regime maintained access for the ACP in the EEC market: it was an arrangement of trade continuation rather than trade development. In addition, Lome maintained EEC access to ACP markets (on the most-favoured nation basis) and encouraged a continuing flow of ACP commodities to the Community.

Where ACP countries could show that their products received less favourable treatment than those of third countries, as in the case of tomatoes, they persuaded the EEC to take action. The Commission consistently maintained that it was willing to review the situation of any ACP products or industries damaged by EEC restrictions; however, it required firm statistical evidence of such damage, which the ACP often found difficult to compile. Where the ACP made a concerted effort to have trade provisions improved for a commodity of importance to some of the least-developed ACP economies and which was not seen as threatening European farmers, as in the case of beef, they also persuaded the EEC to improve trade provisions. But for products of a sensitive nature, such as sugar and textiles, the ACP were less able to obtain concessions. Thus, although the EEC showed itself marginally flexible in the application of the Lome trade provisions, it diluted the free access for ACP goods promised in the Convention with a substantial measure of protectionism.

STABEX results

Review of objectives and provisions   The Lome Convention's STABEX (stabilization of export earnings) scheme was implemented:

> With the aim of remedying the harmful effects of the instability of export earnings and of thereby enabling the ACP states to achieve the stability, profitability and sustained growth of their economies.[15]

In practice, the STABEX system was more limited than this objective: it sought to stabilize export earnings from certain commodities exported by the ACP to the EEC when these earnings fell in accordance with the criteria set out in the Lome Convention. The products covered by the STABEX system accounted for only about 30 per cent of ACP export earnings, leaving 70 per cent 'uninsured'.[16]

An ACP state which experienced a fall in export earnings for one of the listed products, and submitted a request to the Commission, would receive a transfer from the EEC provided that it satisfied four criteria. First, the products had to meet the required proportion of exports (dependence threshold). Second, export earnings had to fall by at least the specified amount below the reference level (trigger threshold). Third, the fall in earnings had to be deemed by the Commission not to have been caused by 'a trade policy measure of the ACP state concerned adversely affecting exports to the Community'. Finally, there had to be funds available for the transfer. For each year of the Convention STABEX received an allocation of 75 million Ecu plus any leftover sums from previous years, and up to 20 per cent of the following year's allocation if required.

The dependence threshold established by the Lome Convention stipulated that export earnings from the product concerned had to constitute at least 7.5 per cent of an ACP state's export earnings for the preceding year. However, in the case of sisal and for the 34 least developed, island and landlocked states mentioned in the Convention, the threshold was reduced to 5 per cent and 2.5 per cent respectively.

In addition to the dependence threshold, a reference level based on export earnings from exports to the EEC for the preceding four years was set for each ACP state and product. If the export earnings from a product covered fell by 7.5 per cent below the reference level (2.5 per cent in the case of the poorest states), a transfer could be requested for the difference between actual earnings and the reference level.

Both the dependence threshold and the trigger threshold — the 7.5 per cent fall below the reference level — had to be met before a transfer could be granted. The European Community's Court of Auditors criticized the dual threshold system, noting that a country heavily dependent on the export of one product might experience a shortfall of less than 7.5 per cent and receive no transfer, whereas a country which just passed the dependence threshold and the trigger threshold, but experienced a smaller absolute drop in earnings would be compensated. The Auditors concluded: 'The result is that the most vulnerable economies of the ACP States, i.e. the less diversified, are those least protected by the STABEX System.'[17]

STABEX was meant to cover losses incurred by the ACP in exporting certain primary and semi-processed products to the EEC. However, for a few of the least developed ACP states which exported only a few of the STABEX products primarily to non-EEC markets, the Community extended 'all-destinations' cover. That is, the EEC guaranteed their exports of STABEX products to all destinations. Originally, this applied to Guinea Bissau, Ethiopia, Rwanda, Burundi and Swaziland, but six other countries were later included.* The European Commission considered that although all-destinations cover could be justified for certain countries, it remained a 'flagrant derogation' of the principle that STABEX guaranteed export earnings from products sent to Europe.[18] Although the extension of all-destinations cover appeared liberal and meant that some countries which otherwise would not have received STABEX transfers became eligible, the soundness of this approach was questionable. The Court of Auditors argued that:

> the extension of the STABEX guarantee to export earnings outside the Community prevents any quantity control by the Community institutions, since there is no possibility of establishing any proper statistical basis.[19]

Although the STABEX provisions of Lome were set out in much greater detail than the export earnings provisions of the Yaounde Conventions, they still left the European Commission considerable discretion in their application. The Commission argued that it needed flexibility to apply the Lome Convention's provisions equitably by taking into account all relevant factors. But the Court of Auditors observed that instead of applying the STABEX rules in a straightforward manner, the Commission frequently bargained with the ACP over them.[20]

The negotiations-like character of the application of STABEX rules, for example, in the selection of the statistics to be used, appeared unbusiness-like to the Court of Auditors, but it was in keeping with the 'close and continuing co-operation' between the EEC and ACP which the Convention was supposed to embody. Although the Commission's flexibility in applying the STABEX rules created some

---

* All destinations cover was granted to Cape Verde, the Comoros, Lesotho, Western Samoa, Seychelles and Tonga.

goodwill among the ACP, it left the Commission open to charges of political influence or favoritism.[21]

All STABEX transfers were interest-free; those to the countries classified as least developed, island or landlocked were in the form of grants. The non-grant transfers had to be repaid into the system if the following two conditions were both met during the five years following the transfer (calculations were the responsibility of the European Commission):

1. The unit value of the export was higher than the reference unit value.
2. The quantity exported to the EEC was equal to or greater than the reference quantity.

If these conditions were met, the ACP state had to pay back a sum equal to the reference quantity multiplied by the difference between the reference and actual unit values, but not exceeding the amount of the transfer.

During the life of Lome I, the ACP paid back 5.9 million Ecu or 1.3 per cent of total STABEX funds.[22] Although at the end of the operation of the Lome Convention the joint ACP–EEC Committee of Ambassadors requested that the unexpended STABEX funds be transferred into STABEX II and that all outstanding loans be transformed into grants, this latter request was denied by the Council of Ministers.[23]

The repayments system was arbitrary in its division of the ACP into grant or loan recipients. It was cumbersome to operate and repayments were not always forthcoming. Only a small fraction of STABEX funds was repaid into the system through this method; thus the hope that STABEX would be self-financing was never realistic. The European Court of Auditors noted that the repayment of a transfer, by being calculated without reference to total export earnings, unlike the CFF system, 'may accentuate the fluctuations in export earnings' rather than stabilize them.[24] Although the repayment of transfers was meant to inject a note of financial realism into STABEX, the difficulties and anomalies involved in obtaining any meaningful level of repayments, and the potentially destabilizing effects of repayments on the ACP economies rendered this objective largely irrelevant.

The operation of STABEX STABEX transfers under Lome I were disbursed for the years 1975, 1976, 1977, 1978 and 1979. Seventeen transfers were approved (for the year 1975) within three months of the coming into force of Lome I in 1976. Over the five-year period of Lome I, 37 out of 59 ACP countries received STABEX transfers for 24 different products.

Of the STABEX funds disbursed, 67 per cent were grants (to EEC-classified least developed countries) and 33 per cent were loans. The transfers were occasioned by loss of EEC demand in 31 per cent of cases (referred to by the Commission as 'unemployment benefit') and 69 per cent were occasioned by local circumstances such as bad weather (referred to by the Commission as 'sickness benefit').

Out of a total of 123 transfers to ACP and OCT dependencies of EEC countries, only eight advances were used. These advances, paid before the earnings shortfall was fully experienced by a recipient country (under Article 19 of Lome I) would have been the most effective way to *stabilize* export earnings, but the limited statistical and administrative capacity of the ACP meant that they did not make full use of this facility.[25]

To the original 375 million Ecu allotted to STABEX under Lome I for the ACP, another 5 million Ecu were added to cover possible transfers to the newly acceding Cape Verde, Papua New Guinea, and Sao Tome and Principe. Another ten states became independent and acceded to the Convention, but these had been covered by the OCT STABEX allocation and remained in this category for financial purposes. Of the 380 million Ecu available for the ACP, 377 million or 99 per cent was spent by the end of Lome I. Of the 20 million Ecu of STABEX funds allocated to the OCT and the former OCT which became independent ACP countries, only 60 per cent was disbursed (86 per cent as grants) making a total disbursement rate of 97 per cent for both ACP and OCT recipients.

Although operated by only nine EEC Commission officials, over one-third of the sums paid out by the end of the Lome Convention were STABEX funds. Thus, in view of its rapid paying out system, and its 99 per cent disbursement rate for the ACP, STABEX was efficient. Yet instead of the envisioned 20 per cent of STABEX funds being paid out in each of the five years of operation, payments varied from 9 per cent to 43 per cent of STABEX funds (see Table 4.5).

Table 4.5 ACP allocation of STABEX over five years

Year	Percentage of allocation
1975	21
1976	10
1977	9
1978	43
1979	17

Source: Comprehensive Report, p. 36, see note 18.

During the operation of Lome I, the Commission allowed two exceptional requests for transfers where the products concerned — groundnuts and cocoa — did not meet the dependence threshold.[26] After following the conciliation procedure set out in Article 81 of the Lome Convention, the Commission also agreed to late requests for transfers by Kenya, Gabon and Mali for the year 1975.[27]

During the operation of STABEX, Western Samoa, Tonga and Lesotho were added to the least developed list, giving them more favourable conditions for STABEX transfers. The Council of Ministers agreed to add cloves, gum arabic, wool, mohair, pyrethrum, vanilla, ylang-ylang and sesame seeds to the covered product list. Only three of these attracted transfers and those jointly accounted for less than 1 per cent of STABEX transfers by value. The ACP requested copper, phosphates, rubber, tobacco, sisal products, cashew nuts and shea kernels to be added to the STABEX list, but the EEC did not agree to these.

Despite the EEC's willingness to offer more favourable conditions to some countries, and to add some marginal products to the STABEX list, 13 per cent of ACP requests, which the Commission found did not meet the dependence and fluctuation thresholds, were refused. In 1978 Senegal — the country which received the most funds from STABEX — forewent a justified transfer of 16.6 million Ecu. Thus, despite STABEX having finished its first five years in credit, it was possible to foresee future problems. Indeed, had Senegal not accepted a reduced transfer or had more ACP requests been approved, STABEX would have run out of funds in its first five years (Table 4.6). Although the Community's Court of Auditors pointed out the dangers of large transfers which might exhaust STABEX funds, the Commission did not accept that the risk of shortfalls in the system was high.[28] It felt that by careful calculations and avoiding products such as minerals which would be too expensive to support, it could keep STABEX operating comfortably within its budget. The danger of a shortage of STABEX funds to meet commitments became apparent under Lome II.

Under Lome I 22 ACP states received no transfers from STABEX. Two countries — Senegal and Sudan — together accounted for over 25 per cent of transfers; and the first three countries listed in Table 4.7 received nearly 40 per cent of STABEX funds.

This unequal distribution of resources led to suspicion within the ACP that the Commission manipulated figures to give more funds to certain countries, notably Senegal, with which it had good relations. Not only in payments, but also in structure, STABEX favoured certain countries. Its export earnings 'insurance' was spread unevenly among the ACP. The Comoros had virtually all exports to all destinations covered by STABEX, while the Bahamas, Barbados, Botswana, Guyana, Suriname and Zambia exported practically no STABEX products.

Table 4.6 Reduction in STABEX transfers by year of application (millions of units of account)

Year	Bases of Transfer*	Transfers Paid	Amounts	Reductions % of bases of transfer
1975	89.5	80.0	9.5	10.6
1976	43.8	37.1	6.7	15.3
1977	36.8	33.7	3.1	8.4
1978	227.5	164.0	63.5	27.9
1979	85.5	62.7	22.8	26.6
Total	483.1	377.5	105.6	21.9

* The basis of transfer is the difference between average export earnings in the four years before each year of application and actual earnings. The basis of the transfer is the same as the transfer except for reductions for changes in the pattern of trade or voluntary waivers.

Source: *Official Journal of the European Communities*, C344, 31 December 1981.

The reply of the Commission to the critics who questioned the uneven distribution of STABEX transfers was that, as in the case of insurance, it could not predict where shortfalls would occur. However, the Community could have ameliorated this problem by altering the list of products covered or restricting the percentage of transfers any one country could normally receive.* But since all the ACP paid the 'premium' of joining the Lome Convention, they should have shared the STABEX funds more equitably.

As well as concentrating on certain countries, STABEX transfers were concentrated on certain products. Groundnuts and groundnut oil occasioned almost 40 per cent of STABEX transfers during Lome I.[29] Through the transfers attracted in particular by groundnuts and cotton (11.57 per cent of transfers), the African countries of the Sahel benefited most from STABEX under Lome I.

The economic effects of STABEX The economic effects of STABEX can be divided into those affecting the sector which attracted the STABEX transfer and those affecting the economy of the ACP country as a whole. In terms of economic effects on particular sectors — groundnut, cocoa, coffee, and so on, — there was no substantial evidence of any particular effect. The rules of STABEX required the recipient to

* The mineral products support scheme of Lome II (SYSMIN) rectified this imbalance to some extent by providing extra resources for Zaire and Zambia.

Table 4.7 Aggregate STABEX transfers for the financial years 1975—9

ACP state	Aggregate amounts (units of account) from 1975 to 79	Percentage
1. Senegal	65 106 389	17.37
2. Sudan*	39 143 441	10.44
3. Mauritania*	37 000 450	9.87
4. Niger*	22 653 960	6.04
5. Tanzania*	20 701 549	5.52
6. Uganda*	20 595 453	5.49
7. Benin*	20 366 720	5.43
8. Ivory Coast	15 000 000	4.0
9. Ethiopia*	14 420 049	3.85
10. Swaziland*	13 224 869	3.53
11. Guinea-Bissau*	11 288 257	3.01
12. Mali*	9 780 903	2.61
13. Central African Republic	7 289 555	2.09
14. Liberia*	7 586 943	2.02
15. Gambia*	7 514 754	2.0
16. Congo	7 361 677	1.96
17. Chad*	7 336 196	1.96
18. Upper Volta*	7 261 902	1.94
19. Gabon	6 703 311	1.79
20. Madagascar	5 747 547	1.53
21. Ghana	5 176 408	1.38
22. Cameroon	4 064 981	1.08
23. Sierra Leone*	3 977 274	1.06
24. Togo*	3 626 614	0.97
25. Western Samoa*	2 837 453	0.76
26. Fiji	2 114 947	0.56
27. Somalia*	1 932 145	0.52
28. Burundi*	1 485 655	0.40
29. Cape Verde*	1 206 564	0.32
30. Tonga*	1 207 990	0.32
31. Rwanda*	608 802	0.16

* ACP state listed in Article 48 of the Lome Convention and therefore not liable to repay transfers

Source: Focke Report, see note 13.

disclose how funds were spent, but there was no obligation for them to be used to support production in the affected sector.

By choosing certain products to support, it seemed as if STABEX was designed to encourage or assure the supply of these to the EEC. However, the interest of the EEC in encouraging the export of products such as sisal, which it recognized as a candidate for diversification rather than for increased production, or coffee, a product in chronic world oversupply, was minimal. Indeed the ACP products of most economic interest to the EEC — oil and minerals — were not covered by the scheme. Furthermore, STABEX transfers in 75 per cent of cases were not used by the ACP for the product which occasioned the transfer.[30]

Although critics of STABEX sometimes charged that it was meant to increase ACP exports to the EEC, the intermittent and often small transfers did not generally result in this.[31] Many transfers were used by the ACP to sustain imports, to pay government officials, or to encourage diversification rather than export production. There were also cases, regarded by the European Commission with dismay, where the funds' use was not clearly reported or funds were used for purposes, such as buying furniture for the Brussels embassy, unrelated to development.[32]

In terms of stabilization of export earnings from particular crops, STABEX had little effect. Because the funds were normally received the year after the shortfall, their stabilization value was minimal. In addition, the repayment of transfers, which might fall due in a shortfall year following an improved year, could itself be a destabilizing rather than stabilizing force. Thus, the Community's aim of 'remedying the harmful effects of the instability of export earnings' (even in the limited number of STABEX products) was not fulfilled through STABEX.

STABEX — which was not meant to be a balance of payments support system — did sometimes have significant if random effects on some ACP countries' balance of payments and the amount of development aid they received from the EEC. STABEX transfers ranged from 150,000 Ecu to nearly 50 million Ecu. The average proportion of STABEX transfers to other EDF aid was 60 per cent, but some countries — Dominica, Swaziland, Mauritania, Gabon, Gambia, Senegal — more than doubled their aid from the EEC through STABEX transfers.[33]

In terms of the ACP countries' overall balance of payments, STABEX payments constituted in the years of the largest transfers, 1975 and 1978, under 0.5 per cent of total ACP export earnings. Nevertheless, for some of the ACP — especially the smaller economies — large STABEX transfers could amount to a large proportion of export earnings. For example, in 1976, Western Samoa and Tonga received transfers of funds equalling more than 25 per cent of their export earnings, while Guinea Bissau received funds amounting to over 100 per cent of its export earnings.[34]

Adrian Hewitt found that STABEX transfers to Western Samoa and Mauritania had allowed those countries to service rather than default on their international debts.[35] Nevertheless, such conjunctions of STABEX payments and balance of payments crises were fortuitous, not planned. The Community's Court of Auditors concluded that although in some cases STABEX transfers had a significant effect:

> the final impact on the economies of the recipient ACP states was probably slight. Sporadic transfers cannot have lasting effect, and the amount of financial resources involved is usually too small.[36]

In some instances the economic effects of STABEX payments were reduced because other aid donors took the transfers into account when calculating their own aid disbursements. The IMF, for example, reduced its balance of payments support to countries receiving STABEX funds.[37] However, in other cases STABEX payments were received by countries not in receipt of CFF or other IMF funds (and therefore, arguably, less deserving of such transfers). But where STABEX transfers were substituted for IMF loans on harder terms, the recipient country still benefited from the interest-free or grant status of the STABEX funds.

STABEX as insurance In an effort to demonstrate that STABEX was not an ill-conceived scheme benefiting a group of arbitrarily chosen countries and products, which failed to take account of the real economic situation of the recipients, the European Commission stressed the similarities of STABEX and insurance. STABEX was not, the Commission noted, a commodity price stabilization system. Nor was it designed for balance of payments support, for funding restructuring or diversification programmes, for aid nor emergency aid, although it might have effects in these areas. STABEX's resemblance to insurance, however, could not be emphasized too strongly.[38]

Like insurance, in the Commission's view, STABEX payments compensated for injury and thus it could not be known in advance where injury would occur. Therefore, large STABEX transfers to a few countries were the natural result of unpredictable injuries (although the Commission had considerable leeway in calculating transfers). Thresholds could be compared to the 'excess' or 'deductible' clauses in insurance, and negotiations over STABEX payments resembled those with an insurance company. Most significantly, transfers occasioned by a particular loss could, like insurance payments, be directed to any use.

However, STABEX in many respects differed from insurance. Unlike insurance, STABEX receipts (except to the least developed) had to be repaid. The dependence threshold functioned not like an 'excess' clause, but as a more fundamental limitation. The bargaining between the European Community and the ACP recipients was much more complex and involved political issues not of concern to an insurance company. The ACP 'policy-holders' of STABEX did not receive equal cover despite their equal standing in the Lome Convention. The Commission considered that the EEC paid the premium for STABEX insurance, but in fact the premium was the political decision of the ACP to adhere to the Lome Convention. Finally, the ACP could only insure certain products — those accepted by the Community.

Although the European Commission used the analogy of insurance to account for some anomalies of STABEX, it also had more ambitious objectives for the system:

> STABEX, on the other hand, is a form of development aid conceived in microeconomic and sectoral terms (the product-by-product approach), the main objective of which should be to stabilize the cash flow to the affected commodity sector, in order to restore its economic viability menaced by natural or economic mishaps.[39]

Thus, the European Commission had two different approaches to STABEX. One compared it to an insurance rather than a development scheme, accepting that its transfers could not be directed to a specific commodity sector or to any necessary restructuring of that sector. The other, more ambitious conception saw STABEX as development aid stabilizing export earnings in a particular sector and thereby encouraging the economic development of that sector. Unfortunately, as has been noted, the more ambitious aims for STABEX were unrealizable and at best STABEX was a restricted form of commodity insurance.

The advantages of STABEX

As well as fundamental flaws, STABEX had a number of advantages. Its principal advantage was its fulfilment, not of its specific objective of stabilizing ACP commodity export earnings, but of the more general objective of furthering 'close and continuing cooperation' between the ACP and EEC.

The European Community was generally satisfied with the performance of STABEX and in the Commission this tended to exuberance:

Heralded as a major innovation in international economic relations, the export earnings stabilization system set up under the first Lome Convention and commonly known as STABEX has performed just as was intended.[40]

The European Parliament's Focke Report more modestly considered that STABEX was 'satisfactory'.

Although STABEX's 'microeconomic' approach to the problem of ACP export earnings was idiosyncratic rather than revolutionary, it was popular with the ACP as well as with the Community. The joint ACP–EEC Council of Ministers found that STABEX 'on the whole proved *satisfactory* both in principle and in practice'.[41] At the 1981 Franco-African summit in Paris, attended by 34 African countries and France, STABEX was held up as a model and the final communique recommended that other industrialized countries implement similar programmes.[42]

The European Community consistently supported the idea of creating a worldwide support system for developing countries' export earnings, recognizing that its STABEX system was limited in both country and product coverage. It was estimated by the European Commission in 1977 that the stabilization of all developing countries' export earnings on a product-by-product basis would have cost US $2,800 million for five years or roughly six times the value of STABEX under Lome I.[43] The EEC itself was unwilling to extend the STABEX scheme to non-ACP countries despite a request from the Association of South East Asian Nations (ASEAN) to have their exports to the Community covered.

The European Community did not follow its self-proclaimed model for relations between developing and industrialized states by extending the STABEX guarantees to other developing countries, but STABEX influenced proposals for other export earnings support schemes. Proposals from the US to the IMF, from Sweden to the UN, and from West Germany to the Conference on International Economic Co-operation (CIEC) borrowed elements of STABEX thinking although none of them were directly derived from it.[44] However, the IMF's CFF, a similar programme operated by the Arab Monetary Fund and STABEX were the only commodity support programmes successfully in operation during the 1970s.

In addition to the political goodwill and the contribution to international debate on commodity problems made by STABEX, it had other virtues. STABEX transfers were on liberal terms. The payments, unlike EDF project aid, were untied and could be used as the ACP recipient saw fit (although this sometimes led to unwise uses). Transfers were interest-free, and in the case of ldcs were grants. Payments, unlike those for EDF projects, were normally quick.

The flexible interpretation of the Convention by the European Commission allowed the ACP to 'negotiate' over the statistics used and hence the transfers received. This gave the ACP an element of participation in the STABEX process. The Commission was able, in some cases, to overlook the rigid threshold requirements or to overlook ACP governments' actions which resulted in export decline and technically disqualified them from transfers.[45] Thus, the STABEX system was flexible enough to allow the Commission to take relevant circumstances into account in its decisions, and to allow ACP input into the system, instead of operating an unyielding bureaucracy. As noted earlier, this same flexibility appeared unbusinesslike to the Community's Court of Auditors. It also allowed suspicions that when a politically friendly country like Senegal received over 17 per cent of total STABEX funds, political influence was at work.

STABEX's structural problems

The major criticisms of STABEX can be divided into those which questioned its criteria of need and those which questioned its economic effects. In addition, criticisms could be made of its selectivity and political aims, its administration, and its lack of sufficient funds.

The Court of Auditors of the European Community roundly criticized the STABEX system under which funds were transferred 'for each individual STABEX product, independently of the state of its (the country's) balance of payments, or of its total export revenue, or even of its export revenue from other STABEX products'.[46] By taking a sectoral rather than an overall view of an ACP state's export earnings, STABEX could give refunds to one country in balance of payments surplus while denying them to a country in balance of payments deficit. Especially since STABEX funds did not go to the producers of the affected sector nor in most cases to remedying its structural defects or improving its productivity, this approach was unjustifiable.[47]

On the positive side, STABEX funds did sometimes provide significant support to a country's balance of payments, or allow it to undertake development projects it could not otherwise afford. However, such effects were intermittent and unpredictable.

A number of negative consequences of STABEX payments have also been alleged. One charge was that STABEX was designed to increase ACP purchases of EEC goods. STABEX aid was not tied to EEC goods, and although it could be used to purchase such goods, this was an indirect and marginal effect. As noted earlier, it was suggested that STABEX directed ACP exports to the EEC and away from other markets, but there was no concrete evidence of this.

It has been argued that STABEX kept the ACP states as commodity

129

producers and prevented their industrialization. The Commission denied this by noting that some processed goods, for example, leather and groundnut oil, were covered. Nevertheless, it was true that STABEX in general supported primary products rather than encouraging manufactures.

Another criticism of STABEX was that it subsidized inefficiency and unprofitable production. The Commission accepted that STABEX was not designed to improve production structures, but because STABEX transfers were largely marginal and sporadic for any sector, they alone were not sufficient either to induce or retard a sector's development. However, it would have been desirable for STABEX not just to have had no effect on productivity or a marginal bias toward maintaining existing export structures, but to have encouraged productivity. The EEC's Development Commissioner Pisani stated that one possible effect of STABEX was to encourage export production at the expense of food crops.[48] But the Commissioner presented no evidence for this proposition.

The selectivity and political aims of STABEX could likewise be questioned. STABEX concentrated on certain products of a group of selected countries with historical links to or of political interest to the EEC. STABEX transfers primarily benefited African countries, the centre of the Community's political interest. Through selecting additional products to cover, or limiting transfers to any one country, the Community could have made a fairer distribution of its funds among the ACP.

Criticisms of the administration of STABEX have also been presented. Although it has been termed 'technically cumbersome, bureaucracy ridden', STABEX was relatively efficient in paying out its funds to the ACP.[49] More justifiably, it was charged that STABEX operated on the basis of dubious statistics. However, owing to the imperfections of import—export statistics in general, and to those obtainable from the ACP in particular, this was not especially the fault of the Commission.

Food aid is often criticized for reinforcing the government at the expense of the private sector. The same could be said of STABEX: it paid funds to the ACP government to compensate for losses incurred by the private sector — the producers. Making STABEX help to maintain producers' incomes would have been a useful amendment, aiding producers to improve their efficiency. This change, although desirable for development, would not have been popular with governments.

Another criticism of the administration of STABEX was that it was undertaken by the EEC alone. The Commission denied this, pointing to the ACP initial request for a transfer, and subsequent consultations with the EEC. But while the ACP countries did play a role in providing information and lobbying the Commission, it was solely the Commission which decided whether to grant a transfer and of how much. The ACP could propose products for inclusion in STABEX, but these had to be accepted by the Community. In terms of product selection, the overall financial allocation for STABEX, and individual transfers, the ACP had only the power of persuasion.

The final criticism of STABEX presented here concerns its insufficiency to solve the problem to which it was addressed. Commissioner Pisani admitted that STABEX alone could not regulate world commodity markets. Action was needed from other industrialized countries.[50] The STABEX scheme was only a partial answer even to the ACP countries' export earnings instabilities, and under Lome II STABEX ran out of funds as it narrowly avoided doing in its first five years.

Despite the political popularity of STABEX's untied transfers to ACP governments, its criteria for assessing need and its economic effects were questionable. Even though the more serious charges levelled against STABEX — that it locked the ACP into outdated production structures or discouraged food production — were not proved, doubts remained about its economic effects.

The challenge of STABEX for the Community was to retain the system's popularity with the EEC states and the ACP, while transforming it into a more effective instrument of development. Making STABEX non-repayable and fairly distributed among the ACP would be a significant advance. A STABEX taking into account overall ACP export earnings, jointly administered by the EEC and ACP, whose transfers were directed to improving the economic situation of the sector which occasioned them, would be a model for other such schemes. During the five years of Lome I, STABEX failed to fulfil its objectives of stabilizing commodity export earnings and furthering the ACP states' economic development.

Aid results

The aid component of the Lome Convention — euphemistically referred to as 'financial and technical cooperation' by the Convention's text — was the pre-eminent 'carrot' offered by the European Community to the ACP. Trade concessions given to the ACP beyond those offered to other ldcs were limited, and the ACP countries were not fully capable of making use of those given. Aid was therefore perceived by the ACP as central to their relationship with Europe.

Archie Mogwe of Botswana, as Chairman of the ACP Committee of Ministers, expressed the idea that all of the other aspects of the Lome relationship — trade, export stabilization schemes, and so forth —

depended on aid. 'Fundamental to all these activities and indeed to every aspect of ACP–EEC cooperation is the overall quantity and quality of the financial resources provided by and through the Convention.'[51]

European Community aid did, over the more than two decades of its operation, establish an independent reputation or identity. It was not — as some argued that it should be — a coordinating agency for the European member states' bilateral aid programmes. The EEC often co-financed projects with its member states, but it had its own separate procedures and objectives.

As a proportion of the member states' bilateral aid, EEC aid was small, amounting to only about 12.5 per cent of their bilateral aid, with roughly the same amount going to other multilateral aid institutions.[52] In terms of the Community budget, aid accounted for less than 3 per cent of spending in 1979. As a proportion of EEC GDP, aid was less than 0.05 per cent, falling far short of the UN's 0.7 per cent target. (Although taken together with member states' bilateral aid the proportion was higher.) EEC disbursements of official development assistance in 1979 were smaller than the bilateral programmes of France, Germany, the UK and the Netherlands.[53]

Nevertheless, despite the modest overall size of EEC aid, it did have a significant impact in some countries. In 1978 Community aid accounted for 4.9 per cent of public aid to the ACP and for a much larger proportion in some states — for instance, 9 per cent in Lesotho and 22.4 per cent in Senegal. In certain sectors of ACP economies, EEC aid was particularly important. For example, EEC funds were responsible for 10 per cent of Senegal's total road network.[54]

In spite of the relatively limited aid flows from the EEC, evidence suggests that these contributions were not completely additional to the member states' total aid programmes. That is, Hewitt and Stevens found no significant increase in member states' aid programmes after the establishment of the EDF in 1958.[55] Community aid was appropriately called 'aid diversion' rather than 'aid creation', indicating that it directed a larger share of the Community states' aid to the ACP without increasing the overall amount of aid given by the member states.[56]

The British government, particularly after 1979, found itself in a dilemma over its aid contributions. It wanted to avoid increasing expenditure on aid, especially multilateral aid, but at the same time it wanted to direct a larger share of its aid to non-ACP countries, to the Asian Commonwealth in particular. However, its reluctance to increase the aid 'pie' overrode its desire to re-direct its aid priorities, thus indicating that in this case policy considerations were subordinate to financial limitations.

Whether, during a time of economic hardship in Europe, all of the aid directed to the ACP countries through the EDF would still have found its way there if that institution ceased to function is a debatable point. That is, although other aid donors such as the World Bank might, as has often been argued, more efficiently have distributed aid than the EDF, governments might well have been tempted not to re-direct the EDF aid allocation in full to multilateral or bilateral programmes. Thus, although a proliferation of aid agencies might not increase total aid amounts available, the abolition of an established aid channel such as the EDF might have tempted a government to trim funds. The funds allocated to the EDF for its objectives — both political and developmental — might not have been inherited by a different aid institution.

Aid objectives

Lome aid had two types of objectives which were interrelated and in some cases conflicting. These can be characterized as political and developmental. The political objectives of EEC aid were not immediately obvious; indeed, one of the outstanding characteristics of Community aid was its claim to be non-political.

The EEC was reasonably successful in having its aid to the ACP accepted as being without political conditions. The Community's Court of Auditors observed that despite its numerous developmental failings:

> Community aid is also generally appreciated by the beneficiaries as being 'generous' (it contains a large proportion of outright grants) and 'non-political', i.e. given without ulterior motives or political strings attached.[57]

The Commission presented its aid as being non-political 'financial and technical cooperation' within an economic agreement — the Lome Convention. Community aid, it argued, was given to the signatory state whatever its regime or political philosophy. However, this argument — in the light of delays in aid to Uganda under Amin, to Equatorial Guinea under Macias Nguema, or the disproportionately large amounts of aid given to certain countries, for example, Senegal — was not completely convincing.*

The apolitical nature of EEC aid was a useful fiction. The Community (a donor which stressed that it had no colonial history) maintained a stance enabling both the donors and the recipients to escape or reduce the stigma of neo-colonialism. But, to the observer of the colonial history of the Lome relationship, the persistent selectivity of the Community in its ldc 'partners', or the unequal distribution of aid

---

* For a fuller discussion see Chapter 6.

among the ACP, the Community's aid was an instrument of its policy rather than an altruistic gift. Furthermore, a pragmatic political observer would, like George Washington, reckon that one nation could not expect disinterested favours from another — or group of others.[58]

The overriding political objective of the Lome Convention's aid programme was to further and maintain the Lome relationship. Thus, an ACP country's signature of the Lome Convention indicated at the minimum its willingness to cooperate with the EEC and to enter into the Community's 'dialogue en famille' with its favoured former colonies and other selected states.

The political objective of strengthening and maintaining good EEC–ACP relations impinged on the more purely developmental objectives of EEC aid in two principal ways: speeding projects which were politically desirable and funding developmentally questionable prestige projects. An example of political urgency causing quick financing of projects can be seen in the case of Uganda after Amin's fall. Following the change of government in Uganda in April 1979:

> the Commission has endeavoured to give this country every possible assistance to enable it to return to normal, and it was able to take prompt and useful action in the very first weeks following the establishment of the new regime.[59]

Thus, between April and June 1979, 500,000 Ecu were given to Uganda from EDF emergency aid funds.

This was a widely acceptable and generally laudable use of EDF funds, but it did show that Community aid was not as politically neutral as the Commission claimed. Some of the large agricultural projects funded by the EDF in Uganda under Lome II — while the Community was still imbued with a sense of urgency to return the country to normality — were questioned on developmental grounds in the EDF Committee, but still approved.

Trevor Parfitt, in his study of EDF projects in Sierra Leone, found that political considerations were paramount in the implementation of the North West Integrated Agricultural Development Project (KIADP).[60] Despite major errors and inconsistencies in the project proposal, the project was quickly approved. This hasty approval was effected largely to deflect criticisms of the EDF's slow disbursement rate. Two years after the implementation of Lome, no major projects were yet under way in Sierra Leone, and the Commission sacrificed technical clarity in the KIADP to remedy this politically unacceptable situation.

The EDF's tendency to finance what Commissioner Pisani described as 'cathedrals in the desert' has been widely recognized.[61] Under the

Lome Convention the ACP were responsible for selecting and preparing projects to be financed by the EDF. Because of the EDF's sensitivity to ACP desires and its lack of hard and fast rules about projects, many of the projects it financed were those desirable to the ACP but incapable of meeting the requirements of a body such as the World Bank. The Makani–Kabala road in Sierra Leone, for instance, was rejected by the World Bank on the grounds that its internal rate of return was too low. It was, however, accepted by the EDF.[62]

The EDF had the reputation of being a soft donor, of accepting projects which were not economically justifiable. The EDF's philosophy (based on the French one) was that a project could be worthwhile for its social or other unquantifiable benefits, even if its economic return were low. These intangible or unquantifiable benefits in practice included keeping or courting the favour of the ACP government involved.*

The funding of prestige projects — under-used railroads and over-equipped schools — by the EDF could in some cases have an indirect developmental effect. Where EDF-financed projects contributed to the standing or power of a government, they contributed to political stability. Political stability, as the experience of Africa showed, was a necessary but not sufficient prerequisite for economic development. The TransCameroon railway, for example, was not completely justified on developmental grounds, but it did assist in maintaining the Cameroonian political status quo.[63]

More extreme critics of Lome aid have referred to it as a bribe; such a characterization was not entirely without foundation. Community aid encouraged ACP governments to have friendly relations with Europe. In some cases it also allowed governments to pass on benefits in the form of a project to a favoured region or group of supporters.

Lome aid was also influenced by political and economic factors exogenous to the relationship itself. These derived from European and third country interests. European interests in selling solar power equipment to the ACP led to an inappropriate concentration on untested technologies for ACP projects. The European Court of Auditors singled out a solar pump which functioned only for a few hours as an example of an unsatisfactory project.[64]

United States' pressure on the European Community resulted in a considerable delay in EDF aid for Grenada (under Lome II). In the spring of 1981 Grenada requested the EEC to hold a co-financing meeting for its airport project. Because of US pressure, the EEC

---

* Although the more economically rigorous governments, notably the British, disagreed with an imprecise idea of social benefits justifying an economically unproductive project, they did not disagree that ACP governments should be encouraged by liberal project aid to look favourably upon Europe.

member states did not participate and the financing proposal for the airport project was long delayed.[65] Community aid outside of the Lome Convention was also politically sensitive: Mozambique and Angola's refusal to recognize Berlin as an integral part of West Germany led to their being barred from receiving EEC aid to non-associates.

The developmental results of Lome aid were less successful than the political achievement of maintaining and expanding the relationship. Developmental aims were in many cases subordinated to political aims. Certain of the developmental failings of EDF aid — unlike the political aspects — were widely criticized by the European Court of Auditors, European Parliament, and the ACP.

Although the official bodies charged with overseeing Lome aid found its administration 'generally satisfactory', independent observers such as the Overseas Development Institute's Christopher Stevens were more critical.[66] In a 1983 speech Dr Stevens called the Community's aid 'one of the worst organized of all aid programmes'.[67] The European Court of Auditors, in spite of its attempts to be more than fair to the Commission, found serious faults in aid administration and projects.

The allocation of aid among the ACP was not based on strictly defined development criteria such as per capita GNP. The Commission preferred to rely on a range of indicators and judgments to arrive at the aid-absorptive capacity of particular countries. This method, described by the House of Lords Select Committee on the European Communities as inconsistent, resulted in the particularly favourable treatment of the original francophone Associates.[68]

The Focke Report noted that at 31 August 1979 the 19 former Associates had received 198 million Ecu, whereas the 38 new ACP states received only 128 million Ecu. The report attributed this to the greater familiarity with EEC procedures of its former Associates; but this was still a definite advantage to them. In the initial allocation of aid as well, the former Associates were favoured. Thus, as Table 4.8 reveals, of the original 19 Associates, 12 remained in the top 19 aid recipients and only 2 — Gabon and Mauritius — were in the lower half. Including STABEX payments would raise the rankings of 13 AAMS and lower 6.

The Commonwealth ACP received the same trade preferences as the former Associates, and some of them were further favoured in the sugar and beef quotas. If the former Community Associates had not done well out of the EEC's aid programme, they might have felt that the Community had not honoured its commitment to preserve their advantages. Thus, the EDF administrative system 'constructed on a French, or Continental, base', provided a substantial flow of aid to the former AAMS.[69] The Commonwealth ACP were less adept at working the Commission's aid bureaucracy, but they were determined in their guarding of and arguing for trade preferences in sugar, beef, and rum.

Table 4.8 Rankings in Lome I indicative programme allocation (disbursements 31.12.79)

	Without STABEX	Including STABEX
Benin	21	15
Burundi	16	21
Cameroon	17	10
Central African Republic	23	29
Chad	18	12
Congo Brazzaville	27	14
Gabon	42	28
Ivory Coast	22	7
Madagascar	8	22
Mali	6	5
Mauritania	25	3
Niger	9	2
Rwanda	15	8
Senegal	14	1
Somalia	13	25
Togo	24	16
Upper Volta	10	6
Zaire	3	12
Mauritius	34	37

Source: Hewitt, Adrian, *The European Development Fund and its Function in the EEC's Development Policy*, pp. 14–15, see note 53.

The EEC's allocation or programming of aid to the ACP was supposed to involve the ACP fully, but in many cases did not. According to Article 51 of the Lome Convention: 'The Community indicative aid programme for each ACP state shall be drawn up by mutual agreement by the competent bodies of the Community and those of the ACP State concerned.' It continued: 'The aid programme shall be sufficiently flexible to enable account to be taken of changes occurring in the economic situation of the various ACP States, and any modifications of their initial priorities.'

Although in some cases the EEC demonstrated 'remarkable donor flexibility', resulting in a well coordinated aid programme geared to the priorities of the recipient states (as in the case of Malawi) the ACP complained about EEC rigidity in making indicative or outline aid programmes and in later changing them.[70] Adrian Hewitt's study of Malawi's use of EDF aid suggested that Malawi's successful relationship with the EDF resulted from its demonstrated competence as an aid-user.[71]

The ACP–EEC Council of Ministers Report of 1980 gave a less sanguine view of ACP–EEC aid cooperation. The ACP Ministers expressed their regret that programming missions sent from the EEC to ACP countries to work out indicative aid programmes:

1. Imposed their points of view on ACP States.
2. Some ACP States found it difficult to get the European Commission to accept additional information concerning individual projects or relevant details.
3. The Commission on many occasions rejected vital technical amendments to projects already submitted to the EEC.

The ACP Ministers further regretted not being fully involved in managing the regional development fund (10 per cent of the EDF) and 'They also hoped that there would be greater participation in the implementation of the provisions on financial and technical cooperation.'[72]

An ACP–EEC experts' report issued in 1980 also noted that the EEC needed to improve its consultation and cooperation with the ACP regarding aid. Specifically, the report recommended that the EEC make more effort to request information from the ACP, consult the ACP more thoroughly over programming aid, consult the ACP over technical changes in any project, try to use ACP consultants when possible, and provide more statistical information to the ACP.[73]

Two of the most frequently made criticisms of EDF aid, which particularly concerned the ACP, were of the slow disbursement of funds and cumbersome procedures of the EDF. These delays were partly due to the double layer of bureaucracy maintained by the Commission. Projects had to be approved by the EEC's delegate in the ACP state as well as the Commission in Brussels. Communication was often slow and the delegate found it difficult to expedite desirable projects although he could slow down questionable ones by requesting further information, delaying correspondence, and so on.[74] Senior officials in Brussels were known to 'forget' project requests they considered undesirable and to try to 'line up' countries to ask for favoured projects.

In addition to the approval of the delegate and the European Commission, projects had to win approval from the EDF Committee. Projects which were selected or identified by an ACP state were often technically (and sometimes politically as in the case of Grenada's international airport) unacceptable to the members of the EDF Committee. The Committee could request further information or studies in the hopes that a project would be improved, substantially altered or withdrawn by an ACP government in favour of a more acceptable one.

As well as delays caused by the delegate, European Commission in Brussels and EDF Committee, some projects experienced implementation delays because of technical problems and supply bottlenecks. Nevertheless, despite the EDF's reputation as a slow spender, the Overseas Development Administration (a department of the British Government) found that the rate of disbursement for EDF projects was not worse than that of other multilateral donors and was, in fact, rather better than the rate for the World Bank's International Development Agency (IDA).[75] In the context of the Lome Convention, however, with its commitment of a limited sum of aid during its five-year duration, the delays in disbursement were particularly serious. The ACP were frustrated when the funds allocated for development projects did not arrive within the five years of the Convention, and delays also meant that inflation reduced the real value of EEC aid. This reduction of aid through inflation affected to a greater degree the countries such as Malawi which relied on slow project aid rather than STABEX or measures such as the Sugar Protocol for the bulk of their EEC aid.

Role of the delegate

Under the Lome Convention the EEC Commission posted a delegate in each of the ACP countries or, in the case of smaller countries, in regional groupings of ACP states. The apparent purpose of the delegate, as outlined in the Convention, was to oversee project implementation and to evaluate completed projects. However, in practice the delegate had two additional functions. The delegate's functions thus fell into three categories: symbolic, information-related, and project-related. Because other multilateral and bilateral agencies did not maintain permanent delegates in aided countries, the precise *raison d'etre* of the delegate must be sought largely in his non-technical functions, in particular in his symbolic role.[76]

As a representative of the EEC, the delegate could be considered as a *de facto* ambassador. Although without formal diplomatic status, delegates were accused of adopting ambassadorial privileges in the ACP states and in some cases of living more grandly than the official ambassadors of EEC states.[77]

The delegate, like US troops in West Germany, was a tangible proof of EEC commitment to the ACP. By styling himself as an ambassador, the delegate emphasized the high level of EEC–ACP relations. The delegate, whose selection by the EEC's Development Commissioner was widely regarded as being a political choice, was thus an important symbol of Euro–ACP cooperation.

The Lome Convention was a political agreement based on the historical links between Europe and its former African colonies. It was portrayed, in keeping with changing international mores, as an economic and trade agreement. In a similar way, the delegate – who was in practice an ambassador of the European Community — was officially presented as a mere technician.

The second role of the delegate, the information-related role, was less crucial than the symbolic one. As the Commission's on-the-spot observer, the delegate could report on political and economic developments in an ACP state. Although communication between the delegate and Brussels was frequently poor, a delegate's reports could influence decisions on aid programming or projects.

The project-related responsibilities of the delegate included co-operating with the National Authorizing Officer (who represented the ACP government in operations related to EDF projects) in issuing, receiving, examining and accepting tenders. He was also, when requested by an ACP state, to assist in preparing and appraising projects. As well as arguing in favour of a project to the European Commission, a delegate, if politically well-connected (as many were), could lobby his own EEC member-state government to support a project. The delegate's role was to transmit information from the EEC to the ACP, to examine completed projects and report on them to the ACP state concerned, and to make a six-monthly report on the operations of the EDF in his state or regional grouping. Finally, 'the delegate shall make sure, on behalf of the Commission, that the projects and programmes financed from the Fund's resources are executed properly from the financial and technical angles'.[78] It was these project-related functions which were most demanding and in which the delegates were most criticized and least efficient.

Most of the criticisms of the delegate system centred on the delegate's lack of authority, his inability to take decisions independently of Brussels. The ACP—EEC Council of Ministers, the House of Lords Select Committee on the European Communities, and independent experts argued that the delegate should have greater power to expedite and oversee the implementation of projects.[79] But instead of an authoritative delegate on the ground with the power to facilitate and expedite projects, the delegate had few powers and often suffered from slow and poor communication with the host government and with Brussels.[80]

Other critics noted that delegations were urban-based, with too little exposure to projects.[81] In addition, rapid staff turnover, excessive daily administrative work, and the failure to report fully on completed projects were cited as problems in the delegate system by the European Court of Auditors.[82]

The House of Lords Select Committee noted, in the delegates' favour, that EDF projects — which were supervised by a delegate — were generally better organized than EEC food aid which was not so supervised.[83] This favourable comparison with the problems of food aid was less than fulsome praise.

Despite the charges that having a European delegate to oversee an ACP project was 'neo-colonial', the ACP wanted to expand the role of the delegate rather than eliminate it.[84] One practice to which the ACP did object was the charging to each country's aid allocation of the cost of the EEC delegation. Owing to ACP pressure, under Lome II the cost of delegations was charged to the EEC budget.

Under Lome I, the technical role of the delegate in EDF projects — his or her ostensible *raison d'etre* — aroused considerable concern. It was in his symbolic presence that the delegate was most effective. Like Lome aid, the delegate was more successful in fostering political co-operation than development.

Management of EDF funds and projects

In its annual report, the EEC's Court of Auditors could examine and make recommendations about the management of EDF funds and projects. Their management in many instances attracted the concern of the Auditors.

In its 1981 report the Auditors complained that they received insufficient information from the Commission and European Investment Bank on some projects. Furthermore, accounts were often presented late and in a form which did not provide the fullest information on the progress of projects. Concern was also expressed by the Auditors that calls for funds from member states to the EDF were handled 'in a most empirical way', resulting in both shortfalls and surpluses. Some member states were allowed to pay their EDF contributions late without being sanctioned. The Centre for Industrial Development was singled out for 'poor budgetary management' and lack of control over mission and entertainment expenses.[85]

The following year's Auditors' report gave the Commission's accounts only a qualified approval. Although improvements had been made in the accounts, they were, said the Auditors, still late and in need of greater clarity. Calls for funds were still 'rough and ready' and member states' contributions to the EDF were still being paid late. Shortcomings were noted in the management of exceptional (emergency) aid, resulting in overpayments. Delays and errors were found in the Commission's accounting of projects and the European Investment Bank's accounts were deemed insufficient to allow the Auditors to assess its management of Community funds. The Court of Auditors also reported that the Commission was unduly lenient with firms which defaulted on their contracts.[86]

In addition to the defects in the management of EDF funds, many problems with the management and implementation of EDF projects were cited by the Court of Auditors and others. Such defects were not in every case the fault of the Commission; the ACP governments, climatic conditions and other factors were responsible for problems in some projects.

The ACP selected and presented to the Community the projects they wanted financed under the Lome Convention:

> Preparation of the projects and programmes which come within the framework of the Community aid programme drawn up by mutual agreement shall be the responsibility of the ACP States concerned or of other beneficiaries approved by them.[87]

The implementation of EDF projects was likewise officially the responsibility of the ACP: 'The ACP States, or the other beneficiaries authorized by them shall be responsible for the execution of projects financed by the Community.'[88] Nevertheless, the EEC bore considerable responsibility for the selection and implementation of projects. The Community made the final decision about whether a project was to be financed, and the Commission often participated in making the project proposals. The Commission determined the aid allocation for each ACP state; it was intimately involved in creating each ACP state's indicative programmes. It also, in the delegate, had a direct observer responsible for overcoming the financial and technical problems to which the EDF projects were prone. Thus, the failings of EDF projects were partly the responsibility of the ACP governments, but they also reflected badly on the EEC's procedures and judgment.

Project criticisms

Agricultural and rural development projects Under Lome I agricultural and rural developments received special emphasis. They accounted for nearly 14 per cent of total EDF IV disbursements at the end of 1979, making them the largest single area of EDF spending after transport. Despite their prominence, the major agricultural projects were seriously deficient.[89]

The catalogue of problems with large EDF agricultural and rural development projects was long. The over-large scale of many projects exacerbated their shortcomings. In the worst cases, not only did projects not produce favourable developmental results, they became a drain on the recipient country's balance of payments. Of four agro-industrial projects in Zaire studied by the Court of Auditors, all of which were at least ten years old, none was viable and all continued to exist only by virtue of government or foreign support.[90]

Many of these large projects were not integrated into the existing rural economy. They neglected the production of food crops and concentrated on export crop production. In many cases land ownership was not fully settled, resulting in hardship to previous owners or the dispossession of traditional women farmers.

The 'narrow technical approach', or failure to consider the human effects of large agricultural–industrial and rural development projects, had serious consequences. In one project the Court of Auditors found poorly paid workers in inadequate housing.[91] A report by independent experts on EDF rural development projects in Africa from 1960 to 1977 concluded that the projects produced a slight or no rise in the standard of living of peasant farmers because of their failure *inter alia* to develop subsistence production or to make lasting changes in the organization of farmers, such as introducing cooperatives. The projects also failed to fulfil the objective of halting the influx of young people from the countryside into the towns. In many instances, the effects of the project disappeared after its completion.[92]

Agricultural and rural development projects had a poor record of fulfilling their objectives – which were sometimes set unattainably high. In a third of the rural development projects studied by the independent experts, production levels were as much as 50 per cent below target levels.[93]

Further difficulties were encountered in agricultural projects which were ill-adapted to local conditions or climate. Palm plantations in Togo and Benin were established in areas of insufficient rainfall. Threshing machines delivered to Mauritania were unsuitable for local crops. Faulty maintenance, difficulties in obtaining spare parts, faulty execution of irrigation works, bad synchronization of investments (developing a processing plant before developing the material to be processed) and creation of excessive processing capacity also plagued many projects.[94]

Large agricultural projects were the most difficult to bring to a successful conclusion because they depended on a variety of natural and human factors, and were often subject to political interference such as the desire of governments to keep agricultural product prices low. The Court of Auditors recommended that smaller-scale projects and technical assistance might have had more positive effects than large rural development projects.[95]

Transport projects The record of EDF transport projects was mixed. Many of the projects created useful rail- and roadways; the Court of Auditors cited a railway project in the Ivory Coast as an example of a technical success.[96] Yet it became a cliche that the EDF financed roads from nowhere to nowhere.

An example of this creation of transport infrastructure without adequate consideration of its use-value was the 7 million Ecu spent on bridges over the Casamance in Senegal. These were under-used because a further bridge over the Gambia river was not built.[97] Cost overruns, inadequate preliminary studies, unjustified use of expensive surfacing, and failure to consider recurrent costs plagued road projects. Togo had to devote 35 per cent of its fifth EDF allocation to road maintenance to repair roads built under previous EDFs.[98]

In his 1979 study of EDF aid to Cameroon, Adrian Hewitt found that over twenty years Cameroon had received half of all EDF investments in the rail sector. Yet, of two EDF railway projects in Cameroon, one, the TransCameroon line, had some success, but the smaller was a 'complete failure'. Hewitt found there were inadequate cost-benefit analyses of the projects and a failure to consider alternatives such as road-building. Moreover, railways in Africa financed by the EDF tended to follow the colonial model of joining a country's interior to its coast to expedite and encourage the export of agricultural products and minerals.[99]

As in road and rail sectors, some airport projects financed by the Community were questionable. Three international airports were built in the Netherlands Antilles, partly financed by the EDF, within a 100 km radius of each other. This was an unnecessary concentration.[100]

Education and health projects The Court of Auditors Report of 1981 contained serious criticisms of EDF-financed health and education projects. Two out of four hospitals examined by the Auditors, and most of the educational projects, were considered satisfactory. The Auditors cited the financing of simple schools in Suriname as an effective project. Nevertheless, many other projects suffered from bad designs and 'incompetent consultants'.

One serious criticism made by the Court of Auditors was that 'Most of the buildings financed by the EDF experience problems, at times serious ones, with the watertightness of the roofs.'[101] The Auditors also criticized the construction of over-modern and over-complex kitchens, sanitary and electrical systems which were soon out of order and difficult to repair. EDF concentration on large urban hospitals benefiting the wealthier sections of society was also condemned. Cost overruns and delays were frequent, and poor synchronization of investments resulted, for instance in Senegal, in schools without furniture.

The report by independent experts to the EEC Commission criticized the general orientation of EDF education and training projects, as well as the poor design, over-equipment and high import content of buildings. Most EDF funds were devoted to general education and training for the public sector, neglecting the private sector. They concluded that EDF programmes suffered from lack of coherence, lack of expertise and limited types of projects. Thus 'considerable reorientation' was needed in EDF training and educational programmes.[102]

Water supply and sanitation projects Water supply and sanitation infrastructure projects were generally considered to be one of the EDF's more successful sectors of investment, providing substantial benefits to both urban and rural dwellers in ACP countries. The European Court of Auditors nevertheless found that these projects suffered from frequent cost overruns and in some cases undesirable social consequences. Where better water supply and sanitation resulted in a more desirable environment, rents were sometimes increased, dispossessing the poorest members of the community.[103]

Energy projects Under Lome I the EEC allocated 190 million Ecu, approximately 0.06 per cent of its aid funds, to energy projects. The EEC recognized that imported energy was a severe drain on ACP resources (only a few ACP countries such as Nigeria and Gabon were major energy producers). Developing domestic energy sources would have been of great benefit to the ACP, but the way in which the Community sponsored energy projects was of dubious value.

Hydro-electric projects accounted for roughly 74 per cent of EEC energy aid. These hydro-electric facilities were mainly over-large 'prestige' projects, although smaller units would have been more useful.[104] Seven and one half per cent of the energy aid was devoted to alternative energy, such as solar and geothermal projects. Some of these projects were also questionable: a solar pump installed in Mauritania functioned only for a few hours and the Court of Auditors concluded that the use of motor pumps in this instance would have been more appropriate.[105]

Hoffman and Birch considered that EEC solar projects were chosen without regard to user needs, and were thus rarely successful. European interest in promoting solar energy projects in developing countries reflected European desires to use the ACP for energy experiments, and also demonstrated the desire of European companies to export solar technology.[106] Given the low success rate of new, unproven technologies in the developing world, the EEC and ACP would have been better advised to concentrate on developing more traditional energy sources, such as fuelwood. Fuelwood has been estimated to account for over 80 per cent of the energy used in the third world.[107] The replacement of fuelwood in the relatively near future with other forms of energy in the developing countries is unlikely; therefore fuelwood has been widely considered as the basis of development and small-scale industrialization for ldcs well into the next century.[108] Thus, the ACP and EEC should have allowed European countries and companies to bear the development costs of new, advanced energy technology, and spent their limited development funds on traditional and proven energy sources.

Coordination of aid among donor agencies and member states Article 44 of the Lome Convention specifically allowed that where the ACP state or states involved consented, EDF projects could be co-financed with international organizations, firms, EEC or ACP states, or third countries. Under the fourth EDF over 20 per cent of projects were co-financed, with Arab organizations being the EEC's main partners. Organizations such as the Arab Development Bank, World Bank, US Agency for International Development (AID) and European government and private agencies also participated in co-financing EDF projects.[109]

Co-financed projects had both some advantageous and some disadvantageous tendencies when compared to projects financed by a single donor. The foremost advantage of co-financing was its potential to increase available development funds by attracting additional financing from other sources. It has been estimated that European Community aid had in this way a multiplier effect of as much as eight times.[110]

Co-financing enabled donors to spread the risk involved in a project. It also facilitated raising large sums which no one donor would be willing or able to invest in a single project. Also, in theory, a project able to satisfy the criteria of a number of different donors would be basically a viable and beneficial project. Nevertheless, a number of problems were experienced with co-financed projects.

Projects could be co-financed in two principal ways: parallel or joint financing. Parallel financing involved each donor in financing a portion of a project, whereas in joint financing each donor contributed part of the financing of the project as a whole. The latter method was generally considered to hold fewer pitfalls.[111] Parallel financing involved the ACP government concerned to a greater degree with each separate donor, increasing the bureaucratic workload. It also required a greater degree of synchronization of investments to ensure that each part of the project was ready at the appropriate time.

Co-financing often resulted in delays, owing to bureaucratic procedures or because donors failed to agree about a policy. Plans for the Gleita dam in Mauritania, for instance, which was financed by the EEC, World Bank and German Kreditanstalt fur Wiederaufbau (KFW) took nearly ten years to process.[112]

As well as the delays which often plagued co-financed projects, co-financing could lead to a tendency to choose uninteresting or excessively large projects. That is, instead of each donor employing its own philosophy in selecting projects (the EDF's philosophy is discussed in the next section), it would choose an uncontroversial or lowest common denominator project for co-financing. In the case of development agencies with little international experience who relied on another agency to select a viable project, this was not a drawback. But for agencies such as the World Bank and EEC which had different development criteria, co-financing could lead to a blurring of the distinctiveness of their individual development philosophies. In terms of size, the EDF has been widely criticized for devoting too much attention to over-large and over-complex projects. Co-financed projects tended to be large ones and thus suffered from the disadvantages of these large-scale undertakings.

The political consequences of co-financing were many. When the EDF co-financed a project with an agency such as US AID, it appeared to cooperate with American foreign policy and presented an image of Euro-American solidarity to the recipient country. When the EDF co-financed a project with European partners, it presented an image of greater European solidarity in Africa. Thus, although in co-financing a development project the European Community might make less of an impression as a distinctive, 'non-imperialist', 'non-political' donor, it could still make a political statement by choosing its co-financing partners.

Although it has often been suggested that the EEC ought to do more to coordinate its member states' policies on development, this proposal was impracticable. The European Commission itself doubted its ability to 'harmonize' aid policies.[113] The EEC member states were traditionally jealous of their independence in this area. The EEC experienced considerable difficulties in managing its own development programme and in co-financing and coordinating individual development projects. This indicated that even if the European member states were less interested in using their development aid to generate political benefits and stimulate exports from their own countries, the European Community would have found the task of efficiently coordinating their development programmes extremely difficult if not completely impossible. Thus, although an agency to coordinate the member states' aid programmes, to eliminate areas of duplication or neglect while preserving the individual character and aims of each country's programme, would be desirable, it was a function the EEC was not fully equipped to perform.

General criticisms of the Lome aid programme

Not all of the failings of EDF aid projects could be directly attributed to the Community. Natural conditions such as drought in the Sahel and the failings of ACP governments also contributed to projects' problems. Nevertheless, a number of recurrent problems arose in relation to EEC development projects. Problems such as cost overruns could, of course, be found in projects in Europe as well as in the developing world. But the failure to use scarce development resources as efficiently as possible, and the frequency of serious problems in EEC projects has been a cause of substantial concern.

One questionable aspect of EEC development philosophy was its refusal to finance a project's recurring or running costs. The objective was to hand over a completed 'turn-key' project to the ACP states. In practice, this policy sometimes involved an ACP government in high recurrent expenses for a project, weakening the country's balance of payments. The European Court of Auditors was severely critical of this policy:

> All these examples show that the principle of only financing capital expenditure is dangerous, and that in practice it is often necessary to finance operating costs if the investments are not to be lost or under-used.[114]

The Community in fact altered this policy under Lome II and accepted that in the case of least developed countries, for a 'start-up' period, or in exceptional cases it would finance running costs on a temporary basis.[115]

The principal types of project failings are summarized as follows:[116]

1. Totally unjustified project.
2. Inadequate preliminary studies.
3. Failure to adapt designs and techniques to local conditions.
4. Narrow technical approach to project.
5. Faulty execution.
6. Faulty maintenance.
7. Unsatisfactory comparison of tenders.
8. Lack of coordination of physical and human resources.
9. Lack of coordination in financing.
10. Objectives not fulfilled.
11. Failure to consider running costs.
12. Little lasting impact on national or regional welfare or productivity.

Of these criticisms, the last was the most comprehensive indictment of the European Community's development efforts. Despite its two decades of special relationship with the ACP, and the large sums of money allocated to aid, there were few positive results. As the Convention's own journal, *The Courier*, recognized:

> In the ACP countries, it was thought — and this is nothing new — that agriculture, industry, trade and of course training are the most important of these priority fields, but 20 years of cooperation have not enabled these sectors to become the framework for a productive and expanding economy . . . . So far, only a few EDF projects have created lasting productive units. Most of them

remain experimental installations which wane after a few years and the ACP countries, overall, remain dependent on the outside world for their food.[117]

Advantages of the Lome aid programme

Despite the serious defects in the EDF aid programme under Lome I, it did have some positive characteristics and advantages over other aid programmes. One advantage of the Lome programme was its variety of instruments. From STABEX to project and emergency aid, the Community was able to transfer resources to the ACP in a variety of ways to meet a variety of needs. The EEC's long experience gave it, at least potentially, the data to enable it to compare, improve and refine its aid programme.

Lome aid was on soft terms. Of the 3000 million Ecu provided under the EDF, 80 per cent was in the form of grants and the rest was in the form of low-interest loans. Interest rates on STABEX funds and European Investment Bank credits were also low. Products selected for EDF funding were not assessed solely on hard economic grounds; the EDF was proud that it tried to consider social welfare benefits as well when assessing a project's viability. Lome aid for projects was tied to purchases in the EEC or ACP, but by giving special preferences to ACP companies, offering a larger market than a national market in which to purchase goods and services, and by its willingness to apply Article 56 of the Convention allowing for third country purchases in exceptional cases, EEC terms were more generous than those of many bilateral donors. The EEC member states did concern themselves with trying to secure their 'fair share' of Lome contracts. The British government, in particular, wished to rectify its small proportion of contracts won (11.23 per cent by 30 June 1980) in comparison with its proportional contribution to EDF IV (18.70 per cent).[118] But the European Commission — which, with the ACP state concerned, was responsible for selecting the most economically advantageous tenders — took the view that:

> The interests of ACP countries in obtaining the most advantageous terms must remain foremost in the award of contracts over and above Member States' interests in obtaining large shares of the available business.[119]

Another creditable characteristic of Lome aid was its special treatment of the poorest ACP countries. It is often considered that multilateral donors are more favourably disposed to least-developed countries than bilateral donors, and the Lome Convention's aid programme did not contradict this view. Of the 46 original ACP, 24 were classified by the EEC as least-developed states eligible for special

149

treatment in terms of financial aid. Thirty-four ACP classified as least-developed, landlocked or island were accorded preferential treatment under STABEX.* These classifications were, if internally inconsistent, even more generous than the UN's which by 1982 classified only 22 ACP (out of 31 ldcs worldwide) as least-developed countries.[120]

Under Lome I, ldcs benefited from special concessions under STABEX, reduced interest rates on loans, and had first call on grants and risk capital. Least-developed ACP states received 56.3 per cent of total Lome I funds committed by June 1981, although they constituted only 44 per cent of the total ACP population. Of the funds allocated to ldcs under Lome, 91 per cent were grants compared with 65 per cent grants to other ACP states.[121]

Although many EDF projects were seriously flawed, the EDF financed some projects with outstanding qualities. The EDF-financed Mopti health centre in Mali won the 1980 Aga Khan prize for architecture.[122] In 1981 the EDF won the Caribbean Tourism Association Prize for aiding Caribbean tourism.[123] Many EDF projects did create useful infrastructure, such as roads and water supply networks, for the recipients.

Regional projects The EDF had a distinctive policy in regional projects. Because of the EEC's own experience as a regional bloc, it was interested in promoting regional organizations among the ACP. This emphasis on regional development was soundly based on economic arguments for the creation of larger markets to promote economic development. It also reflected Europe's desire to export or to foster the development of 'Community' organizations in the ACP. Such regional groupings would, in Commission thinking, be an appropriate complement to their European Community partner.

Other donors also supported regional projects such as inter-state railways, but by expressly reserving approximately 10 per cent of its 3390 million Ecu aid budget for regional projects, the EEC gave them special priority. In some cases, regional projects amounted to more than the specified 10 per cent: under EDF IV 36 per cent of the aid to Fiji, Tonga and Western Samoa went to regional projects.[124]

The Focke Report noted with approval that the full 333 million Ecu of EDF and EIB resources allocated for regional projects were being used for this purpose. However, an analysis of the sectoral composition of the aid reveals that major regional industrial and trade projects were

* Bahamas, Barbados, Botswana, Burundi, Central African Republic, Chad, Dahomey, Equatorial Guinea, Ethiopia, Fiji, Gambia, Grenada, Guinea, Guinea Bissau, Jamaica, Lesotho, Madagascar, Malawi, Mali, Mauritania, Mauritius, Niger, Rwanda, Somalia, Sudan, Swaziland, Tanzania, Togo, Tonga, Trinidad and Tobago, Uganda, Upper Volta, Western Samoa, Zambia.

lacking. Thus, although the Community was willing to help the ACP develop better regional transport and communications infrastructure, it was not eager to promote regional industrial or trade development which could lead to direct competition with European firms and products (Table 4.9).

The emphasis on regional projects in Lome could — where these were properly conceived and executed — be a beneficial aspect of Lome aid. But despite these advantages and their encouragement of cooperation among the ACP states involved, large regional projects such as inter-state railways financed by a number of donors could suffer from the problems of large projects and co-financing described earlier. Also, the European concept of regionalism in Africa at times conflicted with ideals of pan-African, pan-ACP, or third world solidarity.

Table 4.9 Sectoral distribution of regional cooperation activities (as of 31.1.80)

Economic sector	Millions of units of account	% of total
Rural sector	39.5	13.2
Industry, energy	25.9	8.6
Transport	144.1	42.0
Telecommunications	13.3	4.4.
Technical training and assistance	33.3	11.1
Research	6.2	2.1
General activities and activities not broken down by sector	37.7	12.4
Total	300.0	100.0

Source: *Focke Report*, see note 13.

The political aspects of regional cooperation as promoted by the EEC were outlined by the EEC Development Commissioner Pisani. The ACP were, he noted:

> With little inclination to enter into regional cooperation and slow to see the need for trade to promote complementarity between neighbouring countries, they have frequently sought special relationships with powerful partners, and tried to model themselves on those partners rather than looking to themselves, their land, culture, neighbours and human resources for the means to fashion their future.[125]

The EEC's interest in promoting regionalism was not based solely on its analysis of the needs of the ACP: it was a way to counter the influence of the US and Soviet Union and to allow the European model of EurAfrican cooperation to flourish.

Microprojects One innovative feature of Lome aid was its programme of microprojects. Twenty million Ecu were allocated under EDF IV for small projects, mainly in rural areas. These could receive up to 75,000 Ecu each from the EDF. The financing of the projects was from three sources: the EDF (average contribution 41 per cent), the ACP government (average contribution 34 per cent), and the local community which the project benefited (average contribution 25 per cent).[126] For the projects financed by late 1979, the average EDF contribution was 7400 Ecu per project, indicating that the EDF was succeeding in financing small-scale development.

By the end of December 1979, nearly all of the 20 million Ecu set aside for microprojects had been allocated to 1827 microprojects in 29 ACP states. This rate of allocation compared favourably with that of other EDF projects. By late 1979, of the microprojects financed, 39 per cent were social infrastructure (schools, clinics, and so on), 23 per cent were wells and water supply projects, 8 per cent were for production development, 8 per cent for storage facilities and markets, and 10 per cent were for projects such as irrigation and afforestation.[127]

Microprojects were introduced as a two-year 'experiment'.[128] A number of problems were encountered with them, especially in the early stages of the programme. Nevertheless, microprojects were a useful complement to existing Lome instruments. Microprojects were subject to delays resulting from over-bureaucratic procedures: the projects had to be grouped into annual programmes, and it was not clear how these programmes were to be related to the indicative programmes for overall Lome aid. In 1976 only one financing decision for an annual programme was taken. The EEC Council of Ministers approved in November 1977 a simplified procedure for approving the programmes and financing decisions thereafter proceeded at an increased rate.[129]

Despite criticisms of the bureaucratic procedures involved in microprojects, most observers considered that the programme was worthwhile. The House of Lords Select Committee on the European Communities quoted approvingly the European Court of Auditors' assessment of 'the genuine success achieved by the projects and the satisfaction of the communities which benefit'.[130]

The introduction of microprojects by the EEC was designed to meet important local needs and ensure the participation of the local community — through the contribution of money, materials or services

— in the project. In spite of administrative failings and in some cases a lack of innovativeness in the projects chosen, the programme largely fulfilled its objectives.

European development aid: summary

The overriding concern of Community aid was to maintain the stability of the Lome relationship. This was accomplished by providing aid to government-selected projects which often had the effect of benefiting the existing ACP regime. The political support given to regimes by the EDF was in some cases generally acceptable, as in preventing further suffering in the aftermath of the Amin regime in Uganda; but in other cases could have had the effect of supporting a questionable regime as in the then Central African Empire. However, it was unlikely that in any ACP state EDF aid played a decisive role in determining the government.

A further political role of the EDF was to be a visible alternative donor. The EDF provided the Europeans with a presence in ACP countries; it also added to the range of choice the ACP had in financing their development projects. Not only could the ACP seek funds from US and Soviet-oriented organizations, they could see a strong European interest evidenced in the EDF as well as in the member states' bilateral donor agencies.

One unlikely argument was advanced by the Commission that European development aid had the political effect of cementing together the European Community. Development aid was, according to this view, 'a cornerstone of European integration'. But, because of the origins of the Community's development aid policy in French insistence and other EEC states' reluctance, and the different views of development policy since maintained by EEC member states, development aid was not an area of complete agreement among Community members. EEC development policy — overseen from its inception to 1985 by a French national as Development Commissioner — was perceived by other EEC states to reflect in large part French policies. Development aid was in its origins an outgrowth of the commitment to integration by the Six; it continued as a small part of Community expenditure which was largely unknown to the European public. Neither public nor governmental (except for French) support of the Community depended much on development policy. Even British concern to have the Associable Commonwealth enter into an agreement with the Community was an acceptance of existing EEC policy, not a statement of the policy Britain would like. Thus, development aid is better considered as an effect rather than a cause or cornerstone of the European Community.

One advantage or potential advantage of EEC aid lay, as noted earlier, in its long experience in ACP countries. The faults which arose in EDF-financed projects suggest that this experience was not fully employed. The European Court of Auditors suggested that a data bank of past project experience would help to utilize this experience.

Like most international aid agencies, the EDF directed its aid to specific projects, not to programme aid which tried to take into account a state's overall financial position and provide balance of payments support. Nevertheless, as shown in the STABEX section, the EEC did in a general way consider an ACP state's financial status when allocating aid. The British opposed this kind of 'disguised' programme aid, arguing that the project aid policy of the Community should be maintained at least until it was replaced by an overt commitment to programme aid. Of course, supporting a country in balance of payments difficulties — as many of the ACP often were — could prove more expensive and difficult for the EEC with its limited aid resources than project aid. The EEC project aid policy was generally well-received by the ACP, and venturing into full programme aid might have involved the Community in a new field for which it was not fully equipped (and might also have duplicated the activities of the International Monetary Fund, a much wealthier organization). It is questionable whether project aid could ever be completely divorced from considerations of a country's economic and (especially in the case of EEC aid) political situation. However, for the Community to abandon its experience and 'Community presence' through project aid in order to try to develop a policy of purely programme aid would have been technically difficult and in any case would have been unlikely to win the support of the European Commission or most of the members of the EEC.

The Focke Report proposed a compromise between programme aid — untied balance of payments support — and closely supervised project aid. It proposed as a 'third solution' that the EEC try to combine the advantages of freely available programme aid with the benefits of EEC supervision, but without its bureaucratic procedures for projects.[131] But, for the reasons mentioned above, the Community's ability to supply programme aid was limited. The proposal for 'programme' aid contained in the Focke Report really represented a call for a better-integrated and more efficient system of project aid.

The Community was more skilful in maintaining its political relationship with the ACP than in furthering their economic development.[132] It must be concluded from the selective inclusion of certain countries in the ACP and the limitations of Community trade and aid concessions that the political objective was in fact foremost. The challenge for the EEC was to develop the same level of skill in its projects that it had in its political relations with the African, Caribbean and Pacific states.

Conclusion

The results of the Lome Convention were less publicized than its inception. This was not surprising as they were altogether less impressive than the early claims that Lome would revolutionize North–South relations. As had been true of the Yaounde Conventions before it, Lome's greatest success lay in preserving the EurAfrican Association, that is, preparing the way for Lome II. Its achievements in aid and trade were, by comparison, negligible.

In its trade provisions, Lome offered little to the ACP beyond the concessions it gave to other ldc suppliers. The ACP were mainly poor, weak countries dependent on the export of a few primary products. The Community's policies did not transform them into industrially developing economies nor help them to do more than just maintain their trade position in the Community market. The ACP did manage to diversify their exports among the EEC countries and in the case of a few products, such as beef, expanded their share of the EEC market. But overall, the ACP did not fare better than less favoured EEC trade partners.

The Sugar Protocol was modelled on the Commonwealth Sugar Agreement and continued its benefits of market regulation. STABEX was also important to ACP commodity exporters. STABEX was introduced as a great innovation of the Convention, but the Community's conception of it was muddled. The stated objective of remedying the harmful effect of the instability of ACP export earnings was unrealizable and the alternative justification of STABEX as an insurance policy was unconvincing. Neither in balance of payments support nor in sectoral economic terms were STABEX transfers particularly effective. STABEX was an unusual and popular system, but its use of resources was not completely justified.

The aid provisions of the Lome Convention had limited economic results. Many projects had serious faults and were of little lasting value to the recipient state. In the worst cases, instead of benefiting a country, a project became a drain on the government's resources.

Project aid was unequally distributed among the ACP, with the francophone former AAMS particularly favoured. Project approval and aid disbursement were slow, leading to many ACP complaints. Although the ACP were supposed to be integrally involved in planning their indicative programme, in many cases they were insufficiently consulted. The EDF was widely criticized for supporting projects which were over-large or of more political than economic value to the recipient state.

Nevertheless, despite many instances of poor management of EDF funds and projects, Community aid did have some good qualities.

Special concessions were given to least-developed countries. Regional projects were particularly favoured. The programme of microprojects was an innovative addition to Community development instruments.

Where EEC aid contributed to maintaining or improving the political status of a country — such as aiding post-Amin Uganda — it could, if indirectly, assist development. However, EEC aid could also contribute to maintaining a less than desirable status quo, as, arguably, in Ethiopia or Sekou Toure's Guinea. Nevertheless, EEC aid alone — unlike French military intervention — was not a decisive factor in determining ACP governments. The overriding political intention of EEC aid was to maintain the special EurAfrican Association, to cement EEC–ACP cooperation at every level. The effects of EEC aid tended to conserve African regimes as well as the EEC–African alliance.

Lome II and beyond

The second Lome Convention, signed on 31 October 1979, came into force on 1 January 1981. The old Lome Convention expired on 1 March 1980, leaving a nine-month gap to be filled by transitional measures. The third Lome Convention, Lome III, was signed on 8 December 1984, three months before the expiration of Lome II on 28 February 1985. Again, a gap of months followed before the treaty could be ratified and come into force in 1985. Despite having negotiated a series of four earlier associations, the signatories had not achieved a smoother transition.

In sharp contrast to Lome I, Lome II was greeted with substantial disappointment, especially from the ACP side. 'Lome II is a compromise that does not fully satisfy either party', wrote a Commission official.[133] Another experienced EEC *fonctionnaire* referred to the new agreement as a 'dog's breakfast'.[134] But much of the disappointment occasioned by Lome II was the result of misunderstanding the nature of Lome I. Lome II was regarded as a disappointment because it did not radically differ from Lome I and did not seem to promise any fundamental re-structuring of relations between developed and developing countries. However, Lome I itself had not actually been the radical reform which some of its enthusiasts had claimed. It was the 'hard sell' of Lome I, the unduly raised expectations, rather than the inherent defects of Lome II which led to disappointment with the second Convention. A more careful assessment of Lome I, showing it as an incremental change from Yaounde II, would have helped to reduce the disillusionment with Lome II.

Dr Christopher Stevens of the Overseas Development Institute reckoned that while Lome I had been seen as part of the road to a new international economic order (NIEO), it successor, Lome II, was widely perceived as the end of that road.[135] But Lome I, as discussed earlier, neither disposed of the means to accomplish the aims of the new international economic order nor committed itself to achieving them. It borrowed the language of the NIEO and this encouraged unrealistic expectations that after Lome 'between ourselves (ACP) and the developed continent of Europe, all our relationships will be falling into a new pattern'.[136]

Like Lome I, Lome II contained some changes from its predecessor and made some expansive rhetorical claims:

> Resolved to continue and intensify their efforts to establish a model for relations between developed and developing States which is compatible with the aspirations of the international Community towards the establishment of a new, more just and more balanced international economic order.[137]

Like Lome I, it also failed to produce many concrete developmental or economic results.[138] Under Lome II the overriding objective of the Convention, and the one which it most satisfactorily fulfilled, was still the maintenance of the EurAfrican Association.

The political quagmire During the course of the Lome II negotiations, frictions developed over the wish of some EEC states, including Britain and Holland, to insert a declaration of human rights in the Convention. The ACP strongly resisted this, suspecting that the EEC wanted to make aid conditional on their human rights behaviour. The ACP took refuge in the argument that Lome, as a non-political trade and aid agreement, was not a suitable vehicle for this kind of statement, and in any case such a declaration was unnecessary because they, the ACP States, were already committed to human rights through declarations in the UN, OAU, and so on. Because of ACP determination, divisions in opinion on the European side, and what many saw as the Community's insensitive approach to the ACP — failing to offer them anything in return — no human rights declaration was included in Lome II.*

While the European Community focused its attention on human rights in terms of violations such as those of Amin in Uganda and Macias Nguema in Equatorial Guinea, the ACP focused on human rights in terms of Europe's relations with South Africa. Since the signing of Lome II in 1979, the institutions of the Lome Convention became particularly concerned with South Africa. The ACP–EEC Consultative Assembly voted in 1982, for instance, for sanctions on South Africa, but the EEC did not respond. The Community tried to keep political questions over southern Africa out of the official Lome ministerial dialogue. Their ineffectiveness in influencing Community policy on

---

* See also Chapter 6.

South Africa demonstrated the weakness of the Lome Assembly and the ACP states' lack of power within the Convention. ACP determination to bring the South African question to the fore embarrassed the EEC and encouraged EEC verbal and financial support ($675 million under Lome I and $800 million under Lome II) for the Southern African Development Coordination Conference (SADDCC).[139]

Although in Lome III the ACP were unable to get the concessions they wanted on South Africa, the EEC succeeded in their quest for a human rights declaration. This was accomplished despite genuine ACP reluctance. The EEC gave the ACP a *quid pro quo* in the form of a joint declaration condemning apartheid. Lome III asserted that the signatories were:

> Reaffirming their adherence to the principles of the said (UN) Charter and their faith in fundamental human rights, in the dignity and worth of the human person, in the equal rights of men and women and of nations large and small.

And to satisfy the ACP, in Annex I the signatories promised 'to work effectively for the eradication of apartheid'.[140]

Although an increased political debate within the Lome Convention was fervently desired by some ACP representatives, it was doubtful whether its results would have benefited them.[141] The joint institutions were ill-suited to taking controversial decisions; where political questions such as human rights declarations were introduced, the EEC rather than the ACP view carried more influence.

Other provisions The European Community entered the Lome II negotiations with the intention of consolidating and slightly bettering Lome I. The ACP, on the other hand, wanted changes such as vastly increased aid, free entry for all their goods, access to surplus EEC agricultural goods, and co-management of aid. The ACP failure to get more concessions from the Community was mainly due to EEC determination; the ACP were not in a position to wrest major concessions from their powerful 'partners'. Another factor in the ACP's lack of success in securing changes in the Convention was their internal lack of cohesion. They were not united in the way they had been during the Lome I negotiations, and some of the most influential ACP negotiators of Lome I such as Shridath Ramphal and Edward Olu Sanu were no longer involved.

Some changes were made in Lome II, but these were of a minor nature. *The ACP–EEC Courier* singled out the Mineral Products (SYSMIN) provisions as a 'milestone' of Lome II.[142] SYSMIN was designed to supplement STABEX by supporting ACP mineral production. Because it was in the form of project aid to mineral production and export (that is, assuring supplies to the Community) rather than earnings stabilization, a senior ACP official called it 'downright embarrassing'.

Lome II included a few concessions to the ACP on trade, for example, in beef and tomatoes. Total financial resources for the Convention were increased to 5,227 million Ecu. Assessed on a real, annual per capita basis, this meant a fall of 24 per cent.[143] STABEX which had been considered the EEC's Director General for Development, 'perfected' under Lome I was given more funds, more products to cover and more liberal thresholds.[144] The system however, ran out of funds in 1980. Another new feature of Lome II was a slow-starting Technical Centre for Agricultural and Rural Cooperation to disseminate agricultural information (whose potential usefulness was regarded, even by some Commission experts, as minimal).

Lome III

Many observers were surprised that the 1984 Convention was dubbed Lome III rather than finding a new name, for instance, Lagos I.* This reflected the successful lobbying of Togo to remain the site of the elaborate signing ceremony. Although Lome III was again mainly an effort to consolidate the EurAfrican relationship, keeping the EEC at the centre of power and the ACP at the periphery, it contained some innovations such as the human rights clauses mentioned earlier. Nevertheless, in the third Lome Convention, as Claude Cheysson — president of the EEC Council of Ministers during the negotiations — described it:

> the underlying principles of the previous Conventions and the broad outlines of their policy pursued with determination over a number of years have been confirmed.[145]

Having received a generally poor press from its efforts of 'consolidation' in Lome II, the EEC tried to put a new face on Lome III. The presentation of the text of the Convention was better organized than its predecessors, with three parts setting out the general aims of the Convention, the areas of cooperation, and the means or instruments of cooperation. The EEC was successful in its attempts to make the Convention more readable, but the new Convention expressed, especially in its first two parts, many goals and aspirations which it was not clear whether or how it could fulfil.

---

* The new convention was widely referred to within the EEC's Development Directorate as 'Pisani I', indicating the new Commissioner's desire to make noticeable changes.

Whereas the *EEC–ACP Courier*'s (official) presentation of the Lome II Convention in 1979 had contained detailed (and disappointing) trade figures and aid statistics, The *Courier*'s presentation of Lome III emphasized rhetoric rather than data. That is, no trade figures were included but references from both EEC and ACP officials to the 'spirit of Lome', 'the dignity of man', and so forth abounded.

Nevertheless, the purple prose accompanying the Convention was not as influential as it had been under Lome I. Critical descriptions of Lome as neo-colonial or a 'long-running soap opera', were as much in evidence as praise for 'fruitful cooperation'.[146] By late 1984 the Commission's rhetoric had a defensive quality which it lacked in 1975 when Lome was widely interpreted as a possible answer to the problems of North–South relations.

In terms of aid, Lome III disposed of a total of 8,500 million Ecu, (7.4 billion in EDF aid and 1.1 billion through the European Investment Bank), an increase in nominal terms of almost 50 per cent over total Lome II funds. This was a larger increase than Lome II was over Lome I, and it was roughly the same per capita, real aid value as Lome I.[147] The total still fell short of ACP proposals for 10 billion in EDF aid plus 2 billion Ecu from the EIB. The Community tried to persuade the ACP to accept a package with 7 billion Ecu of EDF aid as a non-negotiable *fait accompli*.[148] However, this offer was later increased to 7.4 billion Ecu, nearer the sum originally favoured by France.

The ACP successfully resisted Commissioner Pisani's proposals for a broad 'policy dialogue', that is, greater EEC involvement in making sure that development projects were properly chosen and executed. The ACP feared this as unwarranted interference in their development programmes. They also successfully resisted EEC attempts to require that STABEX transfers be directed to the affected sector; however, the Convention did require them to provide more information and justification of their use of STABEX monies.

Another small ACP victory was the addition of a chapter on cultural cooperation in Lome III. This called for cooperation, that is, aid, for cultural and social projects and programmes in the ACP states including research, cultural exchanges and (more an EEC than a unanimously ACP interest) the enhancement of the role of women. This ACP-initiated change was in keeping with the spirit of the EurAfrican Associations which, as long ago as 1957, referred to promoting the cultural development of the Associates.[149] The most controversial ACP proposals — for the return of ACP cultural items held in Europe — were not included.

In addition, the ACP obtained a joint declaration on ACP migrant workers and students in the Community. This declaration fell short of

ACP aspirations to have their nationals treated within the Community as were EEC nationals. It offered only a framework for consultation, but it at least addressed the problem.

The EEC in Lome I and II had sought to establish a framework for investment guarantees. It finally achieved this in Lome III. In Title IV of the Lome III Convention, the parties agreed to study ways to facilitate private investment and to remove obstacles to it.[150] However, it was questionable whether such a policy really was compatible with the aims of socialist ACP countries such as Mali or Ethiopia and to what extent it could be put into practice. For its part, the EEC had announced as long ago as 1969 that Yaounde II provided 'Great Possibilities for Private Investment in Africa'.[151] Nevertheless, it had failed to reverse the trend away from private investment in Africa, and Lome III might well prove similarly ineffective.

Lome III was not concluded for an indefinite period, with five-yearly reviews and updates of specific provisions, as the Commission had proposed. In this respect the Commission was not able to turn the clock back to the 1957 Treaty of Rome Association. The Commission had stressed the need for long-term planning in terms of food strategies and the fight against desertification. However, the ACP were not willing to commit themselves indefinitely to the Convention, abandoning their 'bargaining card' of completely rejecting an unsatisfactory agreement. But Lome III did offer, to those countries which wanted it, help in preparing multi-annual food programmes, and the Convention also stressed the long-term nature of the fight against desertification.

It is beyond the scope of this study to make an exhaustive analysis of Lome III, but, briefly, other innovations included a fisheries chapter, specific funds to aid refugees, and the EEC's commitment to consider making available surplus agricultural goods to countries with (approved) food policies. STABEX and SYSMIN were continued and liberalized. More funds were devoted to regional cooperation (which covered large, anti-desertification projects) and special treatment continued to be given to products such as bananas. The microproject programme was expanded and the Joint Committee of the Consultative Assembly was abolished.

The number of ACP signatories to Lome rose from 46 in 1975 and 57 in 1979 to 65 (including the much-prized Mozambique) in 1984. Although at the time of negotiating Lome II there had been some talk, mainly from Nigeria, of not joining an unsatisfactory Lome II, by 1984 even this possibility had faded. The stability of what the third Convention called the 'acquis' — the acquired right — of ACP—EEC relations appeared stronger than ever.[152]

Whatever its shortcomings, in the mid-1980s the Lome club remained popular. When delegates to the Lome III signing ceremony in Togo afterwards sang, appropriately in French, 'It is only an au revoir', it was hard to doubt that there would be another meeting in five years to finalize a new ACP—EEC Convention.[153]

Notes

1. Twitchett, Carol, *A Framework for Development*, London, Allen and Unwin, 1981, Ch.2.
2. Moss, J. and Ravenhill, J., 'Trade Between the ACP and EEC during Lome I', in Stevens, C. (ed.), *The Atlantic Rift, EEC and the Third World: A Survey 3*, London, Hodder and Stoughton, 1983.
3. *Report of the ACP—EEC Council of Ministers 1976—1980*, Brussels, EEC, July 1980, p. 32.
4. Twitchett, *op cit*, Ch.2.
5. *Report of the ACP—EEC Council of Ministers 1976—1980, op cit*, p. 34.
6. *Report of the ACP—EEC Council of Ministers 1976—1980, op cit*, p. 91.
7. *Report of the ACP—EEC Council of Ministers 1976—1980, op cit*, p. 86.
8. *ibid*, p. 46.
9. *ibid*, p. 56.
10. *ibid*, p. 60.
11. *ibid*, p. 86.
12. *ibid*, pp. 19—20.
13. Focke, Katarina, *From Lome 1 towards Lome 2*, text of the report and resolution adopted on 26 September 1980 by the ACP—EEC Consultative Assembly, p. 14.
14. *Report of the ACP—EEC Council of Ministers 1976—1980, op cit*, pp. 69—70.
15. *Lome Convention*, Article 16.
16. 'North—South Rift within STABEX', *South*, December 1980.
17. 'Comments on the Operation of the Export Earnings Stabilization System', *Report Adopted by the Court of Auditors of the European Community*, 19 July 1979, p. 3. (Annexed to *Comprehensive Report on the Export Earnings Stabilization System established by the Lome Convention*, Brussels, EEC, 1981.)
18. *Comprehensive Report on the Export Earnings Stabilization System established by the Lome Convention*, Brussels, EEC, Sec81—1104, 1981, p. 40.
19. *ibid*, p. 163.
20. *ibid*, p. 163.
21. Wall, David, *The European Community's Lome Convention*, London, Trade Policy Research Centre, 1976, p. 13.
22. *Comprehensive Report, op cit*.
23. Focke Report, *op cit*, p. 27.
24. Court of Auditors Report, 1979, *op cit*, p. 19.
25. *Comprehensive Report, op cit*, p. 34.
26. *ibid*, p. 45.
27. *Report of the ACP—EEC Council of Ministers 1976—1980, op cit*.
28. *Commission's Comments on the Court of Auditors Report*, Brussels, EEC, COM 80 211 final. (Annex II to the *Comprehensive Report, op cit*.)
29. Focke Report, *op cit*.
30. Court of Auditors Report, 1979, *op cit*. The court noted that 37 per cent of ACP replies about the use of funds were evasive.

31. For instance, Hewitt, Adrian, 'Stabex: Analysing the Effectiveness of an Innovation', in Stevens, C. (ed.), *The EEC and the Third World: A Survey III*, London, Hodder and Stoughton, 1983.
32. Court of Auditors Report, 1979, *op cit*.
33. *Comprehensive Report*, *op cit*.
34. Persaud, B., 'Export Earnings Stabilisation in the ACP–EEC Convention', in Long, F. (ed.), *The Political Economy of Relations with African, Caribbean and Pacific States*, London, Pergamon, 1980.
35. Hewitt, *op cit*. (Note 24).
36. Court of Auditors Report, 1979, *op cit*, p. 20.
37. 'North–South Rift within STABEX', *op cit*.
38. *Comprehensive Report*, *op cit*, pp. 70–82.
39. *ibid*, pp. 70–71.
40. *ibid*, p. 2.
41. *Report of the ACP–EEC Council of Ministers 1976–1980*, *op cit*, p. 82.
42. *Le Monde*, 6 November 1981.
43. *Comprehensive Report*, *op cit*, p. 75.
44. *ibid*, p. 75.
45. Court of Auditors Report, 1979, *op cit*, p. 3, cited the cases of Congo and Ivory Coast's actions in 1975 which resulted in lower earnings from wood exports.
46. *ibid*, p. 1.
47. Wall, *op cit*, p. 13.
48. Pisani, Edgard, Speech to ACP–EEC Consultative Assembly, Strasbourg, 24 September 1981, p. 4.
49. Wall, *op cit*, p. 13.
50. Pisani, *op cit*.
51. *West Africa*, 17 October 1983. p. 2393.
52. Twitchett, *A Framework for Development*, *op cit*, p. 17.
53. Hewitt, A., 'The European Development Fund and its Function in the EEC's Development Aid Policy', London, Overseas Development Institute, working paper no. 11, 1982.
54. Court of Auditors Report, 'The European Development Funds', *Official Journal of the European Communities*, C344, 31 December 1982.
55. Hewitt, A. and Stevens, C., 'The Second Lome Convention', in Stevens, C. (ed.), *The European Community and the Third World: A Survey 1*, *op cit*.
56. Hewitt, Adrian, 'The European Development Fund as a Development Agent: Some Results of EDF Aid to Cameroon', *ODI Review*, 1979, no. 2.
57. Court of Auditors Report, 'The European Development Funds' (1982), *op cit*.
58. Washington, G., 'The Farewell Address', in Commager, H. (ed.), *Documents of American History*, New York, Appleton-Century-Crofts, pp. 169–174.
59. 'Commission Report to the ACP–EEC Council of Ministers on the Administration of Financial and Technical Cooperation in 1979, under the Lome Convention', in *Report of the ACP–EEC Council of Ministers 1976–1980*, *op cit*, Annex IV, p. 21.
60. Parfitt, Trevor, 'EEC Aid in Practice: Sierra Leone', in Stevens, C. (ed.), *The EEC and the Third World: A Survey 4*, London, Hodder and Stoughton, 1984.
61. Hewitt, A., 'The European Development Fund and its Function in the EEC's Development Aid Policy', *op cit*.
62. Parfitt, *op cit*.
63. Hewitt, A., 'The European Development Fund as a Development Agent: Some Results of EDF Aid to Cameroon', *op cit*.

64. Court of Auditors Report, 'The European Development Funds' (1982), *op cit*. See also Hewitt and Stevens, *op cit*.
65. 'EEC Resists US Demands', *South*, June 1981, p. 78.
66. See, for instance, *ACP—EEC Council of Ministers Report 1980—1981*, Brussels, EEC, 1981.
67. Stevens, C., 'Prospects for Lome III', Lecture given 14 October 1983, at the Overseas Development Institute, London.
68. House of Lords Select Committee on the European Communities, *Development Aid Policy*, London, HMSO, 1981, p. xliv.
69. *ibid*, p. XXV.
70. Hewitt, A., *Malawi's First Eight Years of Cooperation with the EEC: The Results of the Lome Conventions*, London, Overseas Development Institute Working Paper no. 12, 1983.
71. *ibid*, p. 63.
72. *Report of the ACP—EEC Council of Ministers 1976—1980*, *op cit*, p. 148.
73. *ibid*, Annex V.
74. Stevens, C., 'Prospects for Lome III', *op cit*.
75. House of Lords Select Committee, *op cit*, p. xxii.
76. Cf. Hewitt, 'The European Development Fund and its Function in the EEC's Development Aid Policy', *op cit*.
77. For the latter charge see Twitchett, *A Framework for Development*, *op cit*, p. 76.
78. *Lome Convention*, Protocol No. 2, Article 30.
79. *Report of the ACP—EEC Council of Ministers 1976—1980*, *op cit*, and its Annex V; also House of Lords Select Committee, *Development Aid Policy*, *op cit*.
80. Parfitt, *op cit*.
81. Hewitt, 'The European Development Funds and its Function in the EEC's Development Aid Policy, *op cit*.
82. Court of Auditors Report, 'The European Development Funds', *op cit*, (1982).
83. House of Lords Select Committee Report, *op cit*.
84. Wall, *op cit*, p. 16.
85. Court of Auditors Report, 'The European Development Funds', *Official Journal of the European Communities*, C344, 31 December 1981.
86. Court of Auditors Report, 'The European Development Funds', (1982), *op cit*.
87. *Lome Convention*, Article 52.
88. *ibid*, Article 55.
89. Court of Auditors Report, 'The European Development Funds', (1981), *op cit*.
90. *ibid*.
91. *ibid*.
92. 'Dossier: Evaluation', *The Courier*, July—August 1983, no. 80.
93. *ibid*.
94. Court of Auditors Report, 'The European Development Funds', (1981), *op cit*.
95. *ibid*.
96. Court of Auditors Report, 'The European Development Funds', (1982), *op cit*.
97. *The Courier*, March—April 1973, no. 78, p. IX.
98. Court of Auditors Report, 'The European Development Funds', (1982), *op cit*.

99. Hewitt, A., 'The European Development Fund as a Development Agent: Some Results of EDF Aid to Cameroon', *op cit.*
100. Court of Auditors Report, 'The European Development Funds', (1981), *op cit.*
101. *ibid.*
102. *The Courier*, July–August 1983, no. 80, p. 85.
103. Court of Auditors Report, 'The European Development Funds', (1981), *op cit.*
104. Hoffman, K. and Birch, D., 'The EEC and Energy Aid to the Third World', in Stevens, C. (ed.), *The EEC and the Third World: A Survey 1*, *op cit.*
105. Court of Auditors Report, 'The European Development Funds', (1982), *op cit.*
106. Hoffman and Birch, *op cit.*
107. *The Courier*, January–February 1982, no. 71, p. 49.
108. *ibid*, p. 56.
109. *Report of the ACP–EEC Council of Ministers 1976–1980*, *op cit*, Annex IV.
110. Twitchett, *A Framework for Development*, *op cit*, Ch.3.
111. *Report of the ACP–EEC Council of Ministers 1976–1980*, *op cit*, Annex V.
112. Court of Auditors Report, 'The European Development Funds', (1982), *op cit.*
113. *Harmonization and Coordination of Development Cooperation Policies within the Community*, Brussels, EEC, COM (76) 358 final.
114. Court of Auditors Report, 'The European Development Funds', (1982), *op cit.*
115. *The Second Lome Convention*, Articles 152–4.
116. *The Courier*, nos 76, 78, and Court of Auditors Reports for 1981 and 1982, *op cit.*
117. *The Courier*, May–June 1983, no. 80, p. 47.
118. *Report of the ACP–EEC Council of Ministers 1976–1980*, *op cit*, Annex IV.
119. House of Lords Select Committee Report, *op cit*, p. xxvi.
120. *The Courier*, March–April 1982, no. 72.
121. *Report of the ACP–EEC Council of Ministers 1976–1980*, *op cit*, Annex IV.
122. *The Courier*, January–February 1981, no. 65.
123. *The Courier*, September–October 1981, no. 69.
124. *The Courier*, March–April 1980, no. 60, p. 42.
125. 'Memorandum on the Community's Development Policy' (Pisani Memorandum), Brussels, EEC, COM (82) 640 final, p. 19.
126. 'Microprojects under the Lome Convention', *The Courier*, September–October 1979, no. 57.
127. *ibid.*
128. *Lome Convention*, Protocol no. 2, Ch.7.
129. *Report of the ACP–EEC Council of Ministers 1976–1980*, *op cit.*
130. House of Lords Select Committee Report, *op cit*, p. xxvii.
131. Focke Report, *op cit*, p. 63.
132. Cf. Hewitt, 'The European Development Fund and its Function in the EEC's Development Aid Policy', *op cit.*
133. *The Courier*, November 1979, no. 58, p. 2.
134. Remarks quoted from a seminar of the University Association for Contemporary European Studies, 24 November 1979.
135. *ibid.*

136. *The Courier*, March 1975, (no. 31), p. 7.
137. *The Second Lome Convention*, in *The Courier*, no. 58, *op cit*.
138. For some of its problems see Lister, M.R., 'The Functioning of the Second Lome Convention', *Journal of World Trade Law*, September–October 1982.
139. *The Courier*, July–August 1982, no. 74, p. IV.
140. 'Third ACP–EEC Convention', *The Courier*, January–February 1985, no. 89, Preamble and Annex I.
141. *West Africa*, 10 January 1983, p. 78.
142. *The Courier*, January–February 1985, p. 32.
143. 'Lome II', London, Overseas Development Institute, Briefing Paper, February 1980.
144. *The Courier*, November 1979, no. 58, p. 24.
145. *The Courier*, January–February 1985, no. 89, p. 17.
146. For instance, *Africa Confidential*, 5 October 1983, p. 4.
147. 'Behind the Screen of New Ideas, an Old Message', *The Guardian*, 7 October 1983.
148. 'EEC–ACP Countries Near Finalising Third Lome Pact', *Financial Times*, 2 November 1984.
149. *Treaty Establishing the European Economic Community*, (1957), (Treaty of Rome), London, HMSO, 1962, Part IV.
150. *The Third Lome Convention*, *op cit*, Title IV, Ch.1.
151. *The Second Yaounde Convention: Great Possibilities for Private Investment*, Brussels, EEC, (undated).
152. *The Third Lome Convention*, *op cit*, Ch.1, Article 2.
153. *The Courier*, January–February 1985, no. 89, p. 3.

5 ACP unity in theory and practice

ACP solidarity, as it emerged during the negotiations for the Lome Convention, was widely remarked upon. This unity among a group of 46 highly diverse states was an outstanding feature of the negotiations and was considered by many observers as one of the most important outcomes of the negotiations. However, the large degree of unity which was demonstrated in the negotiations of the African, Caribbean and Pacific states vis-a-vis the European Community was not continued and expanded in practice during the five years' duration of the Lome Convention.

The ideal of ACP unity had a firm philosophical basis in the tradition of pan-Africanism and in the renewed emphasis on third world solidarity expressed in the UN system. But the broad support among the ACP for the concept of ACP cooperation and self-reliance and the promising start of ACP unity in the negotiations with Europe did not lead to a great broadening and deepening of ACP solidarity. ACP unity under the Lome Convention was impressive at the rhetorical level, but it produced few results.

The Nigerian ambassador, Olu Sanu, noted that after the negotiations ACP political will and effectiveness seemed to disappear: 'I believe that ACP states have made a fundamental mistake in not appreciating that the task of implementing the Convention is as important as the Convention itself.'[1] The ambassador argued that through the weakening of the ACP Secretariat and the transfer of many of the experienced ACP ambassadors after the Lome negotiations, the ACP were less able to deal effectively with the Community than they had been.

In the wake of the extraordinary expression of ACP unity during the Lome negotiations, the obstacles to that unity reasserted themselves. One obstacle was the lack of any *raison d'etre* for the ACP Group other than their relations with the European Community. The African, Caribbean and Pacific states had no history of economic, political, or cultural relations with each other, and in some cases were even largely ignorant of each other's existence. In addition, the new ACP had different relationships with the Community and its member states: some were former Associates; some were Commonwealth countries; and others like Guinea and Equatorial Guinea were new to close relations with both the Community and many of its members. Economic interests among the ACP were different too. The ACP included sugar producers, STABEX-covered commodity producers, and in the case of Nigeria, a country pre-eminently interested in industrial development. ACP states with a particular economic interest, such as sugar, often felt that this interest was insufficiently supported by their ACP partners.

The ACP states' wide diversity of history, culture, political relations and economic interests, despite their common links with the EEC, was observed by an American official who remarked that the ACP contained more centrifugal than centripetal forces. Even the ACP concept of intra-ACP cooperation was not clearly defined or differentiated from the terms 'regional' and 'interregional cooperation' which were mentioned in the Convention.[2] Nevertheless, the ACP did continue to try to enhance their solidarity or 'intra-ACP cooperation' even though they usually failed to implement their own proposals.

Because of the new Lome Convention, the ACP developed a system of cooperation which, although it fell far short of their highest aspirations, was extremely unlikely otherwise to have emerged. By bringing together 46 different countries into the new Convention, the EEC helped to foster their cooperation, especially at the regional levels. In fact, as mentioned in Chapter 4, the EEC liked to see the ACP as emulating the European model of regional cooperation.

The effects of ACP cooperation in the Lome negotiations were particularly noticeable in the impetus given to the creation of the West African Economic Community (ECOWAS) later in 1975.[3] Other regional organizations such as the South Pacific Bureau for Economic Cooperation (SPEC), the executive body of the South Pacific Forum founded in 1972, and the Indian Ocean Commission (Mauritius, Madagascar, Seychelles) received added importance from their role of coordinating activities relating to the Convention.

The history of ACP cooperation

The Georgetown Agreement

The treaty signed by the ACP in Georgetown, Guyana on 6 June 1975 became the formal basis of the African, Caribbean and Pacific Group of States (ACP Group). The Georgetown Agreement, concluded just three months after the signing of the Lome Convention, reflected the idealistic and sanguine atmosphere of the recently completed negotiations with the EEC. The Agreement gave the ACP a legal personality and a formal, independent identity. By establishing their own international organization, the ACP hoped to make themselves more equal to their EEC partners and more able to foster their own interests outside as well as inside Lome.

The objectives of the ACP Group as expressed in the Georgetown Agreement were ambitious. Of the eight objectives set forward in Article 2 of the Agreement, the first three dealt with the Lome Convention while the last four addressed intra-ACP cooperation and third world solidarity.[4] The objectives were:

1. To ensure the realization of the objectives of the Convention of Lome.
2. To coordinate the activities of the ACP States in the application of the Convention of Lome.
3. To determine joint positions of the ACP Group vis-a-vis the EEC on matters covered by the Convention of Lome.
4. To promote and strengthen the existing solidarity of the ACP Group.
5. To contribute to the development of greater and closer trade, economic and cultural relations amongst developing countries in general and, to this end to develop the exchange of information amongst the ACP States in the fields of trade, technology, industry and human resources.
6. To contribute to the promotion of effective regional and inter-regional cooperation amongst the ACP States and amongst developing countries in general, and to strengthen the links between the respective regional organizations to which they belong.
7. To promote the establishment of a new world economic order.

Despite declaring wide-ranging objectives for the ACP, the Georgetown Agreement was itself a brief and sketchy document, consisting of only eight pages in the English version. Compared to the complexity of the Treaty of Rome or the Treaty of Brussels, the Georgetown Agreement was a skeleton document. Whatever its references to the objective of developing effective regional and inter-regional cooperation amongst the ACP in the fields of trade, economic and cultural relations, the Georgetown Agreement did not provide the detailed mechanisms for realizing such cooperation. Through its lack of detail the agreement gave an impression at odds with its ambitious, stated objectives. It showed that cooperation among the ACP was not envisaged, or practicable, on a scale comparable to cooperation within the EEC.

What kind of organization, then, did the Georgetown Agreement establish? The institutions of the ACP group were created as counterparts to the joint ACP–EEC institutions. Like Lome, and like the EEC, the ACP Group was based on a formal contract. Officially, the organs of the ACP were the Council of Ministers and the Committee of Ambassadors, assisted by a General Secretariat. Although the preamble and objectives of the Georgetown Agreement indicated that the ACP aspired to a sphere of action outside of the Lome relationship, the institutional structure of the ACP was based on the structure of the Convention and was therefore most suitable for operations relating to the Convention.

Like its EEC counterpart, the Council of Ministers was the supreme decision-making body of the ACP Group. It met bi-annually and could delegate to the Committee of Ambassadors any of its powers. The Council was also responsible for liaison with the ACP members of the Lome Consultative Assembly. The Assembly itself was the only major Lome institution not re-created by the ACP. This reflected the Consultative Assembly's lack of decision-making power, its cumbersome and expensive nature, and its questionable appropriateness for countries without parliaments. Because of the large number of ACP states, the Council appointed a bureau or executive committee every six months to deal with the Group's business. The bureau consisted of one member from each region: West Africa, East Africa, Central Africa, Southern Africa, the Caribbean and Pacific. The presidency of the Council was elected from among members of the bureau so that it rotated between Africa, the Caribbean and Pacific.

Despite modelling themselves on the institutions created by the EEC, the ACP managed to make some pragmatic improvements in these arrangements. Instead of following the Community's practice of taking important ministerial decisions by consensus (the Luxembourg Compromise), Article 10 of the Georgetown Agreement provided that although decisions of the Council would normally be taken by consensus, in special circumstances decisions could be taken by a two-thirds majority. Another pragmatic improvement made by the ACP was to adopt just two working languages – English and French – thus avoiding some of the battery of problems encountered by the Community with its nine working languages.

Like the ACP Council of Ministers, the ACP Committee of Ambassadors was modelled on the joint Committee of Ambassadors established by the Lome Convention. The duties of the ACP Committee were the same as those of the joint Committee of Ambassadors in the context of Lome: to assist and carry out the instructions of the Council, to oversee the implementation of the Convention, to report on its activities to the Council, and to supervise its committees and working groups. The Georgetown Agreement provided that this last function would be carried out by a bureau of the Committee, composed of a chairman and five vice-chairmen to be chosen every six months. Unlike the ACP Council of Ministers, the Ambassadors were encumbered with the procedure of taking decisions by consensus.

In a report adopted by the ACP–EEC Consultative Assembly, S.R. Insanally of Guyana argued that the ACP Committee of Ambassadors was not sufficiently assisted by the ACP Secretariat, leaving them overworked:

> It may also be fairly said that on the ACP side the Committee of Ambassadors runs the risk of being reduced to a technical body since it is the Ambassadors who constantly grapple with the Commission on the details of every issue.[5]

The report also noted that the preparatory work done by committees and sub-committees of the Ambassadors was not sufficiently utilized and that these committees had therefore lost much of their dynamism and even failed to meet regularly.

The Suva Declaration

The Suva Declaration was meant to be a programme of action for the ACP to follow after they had, in the Georgetown Agreement, established their collective identity. The declaration was made by the ACP Council of Ministers at their meeting in Suva, Fiji in 1977.[6] The preamble of the declaration mentioned 'the political will of the ACP States to strengthen cooperation among themselves for their individual and collective benefit;' considered 'the steps already taken to consolidate and strengthen the existing solidarity of the ACP Group in the conclusion of the Georgetown Agreement formally establishing the ACP Group;' and pointed out 'the need to translate into practical action the principles of collective self-reliance and of self-determination by the ACP countries and to reinforce their unity and capacity for joint action'.

Nevertheless, the Suva Declaration did not fully demonstrate that the ACP had the political will to translate their principles of collective self-reliance into action. Although the Suva Declaration was supposed to be a programme of action for intra-ACP cooperation, it was more a set of general objectives than a detailed plan for achieving practical results. Like the Georgetown Agreement, the Suva Declaration was a brief document — only twelve pages in the English edition. It showed that the ACP were interested in broadening and deepening their cooperation, but it did not show that they were fully committed or knew how to do this.

The action programme for intra-ACP cooperation set forward in the Suva Declaration covered six sectors:

1. Transport, communications and other services.
2. Trade.
3. Development of intra-ACP enterprises and cooperation in production.
4. Development finance.
5. Technology, know-how, and technical assistance.
6. Cultural, scientific and educational cooperation.

Proposals for cooperation in the first area — including shipping, air and land transport, communications and banking, insurance and credit — were extensive but not developed in detail. 'The importance of communications networks between the ACP countries as a basic precondition for the development of intra-ACP cooperation' was recognized as was the equivalent importance of insurance, banking and credit. The main specific recommendations for this sector were to undertake studies into the extent to which the lack of transportation constituted a barrier to intra-ACP trade, how ACP cargoes might be aggregated to reduce shipping costs, and whether regional shipping lines could be established or strengthened.

Trade was the most extensively covered sector in the Suva Declaration. Nine proposals for trade cooperation were presented, although these were set out in general terms or in their early stages of conceptualization. Two dealt with making greater use of Lome provisions. The proposals were:

1. To strengthen the collective bargaining power of the ACP in their trade with the industrialized countries.
2. To liberalize conditions of trade among the ACP and other developing countries.
3. Fully to utilize Lome provisions for supporting the expansion of ACP trade.
4. To adopt active measures of trade cooperation among the ACP such as in the conclusion of medium- and long-term commodity supply and purchase contracts.
5. To undertake joint ACP action to improve and stabilize ACP export

prices; to cooperate in processing, product improvement, technical support, marketing and shipping.
6   Fully to exploit Lome provisions relating to the accumulation of processing and cumulative treatment (under the rules of origin) in respect of exports to the European Community.
7   To identify possibilities for the production and trade of ACP goods and prospects for complementarity between sectors in different ACP countries.
8   To identify and eliminate obstacles to intra-ACP trade.
9   To develop a clearance system for ACP trade payments and closer links between ACP central banks.

The third sector identified for action in the Suva Declaration was the creation of intra-ACP enterprises and cooperation in production. The creation of ACP multinational enterprises — in areas yet to be identified — was envisaged. Financial support would be sought from the EDF initially. It was not indicated whether such multinationals were to be wholly or partly government-owned or private enterprises. In addition, ACP collaboration in the development of hydro-electricity, roads, telecommunications, airline and shipping services, banking and insurance (as was earlier recommended in Part 1 of the declaration), and technology and research were proposed.

In the area of development finance, the Suva Declaration contained several general proposals for enhancing intra-ACP cooperation. These were to provide for balance of payments adjustment assistance, to support the stabilization of commodity prices, and to serve as a framework for long-term development finance. The proposals for balance of payments assistance, and the like, went even beyond the aid intentions of the Lome Convention. How the impoverished ACP countries were to attract financing for such ambitious undertakings was not specified. As more specific objectives, the declaration envisaged the creation of machinery within the ACP Secretariat for maximizing benefits to ACP enterprises from EDF project tenders, and the systematic sharing of information about development finance among the ACP.

The fifth section chosen for action was technology, know-how and technical assistance. This proposed increasing the transfer and sharing of technology and expert services among the ACP countries. This proposal closely imitated or duplicated the functions of the ACP—EEC Centre for Industrial Development. It was, however, unlikely that the ACP had a sufficient amount of solely ACP expertise to make such an overlapping if not duplication of CID activity worthwhile. As the Suva proposal itself did not contain any details about how this technology cooperation should be accomplished — whether through the ACP Secretariat or another body — it may be doubted whether the ACP were entirely in earnest in this proposal.

The final area identified by the Suva Declaration was cultural, scientific and educational cooperation. The ACP interest in creating what could be called a 'UNESCO' section of activity was allocated only one paragraph in the declaration, indicating its rather secondary position in ACP thinking. It did show that the ACP were interested in expanding their fields of cooperation (both with each other and with the EEC, with whom they also proposed to undertake cultural, scientific and educational cooperation).[7] The ACP hoped for a relationship with each other based not only on the aid and trade preferences of the European Community, but one with broader horizons which would be 'a foundation upon which they (the ACP) will strive to build a strong and united brotherhood of nations'.[8]

The scope of the Suva Declaration was extraordinarily broad. It proposed intra-ACP cooperation in fields ranging from balance of payments assistance to commodity price stabilization, insurance, banking, technology transfer and cultural exchanges, but many of the proposals were only sketchily outlined. Those which, like the balance of payments assistance, required extensive funding seemed completely unrealizable.

Although it was impressive in the sphere of declarations, the Suva programme led to little concrete action. The ACP had too many costly, vague and indefinite targets instead of one or a few well-defined and achievable ones, whose accomplishment would then increase the impetus for cooperation. Because of this, as well as owing to the inherent ACP problems of poverty, diversity of views and traditions, and lack of experience in these fields, intra-ACP cooperation remained more of a theory than a reality.

ACP cooperation in practice

The ACP General Secretariat

Although the ACP Secretariat was established during the Lome negotiations as the successor to the Association Secretariat, it was in Chapter III of the Georgetown Agreement that the regulations establishing and governing the ACP General Secretariat were formally set out. Articles 18 to 21 of the Georgetown Agreement specified the location, functions, and government of the Secretariat. Despite its brief treatment in the Agreement and its secondary status (unlike the Council of Ministers and Committee of Ambassadors it was not considered an 'organ' of the Group), the ACP Secretariat was one of the most controversial and potentially the most progressive ACP institution.

The functions of the Secretariat were to 'assist' and 'service' the organs of the ACP. According to Article 19 of the Georgetown Agreement, under the authority of the organs, the ACP General Secretariat was to monitor the implementation of the Convention, service the organs of the ACP Group and the joint Lome institutions, and carry out tasks assigned to it by the Council of Ministers and Committee of Ambassadors.

During its operation under Lome I, the ACP Secretariat encountered numerous problems. In its problems as well as in its limited achievements, the ACP Secretariat can be considered as the foremost example of intra-ACP cooperation during Lome I. The experience of the Secretariat illustrated the problems of the practice, rather than the theory, of ACP cooperation.

The functioning of the ACP Secretariat was not satisfactory; it had difficulties in providing technical and secretarial services to the ACP. With a staff of only 65, 24 of them classified as experts, the ACP Secretariat could not offer the same level of back-up to the ACP as the European Commission and the Secretariat of the EEC Council of Ministers could offer to the Community. This meant that in negotiations with the Community the ACP were generally less well prepared and found it difficult to make their own proposals or take the initiative in discussions. This also produced a high level of dissatisfaction both among the staff of the Secretariat and the ACP diplomats who relied on it.

One senior ACP official remarked that he was embarrassed to attend international meetings as a representative of the ACP Secretariat because of the poor reputation of the institution. A wish to improve the efficiency and standing of the Secretariat, to make it into more than a 'glorified post office' did exist among many Secretariat staff and some ACP diplomats.

The problems of the ACP Secretariat can be divided into three interrelated categories: lack of political will to have a strong, efficient Secretariat; lack of expertise in recruiting and managing staff; and lack of financial resources. To turn first to the ACP Group's lack of political will to develop a strong and effective Secretariat, this stemmed from the ACP ministers' and ambassadors' fear of a rival centre of power and from their failure to appreciate the importance of having a Secretariat able to monitor the functioning of the Convention and provide the technical information and services necessary for the ACP to deal with the Community. This lack of political will to have an efficient Secretariat also showed that the ACP states did not consider that developing a degree of practical equality with the EEC was a readily achievable goal.

The ACP Committee of Ambassadors was reluctant to see the

Secretariat become a potentially powerful and independent ACP institution. Instead of realizing the benefits of having an effective, independent Secretariat able to offer the ACP many of the services supplied to the EEC by the Commission and Council Secretariat, ACP ambassadors were jealous of their own power and unwilling to delegate much of their authority to Secretariat officials. The ambassadors thus became involved in many of the details of ACP—EEC interaction although they were not well suited to this role.

S.R. Insanally of Guyana, in a report to the joint Consultative Assembly, recommended:

> that the ACP Secretariat should be fortified in such a way as to be able to thrash out routine problems and to leave more time to the Ambassadors for their major task of political direction. At the moment, the Committee of Ambassadors is too often ensnarled in a technocratic bind and prevented from dealing with the fundamentally political difficulties.[9]

Without a determined ACP effort to approach the Lome Convention as professionally as did the European Community, that is, by developing the appropriate technical infrastructure, the ACP had little hope of dealing with the EEC on equal terms. The failure of the ACP Group of States to establish the ACP Secretariat as a viable, efficient institution demonstrated the group's lack of political will to achieve intra-ACP cooperation; it also demonstrated that the ACP states were not committed to a steady progression to equality with the EEC.

The lack of ACP expertise in recruiting and managing staff was not entirely separate from the reluctance of the ACP organs, particularly the Committee of Ambassadors, to see a rival centre of power develop. The Committee of Ambassadors liked to keep close control over the staffing of the Secretariat. One of the senior Secretariat officials remarked that he could not even fire a messenger without the permission of the ambassadors.

Recruitment to the Secretariat was based on considerations of geographical balance and often, of patronage. Complaints were common — both within the Secretariat and from ACP diplomats based in Brussels — that many of the Secretariat staff were unqualified. Certainly, the administrative problems faced by the ACP, the failure to have documents prepared in time for meetings, problems with making translations although only two languages were involved, the failure to keep adequate archives of ACP documents, suggest that the management of the Secretariat was slack. On the technical side, the ACP Secretariat was not equipped to prepare detailed studies and it had to rely on organizations such as the Commonwealth Secretariat and the United Nations Development Programme (UNDP) to prepare reports for it.

Notable within the Secretariat was a lack of *esprit de corps*. Neither of the first two secretaries-general of the organization was noted for being particularly effective. Tieoule Konate, the first secretary-general and former finance minister of Mali, was voted out of office by the ACP ministers in May 1980 and replaced by Thomas Okelo Odongo, a former assistant finance minister of Kenya. The voting, which replaced a francophone West African with an East African and left the two top posts in the Secretariat in the hands of anglophone officials, created a good deal of resentment. Mr Okelo, after taking up his appointment, observed in an interview that 'some members of the staff may not be very friendly to the secretary-general', a problem also faced by his predecessor.[10] It may be wondered whether a group of 46 largely poor countries, many without an efficient domestic civil service, and without a strong tradition of an independent, international civil service could have succeeded in creating an effective international civil service to staff the ACP Secretariat.

The tasks of the Secretariat were numerous, as Secretary-General Okelo noted: servicing countries from three different continents with different cultures, gathering data, communicating with members, coordinating the ACP organs, coordinating the ACP with other international organizations, and with Europe and, above all, monitoring the implementation of the Lome Convention.[11] Faced with these extensive tasks which increased as the membership of the ACP expanded during the Convention, yet restricted in its ability to respond by poor management and limited resources, the ACP Secretariat was not able to become a significant factor redressing the EEC–ACP balance of power within the Convention. The sight of a harassed senior ACP official searching for a new ACP state on his map and enquiring what language was spoken there was representative of the difficulties experienced by the Secretariat staff.

The third main reason for the Secretariat's impotence was its lack of funds. This problem derived from the poverty of most of the ACP countries and from the low priority given by the ACP governments to the Secretariat. The annual budget of the ACP General Secretariat was, up to the end of Lome I, under two million pounds sterling. This was paid for by contributions from the ACP Group as provided for in Article 21 of the Georgetown Agreement, supplemented by a smaller contribution from EDF regional development funds. If the ACP organs wanted the Secretariat to be able to provide more services, or to make the ACP more able to negotiate on an equal basis with Europe, then it was clear that the Secretariat needed more resources, more staff and more funds. Despite their countries' poverty, if the ACP had been determined to create a more powerful and efficient Secretariat they could have sought funds from other sources: from regional or international development agencies or loans from member states such as

Nigeria and Gabon which benefited from the 1970s oil price rises. As it was, however, the ACP states' contributions to the Secretariat budget were often in arrears and considerations of holding down the cost of the Secretariat[12] prevailed over complaints by ambassadors such as Monyake of Lesotho and Lewis of Trinidad and Tobago that services were inadequate or resources insufficient.[13]

The ACP ambassadors' Working Party on Intra-ACP Cooperation recommended in 1979 that, *inter alia*, the ACP Secretariat should be strengthened.[14] Also in 1979, the Nairobi ACP–EEC Conference on the Development and Promotion of ACP Trade made a series of specific proposals for extending the role of the ACP Secretariat. The conference recommended that a feasibility study be undertaken into setting up within the ACP Secretariat an export development unit with the task of creating a trade information system, identifying financial and technical assistance sources for export development from extra-Community sources and distributing that information to the ACP states, and helping ACP producers to negotiate international commodity agreements for ACP products not covered by them.[15] Despite the criticisms of the operation of the Secretariat and the ambitious plans for extending its role, little change was made. By the end of 1984, the ACP Council of Ministers was still discussing the problems of poor organization and low staff morale in the Secretariat, while trying to economize on the budget.[16]

The Secretariat was the foremost example of intra-ACP cooperation, but it was an example which showed that the ACP were not entirely committed to this concept. Percival Patterson, former deputy prime minister of Jamaica, deplored the fact that the ACP had made insufficient use of their Secretariat. Although the ACP, unlike the Group of 77 or the non-aligned, had a secretariat, they failed to appreciate its value.[17]

Proposals for a permanent third world or Group of 77 secretariat were often put forward. The ACP did manage to create and sustain a Secretariat, but it was not an effective one. Ironically, many of the arguments put forward by the Commonwealth Secretary-General, Shridath Ramphal, in favour of establishing a secretariat for the 'South' could be adduced in arguing that the ACP ought to render their Secretariat fully functional.

> The South has not organized effectively either for negotiations with the North or for cooperation within its ranks . . . . The South requires sustained, not ad hoc, technical back-up with at least a modest central organization if it is to be effective on either front. We seem to imitate the North save in the really critical areas of organization and management.[18]

The ACP did imitate the North, in the form of the EEC, in many of their institutional arrangements. The establishment of the ACP Secretariat was owed to the existence of similar Community bodies — the Commission and the Council Secretariat. Nevertheless, the ACP were less able than the EEC to make their back-up organization work successfully. In the ACP Secretariat, which could have acted as a model to other organizations, the ACP demonstrated instead how a seemingly desirable institution could become ineffectual. Instead of becoming a model for other developing countries, the ACP Secretariat became something of an embarrassment.

The intra-ACP development bank

The idea of creating an ACP development bank was audacious. It was in keeping with the Suva Declaration's recognition of the importance of banking services and its proposal that:

> measures aimed at improving the availability of capital on terms more favourable to the ACP countries might be contemplated, and whenever possible with the cooperation of other developing countries.[19]

The idea of the intra-ACP bank was proposed in December 1975 and an initial report on the bank was presented to the ACP Council of Ministers meeting in Lusaka in December 1978. Even the normally restrained *ACP–EEC Courier* commented that 'The bank seems one of the most promising means of furthering intra-ACP cooperation and the "collective self-reliance" advocated by all the ACP countries.'[20]

The Lusaka Council requested a study of the ACP trade and investment bank proposal from the UN Department of Technical Cooperation for Development. The study group of seven experts, assisted by a panel of twenty honorary specialists in international finance, began its work in March 1978. The group's report was issued after four meetings during 1978 and 1979. It analysed in considerable detail the need for, purposes, functions and structure of an ACP trade and investment bank.[21]

The experts' report argued that there was a need for an ACP bank. Compared to other developing countries, the ACP lagged behind in growth: from 1970 to 1976 their annual growth rate was 3 per cent whereas non-ACP developing countries achieved a rate of 5.7 per cent. The annual growth of ACP exports to third countries fell from 4.9 per cent in the 1960s to 0.6 per cent up to the end of the 1970s. Neither official development aid flows nor the private capital loans upon which the ACP were increasingly dependent were sufficient to finance a satisfactory rate of ACP economic growth.[22] Thus, the ACP should establish a new institution to attract new sources of private and official finance and to develop fast-yielding, export-oriented manufacturing and processing projects.

The proposed ACP bank would not duplicate the functions of other institutions because no existing institution specialized in financing and promoting trade for the ACP Group. For the purpose of financing current trade and aiding the growth of ACP export capacity, there was a 'financial institution gap'.

The report envisaged the bank having the overall objective of promoting the quick growth of ACP exports in order to help ACP economic prospects and the longer-term objective of increasing intra-ACP trade. It was acknowledged that the precise role of the bank would evolve to fit circumstances, but its functions could include: project identification, initiation and development (particularly projects with a quick export potential); arranging financing for trade-related projects by financing, co-financing or seeking other financing for them; assisting the ACP to create national credit institutions, participating in insurance and reinsurance of trade; and providing multilateral clearing arrangements and expert services.

The report recognized that the creation of an export-oriented trade and investment bank did have some risks. It would need competent, professional management, efficient operations, prudent building of reserves, strict cost controls and reasonable profitability. Developing new markets would have to be a priority. Ultimately, the bank's success would depend on the active participation of the ACP.

It was proposed that the ACP should retain control of the bank but other countries or development institutions could hold equity. In order for the bank to make a meaningful impact it needed a paid-up capital of US 75 million dollars initially with a further 75 million dollar tranche to be paid within three years. The report anticipated that the bank would have a tiered capital structure under which the ACP countries would be placed in groups based on appropriate economic measures. Each group would be allocated a minimum subscription and the ACP countries could participate in the bank by paying the subscription rate for their group or of a higher group. It was recognized that for some ACP countries raising the capital payment would be difficult and they might wish to seek aid for this from other sources.

The bank would be governed by a board of directors, the majority of whom were elected by shareholders. Day-to-day responsibilities would be taken by a full-time executive committee with a qualified staff and consultants.

Having considered the possibilities and problems facing the ACP bank, the experts decided 'It is the unanimous recommendation of the Group of Experts that the establishment of an ACP trade and investment bank is both desirable and feasible.'[23] In accordance with their sanguine view of the bank, the experts recommended further discussions with ACP governments, the preparation of draft articles for the bank and the preparation of technical services in connection with a special conference of ACP ministers or plenipotentiaries to adopt the draft articles.

In June 1981 a meeting of ACP government financial experts considered two reports on the proposed bank. Both reports, one from the UN experts mentioned earlier and one from Roy Jones, a Jamaican consultant, favoured establishing an ACP trade and investment bank. The ACP experts agreed that a flexible ACP financial institution concerned with developing ACP exports and intra-ACP trade should be created.[24]

The ACP ambassadors too, at least overtly, were in favour of establishing a trade and investment bank. They issued a report in November 1981 favouring its creation as recommended by the ACP experts in June of that year.[25] Nevertheless, not all ACP states were convinced of the need for the bank. These reservations became apparent when the ACP Ministers met in Maseru in December 1981 and instead of approving the proposal for the bank, they asked for further reports on its costs and benefits.[26]

Many ACP countries were worried about paying the subscription. Some wanted to prevent a proliferation of institutions when they were not persuaded that existing regional development banks were incapable of fulfilling the role envisaged for the ACP bank. The ACP were not ready to undertake the large commitment of an intra-ACP bank, however desirable it might appear. As one ACP diplomat summarized the situation, 'Politically, cooperation is difficult.'

Thus, at the end of 1981 the impetus for the creation of an intra-ACP bank was lost. In February 1982 Michel Poniatowski, chairman of the European Parliament's Development and Cooperation Committee, suggested the creation of a joint ACP–EEC bank to help the ACP to acquire foreign exchange and foster trade.[27] But the ACP never took this proposal seriously. The intra-ACP bank was not declared formally dead and it persisted as a project which could be further considered or undertaken at a future date.

Other projects

As well as creating the ACP General Secretariat and considering the intra-ACP bank, the ACP contemplated other projects. One such idea was an ACP newsletter or bulletin to give the ACP version of news instead of relying on the joint *Courier* (previously *Association News* in English) or the reports in the Western press. Although the *ACP–EEC*

Courier tried to present information in a generally non-controversial, non-political way, it was housed within the EEC Commission and published and edited by Commission officials. *The Courier* employed ACP journalists and was, at least nominally, overseen by an ACP ambassadors sub-committee. Nevertheless, ACP countries did at times feel aggrieved over some of its contents and it was proposed to have an independent organ. The cost-conscious ACP Council of Ministers decided in 1981 that because of the expense involved, instead of producing an ACP bulletin they would try to make greater use of *The Courier*.[28]

Another proposal considered by the ACP Group was that of establishing an ACP federation of chambers of commerce similar to one existing in West Africa. This was proposed, *inter alia*, at a conference of ACP trade operators in Nairobi in 1979. A subsequent meeting of the trade operators in Lome in 1981 considered the establishment of a federation of ACP chambers of commerce as a longer-term objective to be preceded by the creation of an ad hoc committee of ACP chambers of commerce to assess further developments.[29]

As an organization which was not purely governmental, but involved the private sector, the ACP federation of chambers was an appealing way to further intra-ACP trade and business contacts. It could foster intra-ACP cooperation without involving ACP governments in major expenditure or the creation of extensive new governmental machinery. Nevertheless, the ad hoc committee recognized at its first meeting in 1982 that many detailed discussions would have to precede the creation of an ACP federation of chambers of commerce.[30]

When Secretary-General Okelo Odongo of the ACP was asked in 1980 what progress the ACP had made in increasing their cooperation and cohesion, he cited the Georgetown Agreement, the Suva Declaration and the 1980 meeting at Montego Bay (where it was proposed to strengthen intra-ACP cooperation and the intra-ACP bank and federation of chambers of commerce were discussed).[31] Although the seminars organized by the ACP Secretariat on trade, education, and so on, aided intra-ACP communication, their results were rhetorical rather than concrete.

At the end of 1982 the chairman of the ACP sub-committee on intra-ACP cooperation, Ambassador Monyake of Lesotho, was questioned about the failure of ACP cooperation to produce tangible results. He noted the lack of resources available to the ACP and maintained that the Georgetown Agreement, Suva Declaration and subsequent meetings had laid a framework, defining the goals of intra-ACP cooperation and the ways of achieving them. It was not the case that nothing had been done, he argued, but that 'We are still spelling out the ways and means of doing something.'[32]

Conclusion

Despite Ambassador Monyake's view that the ACP were preparing to make intra-ACP cooperation a reality, many problems stood in the way. The ACP Group was not an impressive international organization. Since 1981 it had observer status at the UN, but the ACP Group had no real diplomatic weight. Unlike the European Community, the ACP Group had no ambassadors accredited to it. Third countries such as the United States would approach individual ACP states rather than the ACP Secretariat or organs.

The ACP bravely maintained that the existence of the African, Caribbean and Pacific Group of States did not depend on the Lome Convention:

> The objectives of the ACP Group extend beyond the narrow confines of the Lome Convention. The existence of the ACP Group does not therefore depend upon the Lome Convention or any successor arrangements to the Lome Convention.[33]

However, it was difficult to see how the ACP Group could be viable without its raison d'etre, the Lome Convention. The efforts that the ACP made toward establishing a sphere of activity independent of the Community remained in the field of declaration; projects such as the ACP bank and bulletin were never realized. Even in its membership, composed solely of Lome Convention members, the ACP did not reach out beyond the Convention. Although the analogy of the ACP as a trade union of the poor failed to subsume the political and historical aspects of the EurAfrican entente, the analogy did illuminate one aspect of ACP solidarity.* To the extent that the ACP Group was a type of trade union of the poor, it was a selectively composed union which had no reason to exist without its 'employers', the EEC.

ACP unity was brought into existence through the European Community. The Community encouraged ACP unity for the sake of strengthening the Lome relationship. In a similar way, an employer might favour a single, strong trade union. The EEC favoured creating a limited replica of the 'Community' model in the ACP Group. However, at sensitive times such as during negotiations for the renewal of the Lome Convention, the EEC tried to divide ACP opinion.

As an organization of developing countries, the ACP suffered from many of the problems common to such organizations: a multiplicity of interests, cultures and languages; and a tendency toward rhetoric rather than action. But the ACP had an additional problem standing in the way of collective self-reliance. This was the central paradox of ACP

---

* See also Chapter 6.

unity. On one hand the ACP needed to develop their solidarity in order to wrest the most advantageous terms from the Community in negotiating and applying the Lome Conventions. It was widely argued that through increasing their coordination and solidarity the ACP could 'achieve a meaningful and equal partnership with the European Community'.[34] But, on the other hand, ACP unity was only partly desirable.

Unity was necessary for the ACP to win concessions from the EEC. But however united, the ACP could not extract, for example, more aid from the Community states than they were prepared to give. Whatever concessions the ACP obtained from the EEC or however they tried to redress the balance of the 'partnership', the ACP could not eliminate the preponderance of EEC power in Lome.

African, Caribbean and Pacific Group unity was in many respects undesirable. It was an artificial unity called into being by the Community. Without its relationship to the Community, the ACP Group would be an unviable white elephant. The ACP institutions and cooperation were useful only in the Lome context. The more effort the ACP invested in creating an ACP Group identity, the more closely they would be tied to Lome. The more cohesion and solidarity the ACP achieved, the greater the waste if the EurAfrican relationship were dissolved.

Thus, the ACP solidarity which was necessary in the context of the Lome Convention was also a reminder of the neo-colonial nature of the relationship. The ACP needed unity in their dealings with the Community, but their unity could not make the relationship equal. ACP unity also had the unwanted effect of dividing the ACP from other developing countries. Solidarity among the ACP could not create an organization which, without its relationship with the EEC, would have a reason to exist.

ACP unity was the only answer the developing countries could bring to the problem of their unequal relationship with the European Community. But given the problematical nature of ACP unity, it was not surprising that the ACP were themselves ambivalent about it. Their doubts about ACP unity were not clearly or openly articulated, but it was apparent that in practice the ACP were less than committed to the ideals of cooperation they expressed, and their efforts to enhance their unity through projects such as the ACP bank were half-hearted.

Notes

1. Olu Sanu, E., 'The Lome Convention and the New International Economic Order', Lagos, Nigerian Institute of International Affairs, 1978, p. 28.
2. Anyadike-Danes, Monya, 'Regional Cooperation and the ACP Group', *Lome Briefing*, no. 19, 1984.

3. Olu Sanu, *op cit*, noted that the Lome negotiations had increased understanding among anglophone and francophone Africans and eased the process of preparing for discussions about ECOWAS.
4. *The Georgetown Agreement*, Article 2, 1975, Brussels, ACP Library.
5. *Report on the Fifth Annual Report of the ACP–EEC Council of Ministers and an Analysis of the Early Experiences of the Second Lome Convention with Recommendations for its Optimal Implementation*, (Insanally Report), 12 October 1981, Document ACP–EEC 29/81/rev.
6. 'Suva Declaration', (1977) text published by ACP general secretariat, Brussels.
7. For instance, *Draft Report on Cultural Cooperation between the ACP and the European Community*, Joint Committee of the ACP–EEC Consultative Assembly, 5 August 1981 (Chasle Report).
8. Suva Declaration, *op cit*, p. 12.
9. Insanally Report, *op cit*, p. 56.
10. *The Courier*, November–December 1980, no. 64.
11. *ibid.*
12. *The Courier*, July–August 1982, no. 74.
13. *The Courier*, September–October 1982, no. 75, and March–April 1983, no. 78.
14. Twitchett, Carol Cosgrove, *A Framework for Development: the EEC and the ACP*, London, Allen and Unwin, 1981, Ch.5.
15. 'Report of the ACP–EEC Conference on the Development and Promotion of ACP Trade', (Nairobi, Kenya, 7–16 November 1979, ACP Document ACP/810/79 Brussels, 31 December 1979).
16. *The Courier*, March–April 1985, no. 90, p. VI.
17. *The Courier*, September–October 1983, no. 81.
18. Ramphal, S., 'South–South: Parameters and Pre-conditions', in *South–South Strategy*, ed. Gauhar, A., London, Third World Foundation, 1983, p. 20.
19. Suva Declaration, *op cit*, p. 10.
20. *The Courier*, January–February 1978, no. 47, p. II.
21. 'Recommendations for the Establishment of a Trade and Development Bank', Brussels, 1979, UN Document TCD/int-77-RO7/1.
22. *ibid.*
23. *ibid.*
24. *The Courier*, September–October 1981, no. 69.
25. 'Presentation Notes by the Committee of Ambassadors on the Conclusions and Recommendations of the Experts' Meeting which was held in Brussels, 22–25 June 1981', ACP Document ACP/859/81.
26. *The Courier*, January–February 1982, no. 71.
27. *The Courier*, March–April 1982, no. 72.
28. *The Courier*, January–February 1982, no. 71.
29. 'Report of the Meeting of Trade Operators from the African, Caribbean and Pacific Group of States Held at Lome, Togo in July, 1981', ACP Document ACP/465/81. The report's proposals included strengthening the ACP secretariat and setting up a centre for ACP trade and development.
30. *The Courier*, July–August 1982, no. 74.
31. *The Courier*, November–December 1980, no. 64.
32. *The Courier*, September–October 1982, no. 75.
33. 'Summary Information of ACP Group of States', ACP, Brussels, 15 September 1979.
34. Twitchett, C., *A Framework for Development*, *op cit*, p. 107, for instance.

6 The discreet entente

The Lome Convention was supposed to establish a partnership among the Community and ACP countries based on complete equality. However, the parameters of the relationship, the value of trade concessions and financial aid, were established by the Community. The ACP were the dependent partners. Just as the language of partnership in the American Alliance for Progress did not eliminate the dominance of the United States in the western hemisphere, the declared partnership of the Lome Convention did not alter the relations between Europe and Africa. Because Lome was an alliance which depended on its traditions, it was not a model which could be replicated elsewhere.

The official Community view of Lome, in keeping with the idea of a partnership of equals, was that it reflected the interdependence of Europe and the developing world, particularly Africa. As Roy Jenkins, former Commission president expressed it, if Europe was to have economic growth, then 'we need the developing countries as much as the developing countries need us'.[1] President Jenkins's view of interdependence was fundamentally economic, stressing Europe's need for the developing countries' demand to stimulate European exports and employment and the need for cooperation with developing countries to reduce international monetary instability, solve debt problems, arrange long-term commodity agreements and foster international mining investments.

Former Development Commissioner Cheysson was more concerned about the political aspects of interdependence. It was not the traditional exchange of benefits — European technology for African raw materials — that he stressed, but the idea that by giving Africa economic benefits, political benefits could be reaped by the Community. He argued that the Community's partners would 'get guaranteed contractual access to the biggest market in the world, the European Common Market, while we in return build up secure and stable relations with these countries'. He observed that the most important sectors of interdependence were energy, raw materials and foodstuffs, but it was 'in all sectors of human activity that interdependence and cooperation must be fostered'.[2]

The Community was interested in securing African raw materials and in exporting European manufactures. But the second view of interdependence — exchanging European trade concessions and financial assistance for influence in the ACP — was the essence of the relationship.

Critics of interdependence pointed out that Africa needed European assistance more than Europe needed Africa. ACP economies were weak and dependent upon European aid and trade. They were not well placed to withhold their raw materials from Europe because they depended upon export earnings and the Community could in many cases find alternative sources of supply. Even the embargo of African strategic minerals such as cobalt, uranium, and so on, would not be crippling to the Community.[3] Thus, interdependence was unequal and involved more dependence on the part of the ACP than that of the Community. Referring to the ACP—EEC relationship as 'asymmetrical interdependence' illustrated the inequality of the partnership in which most decisions were made by the EEC, but did not convey the historical or geo-political aspects of the association.[4]

By 1982, Commissioner Pisani formulated a qualified version of interdependence. It did not entail an equal sharing of benefits, but still contained advantages for both sides. He called for the Community to cooperate with the South to undertake 'development that is interdependent, unequal but in the interests of both'.[5]

The concept of interdependence, especially of an interdependence extending to all fields of human activity, was similar to the older, but vague philosophy of EurAfrica. 'EurAfrican' was often used as a convenient adjective to refer to Europe and Africa jointly. But EurAfrica meant more than a handy, neutral term of reference. It implied the continuation of economic, political, cultural and often military links between Europe and Africa.[6] It was less imbued with the idea of equality between the continents than was interdependence. As a political philosophy it could be contrasted with pan-Africanism, the loosely defined concept of African unity, or the ideas of independence and self-reliance. EurAfricanism was a general orientation which emphasized the need for cooperation between Europe and Africa.

The philosophy of EurAfrica encompassed the idea of mating European technology with African raw materials, that is, economic interdependence. The political geographer Geoffrey Parker described this concept of a EurAfrica which was 'a sort of pan-region which could operate to the mutual benefit of both continents, the one highly industrialized and the other rich in physical resources'.[7]

EurAfricanism, like association, was derived from French political thinking. Especially after the mid-1970s when the Lome Convention introduced new language to rid itself of overtones of colonialism and the Brandt Report of 1980 popularized the term 'interdependence', 'EurAfrica' was seldom officially used in connection with the ACP–EEC relationship.[8]

In 1963 Arnold Rivkin called the Yaounde Association the 'high water mark' of EurAfricanism, because it demonstrated the newly independent former colonies' desire to remain associated with Europe.[9] However, with its increased membership, the return of Guinea to the European fold, and the favourable climate of opinion which greeted its inception, Lome I could now better be considered as the high water mark of EurAfricanism. Although the Lome Convention was less overtly based on the EurAfrican idea than were the Yaounde Conventions, it continued to represent the successful implementation of EurAfricanism. The EurAfrican ideal of maintaining close, if unequal, relations of every kind between the two continents remained the theoretical backbone of the Lome Convention.

As well as the general idea of interdependence, a more specific analogy was also applied to ACP–EEC relations. Former Development Commissioner Claude Cheysson frequently compared STABEX to unemployment insurance and emergency aid to sickness benefit.[10] Thus, the EEC was depicted as an international welfare state in which the ACP were the workers. Although, as noted in Chapter 3, STABEX – with its thresholds, arbitrary list of products covered, and discretionary application – was in many ways dissimilar to insurance, the analogy was mainly used by the Commission to emphasize European enlightened benevolence.

A further metaphor considered the ACP as a trade union and compared the EEC–ACP negotiations to employer–employee negotiations. As mentioned in the previous chapter, this analogy could be used to illustrate some aspects of the Lome relationship. However, not all the ACP were happy with this kind of formulation which depicted the ACP as suppliant workers in the international system rather than sovereign states.[11]

Although the union analogy could be drawn in some instances, its usefulness was limited. Like unions, the ACP needed solidarity to have bargaining power with the Community and like unions they might threaten to 'strike' by walking out of the negotiations or withholding their labour in the production of raw materials for the Community (although as mentioned earlier their ability to do this successfully was minimal). Again, like employers who preferred to deal with one strong union rather than with a multitude, the EEC preferred to deal with a united ACP than with a fragmented group of countries. However, Community support for unity in its developing associates was limited to blocs — the ACP, the Mediterranean littoral countries (whose unity in negotiations the EEC favoured but was unable to accomplish), and non-associates whose unity was not encouraged. The ACP themselves were, as noted in the previous chapter, ambivalent about their solidarity. Thus, the analogy of the ACP as a trade union, with the EEC as a welfare state or as enlightened employers was often made, as was the comparison of the Group of 77 with a trade union of the poor. However, the analogy had limited application to the ACP and failed to represent the importance of the legacy of colonialism and of Europe's political interests in shaping the ACP—EEC relationship.

The non-political alliance

The official European view of the Lome Convention was that it was a non-political trade and aid relationship. This low political profile was one of the great strengths of the Convention. The affectation of political neutrality helped to keep the Convention out of superpower rivalries and distanced it from the discredited era of colonialism.

The claim that the Convention was politically neutral rested on two pillars: (1) the Community's status as a new and civilian power and (2) its willingness to enter into equal, binding contracts with ACP regimes without regard to, and without attempting to exert political influence over, their political orientation.

Commissioner Cheysson developed the reason (1) for the Community's political neutrality, explaining that its lack of military equipment and history (at least *qua* Community) of imperialism made it singular in its relations with developing countries.

> The Community is weak, it has no weapon, it has no aircraft, it has no submarine, it's completely inapt to exercise any domination. This in many ways is a great asset to deal in the Third World, to discuss with the Third World. The European Community is young, it has no past.[12]

M. Cheysson argued that its special nature gave the Community advantages over its member states:

189

> Addressing Africa, the Community has no powers. It was born at the same time in the same years as most of these new independent states. It cannot be suspected of imperialism. It does not meet the same allergies, the same inhibitions as some of our member countries, if not all, do meet.[13]

The second pillar on which the Community based its claims to have a neutral, even non-aligned, relationship with the ACP was its respect for the ACP countries' internal autonomy. The ACP—EEC contract, as discussed in Chapter 3, was to assure that whatever a country's regime or however it changed, relations with the Community were not affected. As Commissioner Cheysson put it:

> we Europeans show very clearly that we have decided not to interfere in internal policies, not to make our aid a means of pressure on them before they choose their political regime. In fact, we support real non-alignment, and I think this is in the interest of Europe as it is in the interests of these countries. Who could deny it at a time when there is so much interference by some foreign countries in Africa?[14]

In practice the Community did concern itself with the internal and foreign policies of its associates and tried to encourage market-oriented development strategies.

In 1979 Fidel Castro shocked the West (as well as strict grammarians) by referring to the Soviet Union as the natural ally of the non-aligned.[15] Though more subtle, the Community's presentation of its relations with developing countries was not fundamentally different. It too claimed that its special style of relationship was naturally appropriate for non-aligned countries.

Commissioner Cheysson emphasized the significance of the non-political nature of Lome: 'What is important in Lome is the general inspiration rather than individual points . . . . It is the rejection of the idea of a sphere of influence, which means complete non-alignment.'[16] The EEC was impressively successful in portraying its Lome Convention as apolitical. This view was widely accepted: Professor J. Moss, for instance, agreed at the end of a study of policy implications of the Convention for the US that, 'the Lome accord is fairly non-political'.[17]

Europe as the middle way

Accompanying the Community's contention that the Lome Convention was not a political agreement was its presentation of relations with Europe as a middle way, avoiding dependence on the superpowers. In strategic terms, Africa was not of primary importance to either the Soviet Union or United States.[18] In fact, the latter was often accused of virtual neglect of the continent. For its part, Africa, having become embroiled in two externally-originated world wars, was well aware of the dangers of being involved in outsiders' political struggles.[19]

Although more in agreement with the US than the Soviets, Europe had its own distinctive policies toward Africa. With its historical connections, its self-avowed political neutrality and its greater tolerance of varied regimes than the superpowers, Europe seemed a safer, more comfortable partner than they. The Community, its proponents claimed, represented a viable third choice for developing countries which wished to avoid joining either the Eastern or Western blocs. After criticizing the attitudes of the US, F. de Schacht, a former Director General in the European Commission, argued: 'the welcome and desired presence of Europe in Africa, even if it is dominating, is better than that of the USSR or Peking China'.[20]

The same argument, that Europe offered a middle way between East and West, was made by the head of the Community's permanent delegation to Latin America, Dr Manfredo Macioti. The EEC and Latin America, he contended:

> offer the world in general and the Third World in particular the 'third way' which so many developing nations are striving to foster against severe odds . . . . Both capitalism — as expressed, for example, by the republican US — and communism — typified by Soviet Russia — appear unsatisfactory models for the world.[21]

Thus, association with the Community was portrayed as a political and economic third way for developing countries, with Europe as a benign model and a suitable partner for avoiding the problems of both East and West.

Former Commonwealth Secretary General Arnold Smith welcomed the adherence of the 46 ACP states to the Lome Convention as an extension of the entente cordiale between Britain and France.[22] The relationship between the Community and the ACP was an 'entente' or understanding between the parties. In view of the powerful French influence on the Lome relationship, the use of the French term, 'entente', was particularly appropriate. But the origins of the Lome entente extended back to the late 1950s, pre-dating Franco-British collaboration in the European Community. The Lome entente was rooted in France's alliance with its former colonies; it was only the Convention's expansion into the Commonwealth which stemmed from France's EEC partnership with Britain.

Unlike a partnership, a political alliance or entente does not imply the equality or complete coincidence of interests of the participants. The Lome Convention was such an unequal entente. It was a well-defined policy on the part of the EEC to foster relations of every kind with Africa. The outstanding feature of the EurAfrican entente was its carefully cultivated low political profile. Thus, the Lome Convention can appropriately be termed 'l'entente discrete': the discreet understanding.

Presenting the Lome relationship as politically neutral was a well-established Community policy. However, the EEC—ACP relationship was in fact politically discreet rather than politically neutral. The Community's overriding political aim was to maintain its presence and influence in the ACP. But by keeping the appearance of political neutrality, disturbing charges of neo-colonialism were minimized and difficult political issues were largely kept at bay.

Political issues in the Lome entente

Despite its efforts to avoid political issues, the Lome Convention did at times encounter them. The main political decisions which faced the Convention fall into three categories. The first of these categories covers the Community's policy of regionalization or bloc politics. A further area of political problems encountered by the Convention concerned East—West relations, particularly with regard to Germany. Last, there were political problems over human rights: how to suspend aid to countries which violated them, how to make declarations in favour of them, and how to deal with their abuse in the Republic of South Africa.

Regionalization

To turn to the first category, there can be little doubt that Europe did think in terms of creating a EurAfrican bloc. Just as Europe had argued that Britain needed the Community to have a major role in world affairs, the Community felt that it needed an associated bloc or sphere of influence to make it as significant an international force as the USA. Writing shortly after the signing of the Lome Convention in 1975, Development Commissioner Cheysson compared the EurAfrican relationship to that of the United States and Latin America. He considered that the wider scope of the Convention — uniting all of Africa (although this was an exaggeration on his part) with Europe in a single agreement and having been negotiated through a single spokesman for Africa — was remarkable. These features, he reckoned, could not be matched by the US in its relations with Latin America.[23]

It was not only Europe which thought in terms of regional blocs. Conservative Africans like former President Senghor of Senegal also favoured this idea. Senghor rejected the globalist approach and approved the development of blocs — Europe with Africa and the US with Latin America.[24]

Many academic writers dismissed the idea that the Lome Convention formed a regional bloc. After all, they argued, the Community itself was non-political and the Convention was a mere trade and aid agreement. Professor Parker argued that because the EEC was not seeking to expand its relations with the ACP it was not creating a neo-colonial bloc.[25] The American professor Miles Kahler considered that the European Community's regional relations were mainly the result of historical accident. He posited that 'the construction of a "mosaic" of ties between the European Community and its regional partners was hardly the result of conscious design'.[26]

However, a careful analysis of the Community's efforts selectively to expand the Lome Convention's membership and an assessment of the similarities of Community and French foreign policy show that the EEC was far from not wishing to extend its regional relationships and certainly did not lack a strategy for doing so. Despite its exalted rhetoric about partnership and changed international relations, the Lome Convention was really about traditional politics; it was about creating a sphere of influence for the European Community.[27]

In geopolitical terms, the Lome Convention was part of a system of continental bilateralism.[28] That is, just as the United States was primarily interested and involved in Latin America, Europe was primarily involved and interested in Africa. This arrangement, which is examined further in the section on superpower attitudes, was highly traditional. Whatever apparently progressive measures the Lome Convention contained in terms of aid and trade, it was a Convention designed to bolster the existing geopolitical system.

The Community's policy of creating a EurAfrican bloc meant that it had to limit the Lome Convention to 'the African countries, to which are added, by an historical accident, some Caribbean and Pacific countries'.[29] Limiting the Convention to this regional plan meant restricting its membership. Early efforts in this direction took place under the first Yaounde Convention. Morocco and Tunisia were discreetly refused admission to that agreement.[30] The EEC saw the north African littoral states (it referred to them as 'Mediterranean' states) as part of another region and tried unsuccessfully to create a Lome-type multilateral pact with them.[31]

As well as excluding the Asian Commonwealth and the north African littoral states from its vision of EurAfrica, the EEC quietly excluded two other countries. Haiti was deemed an undesirable partner in Lome because of its human rights record, although France did not support its exclusion. The Cook Islands were not admitted to the Convention because of concern over their legal status.

While the Community excluded from Lome some applicant countries, it assiduously courted others which were initially indifferent to it. The political strategy of the Lome bloc required gaining as large a membership as possible in sub-Saharan Africa. The Community's efforts in this regard to attract Mozambique and Angola are discussed in the following section.

East—West issues

The Lome Convention was primarily concerned with post-colonial relations, not with East—West conflict. Nevertheless, questions of East—West relations were not completely escapable. The idea of the European Community aiding the ACP to wean them away from socialist influence was a constant if unstated theme of Lome. Overt political problems arose over the question of relations with East and West Germany.

Prior to signing the Lome Convention in 1975, Tanzania's close relations with East Germany gave rise to some apprehension in the European Commission. From the mid-1950s the Federal Republic of Germany applied the Hallstein Doctrine to its foreign relations. This doctrine meant that West Germany would not officially recognize any country (except the Soviet Union) which recognized East Germany. When Zanzibar (which recognized East Germany) and Tanganika (which recognized West Germany) united in 1964 to form Tanzania, the new state had relations with both Germanys. West Germany then cancelled its military aid to Tanzania and Tanzania in turn refused its economic aid.

However, the strict application of the Hallstein Doctrine was gradually weakened. By 1972 a friendship treaty was signed between the two German states and East Germany was able greatly to expand its diplomatic relations in Africa. Thus, the potential problem of West German insistence on not signing treaties with African states which recognized East Germany had been overcome by the time of the signing of the Lome Convention, enabling states such as Guinea and the People's Republic of the Congo to join.[32]

The Hallstein Doctrine was never a major problem in EEC—African relations, but the so-called Berlin Clause became a subject of controversy. In its international agreements the Federal Republic of Germany insisted on inserting a declaration, known as the Berlin Clause, stating that the agreement applied also to Berlin unless the West German government declared otherwise within three months of its entry into force. Associated with this was a declaration that all persons deemed to be German under the Republic's laws were to be considered nationals of West Germany.[33] Although these two declarations had also been inserted into the Yaounde Conventions, it was only with regard to Mozambique and Angola's participation in the Lome Convention that the Berlin Clause became controversial.

When Angola and Mozambique gained their independence from Portugal in 1974, they had good relations with East Germany, which had supported their liberation movements, and poor relations with West Germany which had not. Angola even refused to establish diplomatic relations with the Federal Republic. In 1978 a West German delegation in Mozambique found that the government refused to sign an aid agreement for eleven million dollars because it included a Berlin Clause which was objectionable to Mozambique's friend, the German Democratic Republic (GDR). In 1979 Mozambique and Angola signed friendship treaties with the GDR,[34] and their joining the Council for Mutual Economic Assistance, in which Angola had observer status, was widely mooted.

The European Commission was extremely interested in persuading Mozambique and Angola to join the Lome Convention. It saw them as a natural extension of its sub-Saharan African sphere of influence. However, there were problems standing in the way. Unlike Zimbabwe, which joined the second Lome Convention in November 1980, shortly after its independence, Mozambique and Angola, once colonies of Portugal, did not have the former colonial power present inside the Community to encourage them to join.*

In addition, the Berlin Clause was an obstacle to Lome membership, particularly for Mozambique. From 1976 to 1980, 7 per cent of the EEC's aid to non-associated countries was earmarked for Angola and Mozambique. But even this non-associate aid for Mozambique and Angola was blocked because of their refusal to sign an aid agreement incorporating the Berlin Clause.[35]

Within the Federal Republic there were two strands of thought about aiding socialist-oriented developing countries. The conservative position was that in order to weaken or politically isolate them, economic aid and contacts should be withheld. The liberal position was to give aid to such countries in order to expand West Germany's influence with them.[36] The European Commission was in favour of the latter position, but Germany's insistence on including the Berlin Clause in agreements made it difficult for the Commission to succeed in attracting Mozambique and Angola to join Lome as it had attracted other newly independent African states. Angola and Mozambique never formally objected to the Berlin Clause and the Community never formally stated that membership of the COMECON was incompatible with Lome membership. Nevertheless, it was clear that these countries'

---

* Portugal and Spain joined the EEC in 1986, an important factor in persuading Mozambique and Angola to join Lome III.

close association with East Germany was a major cause of their disinclination to become associated with the European Community.

As for the ACP Group, it had no great enthusiasm for receiving Mozambique and Angola. Some countries saw their accession as causing the aid cake to be sliced yet more thinly. One ACP Secretariat official even argued that their language, Portuguese, would make working with these countries difficult (although this had not been a particular problem with Cape Verde and Guinea Bissau). The strong desire for Angola and Mozambique to join Lome came from the European Commission, not from the ACP.

Both Mozambique and Angola sent observers to the negotiations for Lome II, but some officials believed that the wrangling and bad atmosphere of the negotiations discouraged them from joining. In 1982 Development Commissioner Pisani visited Angola and Mozambique to persuade them to join Lome. President Machel and President Dos Santos explained to him that they preferred to negotiate bilateral agreements with the EEC, similar to Algeria's, rather than join Lome. M. Pisani told them such bilateral agreements would be difficult to arrange and would not provide them with as much aid as they would get under Lome. The Community view was that:

> The most appropriate and natural means of establishing broadly based and effective cooperation between Angola and Mozambique on one hand and the European Community on the other is by accession to the Lome Convention. There are other possibilities, it is true, but they would not open up such a large field of potential.[37]

Bilateral agreements would not have fitted in with the Community's regional political strategy as would the expansion of Lome. The Community was even willing to offer more aid to Angola and Mozambique if they would join. By the time of the commencement of negotiations for Lome III in 1983, both countries sent delegations although they did not promise in advance to sign. Nevertheless the prospect of their joining was a coup for the Community. As *West Africa* commented, 'For the Community their presence is a welcome bonus, since it means that once again it can be claimed that in Lome it has a deal with all the independent states of black Africa.'[38] The EEC finally succeeded in attracting Mozambique and Angola into Lome III, in 1984 and 1985 respectively. This was a great success for the Community's policy of regionalization and its policy of extending its influence in socialist Africa.

Human rights issues

The area of human rights contained some of the thorniest political problems facing the Community. The first problems which emerged concerned how the Community could stop aid to countries which abused human rights. Clearly, the EEC could not apply very stringent standards or it would have to stop aid to a large number of its ACP associates. The Lomé treaty itself contained no legal basis on which aid could be halted for violations of human rights. Nevertheless, three criteria underlying EEC decisions to stop aid discreetly can be formulated:

1 There was particularly gross abuse of human rights.
2 Some fairly early change of regime was foreseen.
3 The concerned state was not, like Zaire or Ethiopia, politically crucial to EEC strategy.

Aid to Uganda and Equatorial Guinea was minimized and mainly directed through international charitable organizations rather than through the governments. As noted earlier, it was not clear that the EEC had the legal power to stop aid to unsavoury regimes. Indeed, part of the EEC's claim to political neutrality rested on the assertion that aid was given to states irrespective of their regime, with Ethiopia often given as an example. Cutting off aid to Lome signatory states was both legally questionable and potentially damaging to the Convention's non-political image.

Despite this, the Community's member states felt that it was desirable to restrict aid to Uganda and Equatorial Guinea. On 26 June 1976, the European Council of Ministers issued a declaration deploring conditions in Uganda and calling for aid to the regime to be directed so that it did not assist the government in oppressing the population.[39] The ACP did express some opposition to the Community's position, particularly in the better-known case of Uganda. But the ACP themselves were not united and the aid cutbacks were carried out discreetly and caused relatively little commotion. As *The Courier* noted in 1979 when Amin had been ousted from Uganda:

> The Community attitude to Uganda under the former regime was essentially reserved and pragmatic. Though the relations founded on the Lome Convention were maintained, the dossiers that were prepared were seldom followed up by commitments.[40]

Only about 5 per cent of the indicative aid programme for Uganda was committed to projects under the Amin regime. The Community found STABEX transfers more difficult to slow down and Uganda received these in 1976 and 1977. Food aid from the Community budget outside the Lome Convention was also reduced.[41]

The full flow of EEC aid was quickly resumed following the overthrow of Amin in Uganda and the overthrow and subsequent execution of Francisco Macias Nguema in Equatorial Guinea — both in 1979. Little resentment over the Commission's actions was felt afterwards, and some Ugandan officials expressed gratitude that the Community's actions might have helped to shorten the Amin regime.

Although the Community could be accused of overstepping its authority in cutting off aid to undesirable regimes, many ACP officials themselves felt sympathy for its actions. Because the Community acted discreetly — maintaining the formal commitments of Lome — and selected its countries carefully, criticisms of its actions in stopping aid to two genocidal dictators were few.

It was when the Community tried to incorporate a formal declaration of human rights in the second Lome Convention that it met determined ACP opposition. Although the ACP were tacitly prepared to accept the Community's actions in restricting aid to Uganda and Equatorial Guinea, they were unwilling to accept a declaration of human rights which might be applied much more broadly. For the Community's part, a formal statement of respect for human rights seemed desirable because it could be used to justify past and future curtailments of aid.

In the second Lome Convention the EEC wanted a 'human rights clause' which referred to basic human rights and allowed the EEC to suspend aid to ACP states which violated them.[42] The ACP viewed this as a charter for unwarranted interference in their internal affairs and argued against it with unity, determination and considerable eloquence.

The proposal for a human rights clause was introduced by the British Labour government. The British believed that their people should not be asked to support financially a regime such as that of Amin which grossly violated human rights.[43] While the British and the Dutch supported the inclusion of a human rights clause, the other EEC member states were less enthusiastic. Within the Commission many officials also doubted the wisdom of pushing this demand. The ACP arguments opposing the human rights reference can be grouped into three main categories: opposing the Convention as a forum, opposing the declaration as unequal, and questioning the interpretation of human rights implied therein.

When the ACP opposed using the Lome Convention as a forum for a human rights declaration, they employed the Community's own arguments that the Convention was non-political. There was no place, the ACP considered, for a human rights clause in what was supposed to be a simple trade and aid agreement.

The ACP further contended that the proposed human rights clause was unequal because it allowed for the EEC to examine ACP activities in this field without allowing the ACP to examine EEC behaviour. The declaration would give the EEC power to suspend aid to the ACP without giving any reciprocal power to the ACP.

The final ACP argument centred on the meaning of human rights. Human rights, in the ACP view, meant economic and development rights in addition to the traditional liberal view of civil rights. It was in this area of human rights that the Community largely failed, and therefore the Community had little justification to criticize the ACP.

Bernard St John, President of the ACP Council of Ministers at the time of the signing of Lome II, skilfully put forward the three arguments outlined above.

> We of the ACP have never concealed our strong and unfailing commitment to that (human rights) ideal. The record of the Lome II negotiations confirms this. That we have not considered it desirable, however, to enshrine this concept in the Lome Convention is due rather to the inappropriateness of the Lome Convention as an instrument for its expression and implementation than to the irrelevance of the concept of any attempt on our part to evade its imperatives. But if the Community so wishes, we are prepared to discuss this question just as we stand ready to discuss the nature of the Community's relations with South Africa.
>
> For ACP States, human rights include, in addition to civil and political rights, the right to economic, social and cultural development. The indivisibility of these rights is now being recognized by the international community.
>
> For us, therefore, any discussion of this subject must be primarily concerned with the question of how to give substance to the right to development, as well as to the civil and political rights of ACP *and* EEC citizens. This means, among other things, the adoption, where appropriate, by the ACP and EEC states, both collectively and individually, of policies conducive to development, the removal of obstacles — economic and political — which hinder the effective enjoyment of all human rights, the condemnation of all attempts to perpetuate the denial of such rights, the cessation of relations — economic, political and cultural — with those who so persist, and finally the destruction of the perpetrators of such policies. This means, first and foremost, South Africa.[44]

The Community found it difficult effectively to counter the ACP arguments against a human rights clause in Lome II. In the face of ACP opposition and a lack of solid EEC support for the proposal, the Community quietly dropped its insistence on the human rights clause and did not attach its own unilateral human rights declaration to the Convention.[45] Although the Lome relationship did have a legal basis, it was clear that not all of the political aspects of the Convention, for example, the tacit acceptance of aid curtailment for human rights reasons, could be readily fitted into it.

The question of EEC relations with South Africa was an increasing problem under Lome I and its successors. The ACP felt strongly that human rights violations by the South African system of apartheid ought to be condemned in the forum of Lome.

Particularly after the Community brought up human rights in the Lome II negotiations, the ACP criticized the EEC's considerable trade and investment contacts with the Republic of South Africa. The Community was South Africa's largest trading partner and biggest source of foreign investment.[46] The ACP also objected to Community arms sales to South Africa and the EEC's failure to enforce its code of conduct for European companies operating there.[47]

As early as 1978 the EEC–ACP Consultative Assembly discussed the problem of relations with South Africa.[48] Although the Assembly passed a resolution in 1981 condemning South African aggression against neighbouring states and calling for self-determination for Namibia, and a resolution in 1982 in favour of sanctions against South Africa, these had little effect. Getting the Council of Ministers to consider South Africa was much more difficult. In May 1982 the ACP tried to debate EEC relations with South Africa in the joint Council of Ministers, but succeeded in having only an informal discussion with no resolutions taken. This topic, maintained the Commission and EEC Ministers, was a political matter; it did not fall within the purview of the Lome Convention.[49]

The ACP, particularly Nigeria, were not happy with the EEC's taking refuge in the apolitical image of Lome. They wanted the subject of EEC relations with South Africa to be confronted openly. A Nigerian government minister argued that: 'It is unimaginable for an economic organ like the Lome Convention to exist and function and even be meaningful without political dimensions.'[50] A still more radical statement was made by the Nigerian ambassador to Brussels in 1982. He insisted that the EEC would have to choose between its special relations with the ACP or its relations with South Africa.[51]

Some observers have seen the ACP expression of their views on South Africa as a positive way for them to put pressure on the EEC.[52] It was also argued that a constructive dialogue about South Africa within Lome could help to reduce tensions in the southern African region.[53]

The success and durability of the Lome relationship owed much to its non-political image. The ability to avoid questions of East–West politics and of neo-colonialism was a great asset to the Convention. Making the politics of the Convention more overt would certainly increase disputes between the signatories. The introduction of a heated dialogue about South Africa might well damage the ACP–EEC relationship.

Despite its quasi-federal institutions, the Lome framework was not well-suited to resolving political disputes. Decisions by the Consultative Assembly had little weight and decisions in the Council of Ministers could be blocked by either side or by determined opposition from one or more states. Thus, the increased politicization of the Convention could result in greater polarization of the two sides without any effective method of compromise.

Likewise, it might be wondered whether airing difficult political issues in the Convention would add anything to debates in international fora such as the UN. It might merely worsen relations in the Convention without producing any meaningful results. It was doubtful whether any political activity of the ACP within the Lome framework could induce the Community member states to change entrenched attitudes or sever profitable trade and investment links with South Africa.

Nevertheless, the ACP should continue to express their condemnation of South Africa's policies, while realizing that the Lome Convention by itself did not offer them an effective means of redressing their grievances and upholding their views of human rights.* The continued articulation of ACP views about South Africa within the Lome relationship might slowly have some influence on the Community, but the chances of using the Convention to make major changes in the international economic order or in North—South politics were remote.

French policy and Lome policy

The importance of French post-colonial policy in the development of the Treaty of Rome Association has already been shown. French policies in the French Association and French Community foreshadowed the development of the Community's 'fresco' of relations with developing countries, as discussed in Chapter 1. French influence did not end with the formative stages of the Association. By analysing continuing French policy towards Africa, the questions of whether the EEC had a definite policy in Lome and whether or not the Community was seeking an African sphere of influence can be answered. French policy influenced EEC policy through the French government and ministers, and through French EEC officials, notably the Development Commissioner — a post held by French nationals until 1985. Indeed, former Commissioner Pisani was quoted in a lapse at the beginning of his career at DG VIII as identifying himself as a French minister rather than an EEC official.

Four themes of contemporary French foreign policy can also be found in Lome policy. These were:

1 The priority given to Africa.
2 The interest in African minerals.

---

* The ACP in Lome III agreed to a 'human rights' clause and obtained a Community declaration opposing apartheid, but the impact of these declarations is likely to be limited. See also Chapter 4.

201

3   The even-handedness of having relations with African states of different political complexions.
4   The portrayal of a middle way between the two superpowers.

The priority given to Africa within the Lome Convention was clearly expressed by former Commissioner Cheysson — afterwards French foreign minister — in the statement quoted earlier in this chapter. The enthusiastic efforts of the Commission to entice Angola and Mozambique into Lome, which were not equalled for Caribbean or Pacific countries, also showed the 'Africa first' policy. The ACP themselves perceived that Africa had first place in the Community's plans. France too followed a policy of 'Africa first'. Although French foreign policy differed from Lome in considering north and sub-Saharan Africa together, in openly singling out francophone Africa for special treatment, and neglecting the Pacific, in other respects the resemblance was striking. Former French Development minister Jean-Pierre Cot explained the priorities of French development policy in 1982:

> Firstly the countries of Francophone Africa both North and South of the Sahara, for whom the effort of public development aid will be maintained and increased .... The second priority is Africa as a whole .... Lastly, the third priority goes to the Central American and Lesser Antilles zone.[54]

The second shared policy theme concerned the European Community's interest in African minerals and raw materials. The Community's interest, described earlier, closely resembled France's interest. 'Strategically, successive French presidents in the post-war period', noted one Africanist, 'tended to view Africa as an extension of Europe with its untapped reservoirs of raw materials vital to the economies and the strength of the Old World.'[55] The French military depended on African uranium, and Africa's oil, cobalt and other minerals were likewise seen as essential to France.

The EEC's interest in African raw materials was concretely demonstrated in the Sugar Protocol and (although it was an aid mechanism as much as an attempt to increase raw material supplies) STABEX. The Community's particular concern for encouraging mineral supplies was manifested in Lome II's SYSMIN aid to mineral production.

The political neutrality of the Lome Convention rested on its claim to deal with regimes of any political hue. Although in the case of the EEC political neutrality was more elaborately conceived and overtly presented as a virtue, France, too, practised a similar kind of neutrality. It associated with both right- and left-wing regimes in Africa. Arthur Gavshon reported that 'the French did not care much about the nature of the regime they were prepared to support and generously aid, provided only that it was pro-French'.[56]

Like Lome's, French neutrality veered to the side of conservatism. It tended to support the status quo and strengthen the allied and aided government. One French official described this as taking Africa as it was and doing the best 'politically and economically, to keep the regimes we deal with in place against sudden or radical change'.[57]

The final similarity in Lome and French policy was their image as a third way between an alliance with the US or Soviets. France portrayed itself as a third force in Africa which wanted to keep Africa for the Africans, not allowing US or Soviet dominance there. Both Lome and France stressed that associating with them was compatible with non-alignment. 'France,' said Foreign Minister Cheysson, 'although a member of an alliance, supports non-alignment in the South.'[58]

Although French policy towards Africa was more overtly political than Lome policy, the Community borrowed many of its themes. By observing these themes, it is clear that the Community's contention that 'it is still open to question today whether Community activity in the development field, rich in instruments and potential though it may be, has really acquired the coherence and consistency of a policy' was a part of building a non-political image and not a tenable assessment.[59]

Among Africanists there is little dispute that France has a sphere of influence in Africa which is enforced when need be with military action as in Gabon, Shaba, the Central African Republic and Chad. The European Community had no military forces, but it used its political and economic policies to maintain a political and economic sphere of influence in the ACP.

Superpower attitudes to Lome

The Lome Convention did not openly engage in a dialogue or confrontation with the USA or Soviet Union. Nevertheless, it evoked opposite reactions from the superpowers. The Soviet view of the Lome Convention was straightforwardly competitive. They considered the EEC as the political extension of their military enemy, NATO. To the Soviets, the Community's Lome policy was just an attempt by European imperialists to exploit developing countries.

The end of colonialism, in the Soviet view, did not change the basic nature of European relations with their former colonies. The EEC wanted to keep the ACP as raw material suppliers and markets for monopoly capital. The Community was seeking political and economic influence in the ACP.

To the Soviets, the Lome Convention had 'progressive features' such as tariff concessions and STABEX, but these, it was argued, resulted from ACP bargaining power. In any case, their purpose was merely to divide Lome countries from other ldcs and to keep them from being attracted by other capitalist countries such as the US and Japan. Although bourgeois propaganda portrayed Lome as a great step forward, its function was to allow greater exploitation of the ACP by the EEC in the future.[60]

The Soviets saw the EEC not as a unified force, but as 'a pack of imperialist wolves, whereby each endeavours to gain advantages at the expense of the others'.[61] They approved of the treaty basis of the Convention as they often employed this legal form in relations with their allies.

In broad geopolitical terms, the Community and the United States were on the same side in their relations with developing countries — the side of preserving the existing international order. The Soviets, on the other hand, stood for revolution and change in these relations.

Despite their similarity of views, the interests of the United States and the European Community in Africa were not exactly the same. Assessing the state of the Atlantic Alliance has been a major occupation for academics and policy makers in Europe and the United States. Whether US and European interests are basically the same or rapidly diverging remains a subject of considerable, if inconclusive, debate.[62] But whatever interpretation is placed upon other US—European differences, up to the present the US and the Lome Convention established a relatively harmonious *modus vivendi* which seems likely to continue, at least in the near future.

Traditionally, the United States considered Latin America as its appropriate sphere of action and influence and largely neglected Africa. The main American interest in Africa was to prevent the spread of Communism, not to expand its relations with the continent. It reacted to perceived crises in Africa without having a consistent policy of its own.[63]

The low priority Africa had in American eyes was unsuccessfully challenged by President Carter's Ambassador to the UN, Andy Young. His policy of African solutions for African problems found little support in a government accustomed to seeing Africa as important only in terms of East—West conflict. Andy Young vividly described the attitude he found in the United States: 'The Senate doesn't give a damn about Africa and it doesn't know a damn about Africa.'[64]

The United States, during the Yaounde and Lome Conventions, was generally satisfied with the system of continental bilateralism, accepting Africa as primarily a sphere of European influence. This acceptance of European influence in Africa held good both for unilateral military interventions such as the 1983 French intervention in Chad and for the more subtle presence of the European Community.[65]

A senior US official in Brussels noted that America respected

Europe's historical ties with Africa. They welcomed European influence in the continent as a stabilizing force. A great deal of consultation between Washington and the Community was carried on, particularly in the case of sensitive countries such as Ethiopia and Grenada. Washington maintained close political contacts with the Community, but it had no relations with the ACP as a group.

Washington was less happy about EEC–African relations in the area of economic ties. It wanted to make sure that African markets remained open to US trade and investment. Specifically, the US worried about the proliferation of preferential agreements between the EEC and developing countries, the existence of reverse trade preferences under the Yaounde Conventions (abolished under Lome), and felt that the EEC sugar policy interfered with the free market. However, the US and the EEC were able to reach an agreement about Community trade relations which operated until the mid 1970s. This secret, informal arrangement was known as the Casey–Soames Understanding.

According to the Casey–Soames Understanding, the US would not challenge EEC trade agreements as being inconsistent with GATT requirements. In exchange, the EEC agreed not to seek further reverse preferences from ldcs and not to conclude preferential trade agreements with countries outside the African, Caribbean, Pacific and Mediterranean areas. Where the US encountered any obstacles to its trade caused by EEC preferential agreements, the EEC would try to resolve these. Thus, although American and European economic interests diverged regarding trade, their basic political understanding enabled them to overcome their differences. There were, according to the American diplomat mentioned above, no really significant problems over the Lome relationship.

To the Community as well as to the United States, their world roles were mutually reinforcing. A European Commission survey maintained:

> The European Community and the United States of America are today the two principal pillars of the western political and economic systems. Their relations at all levels are particularly intense, and their world roles largely complementary.[66]

The First General Report on the EEC, issued in 1958, praised the support given by the USA to European integration. It announced that the EEC would 'reinforce the coherence of the free world'.[67]

The Community's foreign policy was to cooperate with America, but also to be independent. The EEC portrayed its African policies to the US as being closely allied to US policies and interests. It was as 'the second pillar of the Atlantic Alliance' that the EEC depicted its activities in developing countries to Washington. However, to the developing countries the European Community portrayed itself differently. To them it, like France, stressed its ability to withstand and even protect them from superpower interference: the idea of Europe as the middle way.

Thus, in respect of its relations with Africa the Community was largely able to have its cake and eat it, too. To the US, Community policies such as Lome were extensions of Western influence; to the Africans, relations with the Community such as Lome were presented as alternatives to US and Soviet influence.

US—EEC competition over Latin America

The system of continental bilateralism — the US pursuing its interests in Latin America and Europe pursuing its interests in Africa — allowed for a fairly harmonious relationship. Nevertheless, points of friction arose and potential problems loomed on the horizon. These involved Europe's steadily growing involvement in Latin America rather than the United States' sporadic bouts of interest in Africa.[68]

The European Community was critical of the American tendency to view the world in black and white terms, to see everything as a question of East—West conflict. Commissioner Pisani went as far as accusing the US of seeking supremacy in its third world relations while Europe wanted only harmonious interdependence.[69] These different approaches were manifested in the case of the Caribbean island of Grenada, an ACP country.

In the late spring of 1981 Grenada requested the EEC, under Article 100 of the second Lome Convention, to hold a co-financing meeting for its airport project. The US claimed that the airport was intended to transfer Cuban troops to Angola, but Grenada firmly denied that the airport would have any military use. Because of US pressure the EEC member states did not participate in the aid conference. Although the US managed to have financing for Grenada's airport project delayed, it did not change the basic EEC approach of 'political neutrality'. The US invasion of Grenada in 1983 further underlined the differences between the US approach to countries it considered part of its backyard and the more tolerant European Community style of relationship.[70]

The Latin Americans themselves were eager to use European influence to counter-balance US influence. They initiated the process which later led to growing EEC interest in their region. The European Community response to early Latin American approaches such as the Latin American Memorandum of 1966 was sluggish and inter-regional relations by the end of the 1960s were virtually in abeyance. However, the Community responded positively to the Buenos Aires Declaration of 1970 which proposed closer relations between Europe and Latin America. Bi-annual EEC—Latin American discussions were established and non-preferential, bilateral trade agreements with Argentina, Uruguay, Brazil and Mexico were negotiated.[71]

Initially, the Community was primarily interested in Africa and tended to regard Latin America as 'middle-class' and the sphere of influence of the USA. But the Community gradually became more interested in Latin America as it recognized the possibility of developing closer ties and the importance of the region economically. Latin America received the highest proportion of Europe's direct investment in the third world.[72] It was also an important trade partner of the Community, supplying as much as 11 per cent of the Community's raw material and 10 per cent of its food imports.[73] An exhaustive analysis of EEC—Latin American trade is beyond the scope of this chapter, but it is nevertheless clear that Europe had strong commercial reasons for its interest in the region, and Latin America likewise had commercial reasons for wishing to expand its relations with Europe.

As well as geopolitical reasons — looking to the Community as a less domineering 'partner' than the United States — and commercial reasons, the Latin Americans had cultural and historical motives for wishing to associate themselves more closely with Europe. The Commonwealth ACP in the Caribbean region and Belize, for example, still had strong ties to Britain. Britain itself encouraged its former dependencies — even when they, like Belize, were initially reluctant — to join Lome and get their share of its financial benefits. The accession of Spain and Portugal to the European Community in 1986 further intensified the links between the Community and the former Spanish and Portuguese colonies in Latin America.

Whether the future form of EEC—Latin American relations would take the form of a multilateral pact or continue, as seems more likely, through bilateral agreements remains unclear. The American Monroe Doctrine may not yet be dead, but it is certainly being challenged by a growing European Community interest in Latin America.[74] However forcefully the US tries to reassert itself in Latin America, it will not be able to exclude the Europeans' interest in the region or prevent the growth in Latin America's contacts with the EEC.

Increasing European influence in Latin America could become the cause of friction between Washington and Brussels. It would not be a friction over long-term objectives, but over methods, policies, and the change in the balance of power embodied in the old system of continental bilateralism.[75]

Whether its growing relations with the European Community lead Latin America to a subordinate partnership with Europe or to a real independence in international politics, they still challenge the old system. It seems unlikely that EEC—Latin American relations will be able to adopt the uncontroversial, non-political facade or benefit from the long history of intimate, stable relations which helped the Lome alliance to weather three decades of a rapidly changing international political climate. Thus, expanding EEC contacts with Latin America — like French arms sales to the Nicaraguan government — could challenge the traditional system of continental bilateralism — Europe with its sphere of influence in Africa and the United States with Latin America.

The Lome Convention and neo-colonialism

This study of the Lome relationship has concluded that it was founded on political goals — principally those of the European Community. It was nevertheless presented by the Community as politically neutral and thus can be termed 'l'entente discrete'. The EEC—ACP relationship was deeply rooted in the colonial past — in the theory of EurAfrica and the colonial policy of association. This remained the case despite its official transformation in 1975 into a 'partnership'.

The Ghanian leader, Nkrumah, was particularly emphatic in his criticisms of the new colonialism which he saw as insidiously manifesting throughout the West's relations with Africa. 'The essence of neo-colonialism,' Nkrumah wrote, 'is that the State which is subject to it is, in theory, independent and has all the outward trappings of international sovereignty. In reality its economic system and thus its political policy is directed from outside.... Neo-colonialism is also the worst form of imperialism. For those who practise it, it means power without responsibility and for those who suffer from it, it means exploitation without redress.'[76] In this view the neo-colonial domination of one ostensibly independent state by another could be accomplished through military, economic, or monetary control or by controlling key civil servants. The neo-colonialist powers sought to divide, exploit and impoverish the developing countries.

In Nkrumah's view the Yaounde Association was neo-colonialism in practice. It was an extension of the colonialist policy of indirect rule. Just as the Berlin Treaty of 1885 was the prelude to colonialism in Africa, the Treaty of Rome signalled the beginning of neo-colonialism. The Association was 'a new system of collective colonialism which will be stronger and more dangerous than the old evils we are striving to liquidate'.[77] Nkrumah's criticisms of the Association providing Europe with cheap raw materials while hindering African economic development and unity were accompanied by those of countries such as Guinea and Tanganyika. Charges of neo-colonialism featured large in discussions in international fora in the early 1960s.[78]

Neo-colonialism is difficult to define precisely. Like 'imperialism', it has been used as a general term of opprobrium to cover a variety of political and economic evils.[79] It referred to the general disappointment among newly independent states that they were unable to escape the political, economic and at times military domination of the developed countries. Neo-colonialism meant that the old dependence upon the metropolitan countries had, contrary to third world aspirations, not disappeared. In African terms it meant that, as William Zartman put it, Africa was a subordinate state system in which countries had little power to influence the decisions of other states inside or outside the continent whereas the decisions of outside states could profoundly affect Africa.[80]

Since their heyday in the late 1950s and the 1960s, charges of neo-colonialism have been less in evidence. By the 1980s, leaders such as Commonwealth Secretary-General Ramphal called for an end to the use of counterproductive, confrontational tactics by the South and an increased attitude of cooperation.[81] A *Times* editorial in 1983 proclaimed that in political terms anti-colonialism was 'a spent force'.[82]

The use of the term 'neo-colonialism' has dwindled in popularity in international dialogues, and the early charges of 'neo-colonialism' which dogged the EurAfrican Association are now less frequent. Nevertheless, the epithet 'neo-colonial' can still be applied to the Lome Conventions, not in this case as a term of abuse, but to illustrate some of their characteristics.

Both the European Commission and some independent observers such as Carol Cosgrove Twitchett maintained that the Lome relationship was not a neo-colonial one. Eight reasons for this view, which have been advanced at different times by various authorities, are assessed below. These are followed by a summary of the principal reasons for concluding that the European Community's 'entente discrete' was a neo-colonial relationship.

1 The Lome relationship was not neo-colonial because it was originally sought by the Yaounde Associates.

This view was advanced by Carol Twitchett who argued, 'In reluctantly acquiescing to the Associates' demands for maintaining association, the Community could hardly be said to have embarked on a course of neo-colonialism.'[83] According to this argument, the Lome relationship was not neo-colonial because the developing countries were free to choose to join or reject it.

The Community's new colonialism can be traced back to the Treaty of Rome in which the dependencies of the member states were, at the instigation of France, first grouped into an 'Association'. That the Associates wished to continue the Association showed their weakness and dependency on Europe and their lack of what Sekou Toure called confidence. It also demonstrated the acceptance of the idea of EurAfrica by leaders such as Senghor.

In the sense that the post-independence Associations were continuations of a policy originally imposed on the Associates by their former colonial rulers without any consultation, they were neo-colonial. The position of the developing countries in the Yaounde and Lome Conventions was still inferior to that of the European states, as had been the case in the Treaty of Rome Association (and also in the French Association and French Community). The EurAfrican relationship was neo-colonial because it demonstrated not principally the freedom the developing countries had with regard to it, but the continuing dependence of the former colonies on Europe. For the remaining dependencies of the EEC member states, the Overseas Countries and Territories (OCT), which were joined to the Yaounde Association and later to the Lome Conventions by decisions of the EEC Council of Ministers, the relationship was still colonial.

2   The EEC was not a superpower capable of practising neo-colonialist policies.

There are two aspects of this view. First, it was maintained by former EEC Commissioner Cheysson and others that the EEC had no military power and therefore could not exercise domination over its 'partners'. However, the theory of neo-colonialism did not restrict domination to military means, and thus the Community's civilian status did not preclude its ability to practise neo-colonialism.

The second aspect of this argument was that the Community states, unlike the superpowers, did not have a coherent policy towards the third world.[84] They were not united enough to produce and implement a common, neo-colonialist policy. However, as the study of the similarities between EEC and French policies earlier in this chapter revealed, its internal differences did not prevent the EEC from having a definite, though discreet, policy towards the ACP.

3   The European Community *qua* Community had no colonial history. Several of its member states like Ireland and Denmark, and Germany after World War I had no African colonies. Some of the Lome signatories like Ethiopia were not formal colonies. Other ACP states like Equatorial Guinea were not former colonies of member states.

Stating that the Community had no colonial history overlooks Part IV of the Treaty of Rome and the continuing Association of the OCT. Although some of the ACP were not former colonies of EEC states, most of them were. Theorists of neo-colonialism like Nkrumah accepted that dependencies might change from being neo-colonies of France or Britain to those of another state (in this case to a group of states).

The biggest change in the Association, the addition of the Commonwealth ACP in 1975, was caused by the entry into the EEC of their former colonial power. Although some of the participants were not directly linked through colonial ties, the general inspiration behind Yaounde and Lome was to maintain and expand the relations which colonialism had established.

4 The European Community did not follow a neo-colonialist policy of 'divide and rule'. It encouraged cooperation among the ACP at every level and the creation of customs unions such as ECOWAS.

Although the Community did generally foster and facilitate cooperation among the ACP states, its policy was divisive with respect to developing countries as a group. This was particularly apparent in the early days of Association when francophone and anglophone African states quarrelled over trade preferences accorded by the Community to the Associates. It was also the case when the ACP opposed the Community expanding its trade preferences for all developing countries under the generalized system of preferences (GSP).[85]

In some cases the Community practised divisive tactics. In the Lome II negotiations, the EEC did not hesitate to approach ACP countries individually in order to persuade them of its viewpoint. Commission officials, a senior Commonwealth diplomat noted, would at times criticize Caribbean or Pacific ACP countries when speaking to Africans in order to create a sense of community of interests between the EEC and Africans rather than among the ACP.

Carol Cosgrove Twitchett concluded that:

> Since the signature of the Lome Convention, however, both English- and French-speaking African states have been linked to the European Community, so the question of the divisive impact of Yaounde Association has no continuing relevance now.[86]

Even though the Lome Convention united francophone, anglophone and lusophone countries in Africa, the Community's policy of regionalization or fragmentation continued to divide ACP countries from north African, Asian and Latin American ldcs.[87]

5 The Lome Convention was not neo-colonial because it led to the gradual weakening of ties between the former metropolises and the former colonies.

This thesis was advanced by William Zartman.[88] The 'decolonization theory' Professor Zartman put forward depicted the Lome Convention as an intermediate stage in full decolonization. The Convention replaced the old bilateral, colonial relations with multilateral ones. By strengthening African economies and states, the Convention helped them gradually to take charge of their own affairs. The replacement of bilateral relations by relations with the Community as a whole meant a general dilution of ties between former metropoles and former colonies. The Lome Convention was thus a natural stage in the process of decolonization.

This sanguine view of the Convention did not take into consideration the forces within the Convention promoting the continuing dependence of the colonies and former colonies on the metropoles. Some multilateralization occurred in economic relations as the ACP broadened their trade relations and lessened dependency on one European trade partner. Nevertheless, the trade preferences and aid of the Lome Convention did not free the ACP from economic dependency on Europe.

In political terms, even less multilateralization was evidenced. The former colonial powers maintained special links with their former dependencies within the Convention. The former colonial powers acted as champions of the interests of former colonies. Within the EDF Committee, delegations tried to make sure that projects in their client developing countries were approved. Instances where, for example, Britain voted on technical grounds against a project in a francophone African state were deeply resented by the French. On occasion delegations whose client state's projects were challenged responded by challenging a project in the objecting delegation's client states.

This patronage relationship also existed in regard to the dependent territories included under Lome. Although projects in the dependent territories which were to be funded by the EDF were discussed by all the EEC member states, they were primarily the concern of the colonial power. As one diplomat noted, his country would not take too kindly to too much interest or interference from other EEC states in the projects in its dependencies.

Later members of the European Community looked forward to using their patronage power on behalf of former colonies. Portugal, for instance, which joined the EEC in 1986, wanted to mediate between the Community and the lusophone African states.[89]

This patrongage exercised by former colonizers on behalf of former colonies within Lome could become the cause of future friction. Spain was deeply concerned about growing French links with its former colony, Equatorial Guinea, and Portugal might try to reduce the influence with its former colonies gained by other EEC member states through the Lome Convention.[90]

Thus, the multilateralization of relations, the full decolonization foreseen by Professor Zartman and others, was unlikely to be fulfilled through the Lome relationship. Instead, dependency on the patronage of the former colonial powers remains a feature of the Lome association.

6   The Lome Convention was not neo-colonial because it gave substantial economic benefits to the ACP.

According to this argument, the Lome Convention did not exploit the ACP, but encouraged their economic development. Any suspicion of neo-colonialism was unfounded because Lome even did away with reverse preferences, allowing the ACP to receive unilateral trade preferences as well as financial and STABEX aid.

In response to these points, the limited value of the Lome trade and aid concessions can be cited. Lome preferences were given to economies largely unable to take full advantage of them; where advantage was taken the Community imposed restrictions, as in the case of textiles. Financial aid itself could be seen to have fallen in value in real, per capita terms from Yaounde II.

Trade preferences under Lome were not very much greater than those offered to all ldcs under the generalized system of preferences operated by the EEC. The much-applauded STABEX system too had its drawbacks in arbitrary application, limited funds and the potential economic effects of discouraging agricultural diversification or industrialization. The Community's efforts to aid the industrial development of the ACP through the Centre for Industrial Development were on a very limited scale.

The Community, by placing higher tariffs on ACP-manufactured rather than primary products, sought to promote the ACP as suppliers of the raw materials it regarded as essential to European industrial production. EEC development assistance did little to change the unequal international division of labour between poor primary producing countries and the rich industrialized nations.[91] Three decades of association with Europe failed to make any great impact on the major development problems of Africa.

The aid and trade concessions of the Lome Convention did not alter the basically neo-colonial foundation of the discreet entente. It did serve to make the relationship attractive and more economically beneficial to the ACP. In the light of the Community's concern to foster — in non-competitive directions — the ACP's social and economic development, to provide what former Commissioner Cheysson described as sickness and unemployment insurance for the ACP, the Community's relationship with these developing countries could be called welfare neo-colonialism.

Welfare neo-colonialism tried to soften the harsher aspects of the ACP—EEC relationship. Unlike association, it accepted in principle the formal equality of the dependent states. Welfare neo-colonialism tried — through aid, trade preferences and STABEX — to alleviate gross conditions of ACP poverty and economic distress. It alluded to the restructuring of the international economic system without engaging in it. Compared with the old colonial system, welfare neo-colonialism was progressive; but it was far from an equal partnership.

7 The Lome Convention was not neo-colonial because ACP governments and the European Commission said that it was not.[92]

Because 'neo-colonial' is generally a term of abuse, it is not surprising that parties to the Lome Convention should deny its applicability to the Convention. Both the ACP and the EEC took pains to distance themselves from colonialism. They made special efforts to abandon terms such as 'Association', which had colonial implications. Nevertheless, many ACP diplomats, EEC diplomats and Community officials have privately acknowledged the neo-colonial nature of the Convention.

8 The role of the EEC delegate was not neo-colonial.

Dr David Wall maintained that the role of the EEC delegate as a permanent representative of the Commission in the ACP countries constituted neo-colonialism. No other aid agency felt compelled to keep an on-the-ground supervisor in countries where it had projects.[93]

However, the ACP themselves, as noted in Chapter 4, were not opposed to the role of the EEC delegate. They favoured enhancing his role in expediting their claims and petitions to the Brussels bureaucracy.[94] Because the ACP accepted the practical value of the delegate, it is easier to interpret his symbolic rather than his technical role as neo-colonial.

In addition to his practical role in supervising EDF projects, the delegate played a political role. He kept track of the political and social conditions in the country or countries to which he was assigned. Because the Community had no ambassadors, the delegate served as a symbol of the Community's commitment to the ACP. Since the Community's relationship with the ACP was neo-colonial, the delegate could be considered a symbol of this neo-colonialism.

In summary, the arguments refuting allegations of neo-colonialism are unconvincing. The weight of evidence demonstrates that the Lome relationship was not, as one senior Commission official doggedly maintained, a simple relationship with a simple job: development. It was a complex political relationship which can be characterized as neo-colonialism. A summary of the reasons for concluding that the Convention was neo-colonial is given below.

1 The Lome Convention was neo-colonial because it carried on the policy of association between Europe and Africa. It sought to continue links between Europe and Africa at every level to further European political and economic goals, establishing a EurAfrican alliance.
2 The Convention was neo-colonial because the parameters of the relationship were set by the Community. Major provisions such as the amount of aid, trade concessions, and programmes such as STABEX were offered to the ACP on a take it or leave it basis.
3 The Lome Convention was neo-colonial because it attempted to regionalize selected African, Caribbean and Pacific states. It created divisions between the ACP and other less-developed countries in Asia, Latin America and North Africa.
4 Instead of weakening ties between the former metropolises and the former colonies, the Convention fostered them. Within the relationship the ACP largely relied on the patronage of the former colonial power to obtain a fair share of aid, trade opportunities, and STABEX payments.
5 The Convention was neo-colonial because its provisions did little to change the economic weakness and dependency of the ACP. Trade preferences and STABEX payments favoured ACP exports of primary products. EEC attempts to industrialize the ACP were minimal. The trade preferences and financial aid which did little overall to ameliorate ACP underdevelopment nevertheless attracted the ACP to the relationship and produced some successful development projects. This softening of EEC interests in ACP markets and raw materials with concessions could be termed 'welfare neo-colonialism'. However, the EEC's pursuit of welfare neo-colonialism did not create a new international economic order or raise the ACP from their traditional status of hewers of wood and drawers of water for industrial Europe.[95]
6 The Lome Convention was neo-colonial because it relied on what Johan Galtung called a bridgehead of the Centre in the Periphery.[96] That is, the relationship was handled on an elite to elite basis, and was largely unknown by the EEC and ACP populations. As noted earlier, the Convention tended to support regimes in power. This was not only an effect of government to government aid, it was also cultivated by successive development Commissioners. Former Commissioner Cheysson was described in *Jeune Afrique* as the confidant if not the accomplice of most of the African heads of state.[97]

The six reasons listed above indicate that the Lome Convention was an example of neo-colonialism — or welfare neo-colonialism. Supplementary reasons why the Convention was neo-colonial such as its widespread reputation for neo-colonialism, the quasi-ambassadorial role of the delegate, and the racial differences between the EEC and ACP populations could also be adduced.[98]

'To colonize,' said a French colonial governor-general in 1941, 'is essentially to cause the indigenous societies to advance down the paths that we have chosen for them.'[99] In conclusion, the Lome Convention was neo-colonial because it was a path chosen for the ACP by the European Community.

The prospects for Lome

V.S. Naipaul's contention that 'Africa has no future' was as unrealistic as Hegel's and Marx's view that Africa had no history.[100] The Lome Convention too had a history, traceable back to European colonialism; it also has a future whose general outlines can be perceived.

Although the preceding section argued that the Lome Convention was neo-colonial, this was not to condemn it utterly. Any alliance between the politically (relatively) stable and economically powerful European Community and the weak, unstable and economically dependent ACP states was bound to produce mixed blessings. The Lome Convention was neo-colonial, but its brand of welfare neo-colonialism was still generally preferable to the military domination practised by the USA and USSR or the sufferings of isolation of pre-1975 Guinea.

The Lome Convention had numerous shortcomings as the analysis of its trade and aid provisions and its neo-colonial nature indicated, yet in many ways it was remarkable. The Convention was remarkable for the way it built upon the colonial legacy and still managed to present itself as something new in international relations. This skilful management and development of the policy of association enabled it to be presented as a partnership among equals, a step towards the new international economic order, a breakthrough in North–South relations. Although the image of the Convention shone more brightly at some times, particularly at the beginning of Lome-I, than others, the actual neo-colonial nature of the treaty was generally obscured.

The skilful development of the Lome policy made it attractive to a growing number of developing countries. By including virtually all of sub-Saharan Africa in the relationship, Lome represented the fulfilment rather than the abandonment of dreams of EurAfrica.

Lome did not reduce European political influence, abolish the economic dependence of the ACP, encourage their rapid industrialization, reduce the power of the ACP elites or accomplish any profound structural changes in EEC–ACP relations. But with its STABEX payments, financial aid, trade concessions, and progressive rhetoric, Lome (and the earlier Yaounde Conventions) achieved a refined policy of welfare neo-colonialism.

Another noteworthy feature of the Lome relationship was its ability to keep a low political profile. By portraying Lome as an economic agreement, the Community largely avoided political problems such as the human rights debate and enhanced the durability of the Convention.

Again remarkable was the Community's presentation of its Lome alliance, *l'entente discrete*, as a middle way between the superpowers while avoiding conflicts with the US. If the Lome Convention was not exactly equivalent to non-alignment as the EEC Commission claimed, it was nonetheless the nearest practicable alternative. With its stated policy of political neutrality, the EEC posed less threat of intervention or domination to the ACP countries than their principal alternative allies, the USA, USSR, or even France.

The option of disengagement from the international system was, as the example of Guinea demonstrated, one which was not generally viable for the ACP. As poor and weak countries heavily dependent on EEC financial aid and the export of primary products, the ACP could not readily afford to pass by EEC assistance, however little real improvement it caused. As sources of substantial financial aid were few and the ACP states' ability to generate autonomous development was limited, they were right to accept the relatively benign partnership of the European Community.

It has been argued that the Lome Convention was 'overrated', that it would soon pass into oblivion, and that attention to it merely diverted interest from more important subjects.[101] However, it is not possible to dismiss the EEC–ACP entente in this way. To paraphrase Professor Emerson, the Lome Convention was at least one pillar of the international order of its day.[102] The ACP–EEC relationship was significant in that it was a long-standing, unique and sophisticated policy which involved a large and growing number of countries.

As to the assertion that the Lome Convention would soon sink into oblivion, no signs of this are evident. Indeed, the past thirty years of the relationship reveal its ability to adapt to new circumstances without losing its essence. Lome — now in its third incarnation — still addresses itself to ACP poverty and dependence and to European political and economic aspirations.

Community interest in areas such as the Mediterranean and Latin America has increased, and interest in the ACP is no longer as overriding in EEC thinking as it was in the mid-1970s. But the Community still considers Lome as the cornerstone of its development policy.[103] It is thus apparent that Europe will continue to seek an *entente discrete* with the ACP.

For many ACP countries, development prospects in the 1980s are bleak. Thus, the ACP will remain largely poor, weak and in need of European help. It is unlikely that the ACP would sacrifice the economic rewards of Lome for the sake of their political principles over South Africa or other issues. It is also unlikely that the ACP will be able to effect more than marginal changes in future Lome treaties.

Potential areas of conflict within the Lome relationship have been outlined earlier in this chapter. These include rivalry among EEC member states over influence in Africa. Potential extenal conflicts regarding growing Community interest in Latin America have also been described. ACP expressions of disquiet over the Community's continuing relationship with the Republic of South Africa are likely to remain a source of conflict. However, the Lome relationship has in the past demonstrated its ability to avoid and withstand such conflicts.

It is likely that the Lome entente will continue to overcome its near- and medium-term problems for five major reasons. First, it has a well-established network of relationships which will, because of political inertia or the tendency for governments to engage in incremental rather than comprehensive decisions, tend to persist rather than be disrupted. Next, as long as the EEC remains a major (and slowly increasing at least in nominal terms) source of financial aid and preferential trade arrangements for the ACP, they are unlikely to reject its Lome Conventions. Third, the Community is unlikely to abandon its long-held interest in Africa's polities and economies. Also, the Convention's low political profile as a discreet entente will continue to help it to escape international criticisms and internal divisions. Finally, the alliance has an ability, most clearly demonstrated in Yaounde I and Lome I, to adapt to changing international political norms.

Having concluded that the Lome relationship is likely to continue for the reasons mentioned above, it remains to consider the probable form of such a relationship. It is not possible to foresee in detail the future development of the Convention, but certain developments are highly improbable. Thus, the foreseeable future of Lome holds no true partnership between the EEC and ACP. The ACP are likely to remain weak, dependent and unable to achieve equality within the relationship.

Community strategy will not permit a globalization of the relationship, extending its aid and preferences to all ldcs. Such a globalization might be favoured by EEC member states such as the Netherlands, but it would destroy the Community's cherished plans for region-to-region relations with the ACP and the Mediterranean littoral states.

Also not discernible in Lome's future is any widespread multi-lateralization of post-colonial ties. Thus, former colonies will continue to need and seek the patronage of the former colonial power in obtaining Lome benefits. Competition for influence in Africa may emerge between EEC states, but such competition is unlikely to lead to a general dilution and eventual elimination of the special links between former colonies and former colonizers.

Another prospect not on the Lome horizon is the rapid economic development or industrialization of the ACP. But, as noted in Chapter 3, there is hope for the continuing development and practical improvement of Lome's aid and trade provisions.

Real ACP unity is also unlikely to emerge from the Lome relationship. Some ACP cooperation and coordination will continue, but divisions between Commonwealth anglophone and francophone, between African, Caribbean and Pacific states will remain important. The ACP ambivalence towards Lome-fostered unity will not quickly be overcome.

The neo-colonial characteristics of the Convention described here will not readily be eliminated. Nevertheless, the Lome entente is well situated to continue, to expand its membership, and to develop its 'welfare' provisions. But after three decades of EurAfrican cooperation, the Lome relationship has not fulfilled the economic, social, cultural or political aspirations of the ACP peoples and seems unlikely to be able to do so in the future.[104]

Notes

1. Jenkins, Roy, 'Europe and The Third World: The Political Economy of Interdependence', *Round Table*, October 1978.
2. Cheysson, Claude, 'Preface' to *Europe and the Third World: A Study on Interdependence*, Brussels, EEC Commission, Dossiers, 1978, no. 2.
3. Alford, Col. J., 'The Strategic Relationship', in *Europe and Africa*, London, Overseas Development Institute, 1980.
4. Ravenhill, John, 'Asymmetrical Interdependence', in Long, F. (ed.), *The Political Economy of EEC Relations with the African, Caribbean and Pacific States*, London, Pergamon, 1980.
5. 'Memorandum on the Community's Development Policy', Brussels, EEC, 1982, COM (82) 640, (Pisani Memorandum), p. 11.
6. Rivkin, Arnold, *The African Presence in World Affairs*, London, Free Press of Glencoe, 1963.
7. Parker, Geoffrey, *A Political Geography of Community Europe*, London, Butterworths, 1983.
8. The decline of the term 'EurAfrica' was also noted by a then senior EEC official, Kaye Whiteman, in an address to the Royal Institute of International Affairs, London, 'France's New Role in Africa', 15 January 1981.
9. Rivkin, *op cit*.
10. Cheysson, C., 'The Relationship Between the European Community and Africa', in *Europe and Africa*, London, Royal African Society, 1978.
11. See remarks of Ambassador Rainford in *The Courier*, November 1979, no. 58.

12. Cheysson, C., 'Security and Development, A View From Europe', address to a World Bank seminar, Annapolis, 3 April 1981.
13. Cheysson, C., 'The Relationship between the European Community and Africa', *op cit*.
14. *ibid*.
15. 'Realigning the Non-Aligned', *The Times*, London, 7 March 1983.
16. Address in Maputo, 1980 (Source: European Commission).
17. Moss, J., *The Lome Conventions and their Implications for the United States*, Boulder, Westview, 1982, p. 147.
18. See, for example, Alford, J., *op cit*.
19. Robert Lemaignen, first development Commissioner, argued that 'This sentiment, this diffuse aspiration for the disappearance of the cursed European war in which the Africans were mixed more intimately than we can imagine, is the most solid basis on which EurAfrica can rest.', in *L'Europe au Berceau*, Paris, Plon, 1964, p. 130.
20. de Schacht, F., 'Le Contexte Politique de l'Association', *Revue du Marche Commun*, May 1969.
21. 'Latin America—EEC Links Urged', *Financial Times*, London, 25 March 1983.
22. Smith, Arnold, *Stitches in Time*, London, Andre Deutsch, 1981, p. 183.
23. Cheysson, C., 'An Agreement Unique in History', in *The Courier*, no. 31, March 1975.
24. See Smith, *op cit*, 'Dealing with Europe'.
25. Parker, *op cit*.
26. Kahler, Miles, 'Europe and its "Privileged Partners" in Africa and the Middle East', in *The European Community*, Tsoukalis, Loukis, ed., Oxford, Blackwell, 1983; for a similar view see Bailey, Richard, *The European Connection*, Oxford, Pergamon, 1983, Ch.14.
27. For a similar view see Dolan, Michael, 'The Lome Convention and Europe's Relationship with the Third World', *Revue d'integration europeene*, (I) 3, 1978.
28. See Curzon, G. and V., 'Neo-colonialism and the European Economic Community', in *The Yearbook of World Affairs*, London, 1971, for a discussion of this point.
29. Cheysson, Claude, interviewed in *Jeune Afrique*, no. 1022, 6 August 1980.
30. Lemaignen, *op cit*.
31. See the Pisani Memorandum, *op cit*.
32. Kuhne, W. and von Plate, B., 'Two Germanys in Africa', *Africa Report*, July–August 1980.
33. *Lome Convention*, Annex XXII and Annex XXIII.
34. Kuhne and von Plate, *op cit*.
35. Statistics from European Commission.
36. Kuhne and von Plate, *op cit*.
37. *The Courier*, March–April 1982, no. 72, p. XI.
38. *West Africa*, 17 October 1983.
39. von der Ropp, Baron Klaus, 'Lome II: The European Community and the North–South Dialogue', *International Affairs Bulletin* (South Africa), Summer, 1980.
40. *The Courier*, July–August 1979, no. 56, p. viii.
41. *ibid*.
42. 'Lome II', Overseas Development Institute Briefing Paper, London, February 1980, No. 1.
43. Twitchett, Carol, *A Framework for Development*, *op cit*, p. 98.

44. Quoted from *The Courier*, March—April 1984, no. 84.
45. Twitchett, C., *A Framework for Development*, *op cit*, p. 127.
46. *The European Community and Southern Africa*, Brussels, EEC, December 1981, p. 10, (statistics compiled for the EEC by M. Lister). Nevertheless, ACP trade with the ACP, and with Nigeria alone, exceeded the value of EEC trade with South Africa.
47. 'SA to get EEC Arms', *The Guardian*, 3 December 1983.
48. Shaw, T.M., 'EEC—ACP Interactions and Images as Redefinitions of Eur-Africa: Exemplary, Exclusive and/or Exploitative', *Journal of Common Market Studies*, 18 (12), December 1979.
49. *West Africa*, 17 May 1982.
50. *West Africa*, 10 January 1983.
51. *West Africa*, 17 May 1982.
52. Shaw, *op cit*.
53. von der Ropp, *op cit*.
54. Press and Information Service, French Embassy in London, 'Excerpts from a Press Conference Given by M. Jean-Pierre Cot', 9 September 1982.
55. Gavshon, Arthur, *Crisis in Africa*, London, Penguin, 1981, Ch.8.
56. *ibid*.
57. *ibid*.
58. Press and Information Service, French Embassy, London, 10 February 1983.
59. Pisani Memorandum, *op cit*.
60. Kazakevicus, V., 'The Common Market and the Developing Countries', *International Affairs* (Moscow), no. 6, 1979.
61. *ibid*.
62. For opposing views see Carrington, Lord, 'Reflections on the Alliance', in *Nato Review*, June 1984, and Kissinger, Henry, 'Britain and the United States: Reflections on a Partnership', in *International Affairs*, Autumn 1982, vol. 58, no. 4.
63. See for example, Rivkin, Arnold, 'Lost Goals in Africa', *Foreign Affairs*, October 1965.
64. Gavshon, *op cit*, p. 157.
65. 'Mitterand Finds a Friend in Reagan', *The Guardian*, 23 March 1983.
66. 'The European Community and the United States', Brussels, EEC Publication, DGI, November 1980.
67. *First General Report on the Activities of the Communities*, EEC, Brussels, 1958, p. 110.
68. Although the French were intensely concerned about any kind of increase in US influence in Africa. See *West Africa*, 7 May 1984, p. 965.
69. *The Courier*, September—October 1981, no. 69.
70. The Community generally resisted US pressure to use aid as a weapon and continued, despite US objections, with its humanitarian aid to El Salvador and Nicaragua. See *Le Monde*, 13 March 1981.
71. Mower, A.G., *The European Community and Latin America*, Westport, Greenwood Press, 1982, Ch.2.
72. Muniz, Blanca, 'EEC—Latin America: a Relationship to be Defined', *Journal of Common Market Studies*, September 1980.
73. Mower, *op cit*.
74. For the view that the Monroe Doctrine is moribund see Grabendorf, Wolf, 'The United States and Western Europe in Latin America', *International Affairs*, vol. 58, no. 4, Autumn 1982.
75. See Vosskuhler, K., 'The EEC and the USA — Differing Politico-Economic Approaches', in *EEC and the Third World: A Survey 3*, Stevens, C. (ed.), London, Hodder and Stoughton, 1983.

76. Nkrumah, Kwame, *Neo-Colonialism: The Last Stage of Imperialism*, London, Heinemann, 1965, 'Introduction'.
77. Quoted from Gruhn, I.V., 'The Lome Convention: inching towards interdependence', *International Organization*, Spring 1976, p. 244.
78. For an account of these see Zartman, I.W., *The Politics of Trade Negotiations between Africa and The European Economic Community*, Princeton, Princeton University Press, 1971, Ch.1.
79. See Twitchett, K., 'Colonialism', *Political Studies*, October 1965.
80. Zartman, I.W., 'Africa as a Subordinate State System in International Relations', *International Organization*, Summer 1967, vol. 21, no. 3.
81. *West Africa*, 22 November 1982, p. 3043.
82. *The Times*, London, 7 March 1983.
83. Twitchett, C., *Europe and Africa: From Association to Partnership*, Westmead, Saxon House, 1978, p. 123.
84. *ibid*, p. 123.
85. Dolan, M. and Caporaso, J., 'The External Relations of the European Community', *Annals of the American Academy of Political and Social Sciences*, November 1978.
86. *Europe and Africa: From Association to Partnership*, *op cit*, p. 124.
87. The term 'fragmentation' was used by Johan Galtung in his study, *The European Community: A Superpower in the Making*, London, Allen and Unwin, 1973, Ch.3.
88. Zartman, I.W., 'Europe and Africa: Decolonization or Dependency', *Foreign Affairs*, vol. 54, no. 2, January 1976.
89. *West Africa*, 10 May 1982.
90. *West Africa*, 2 May 1983.
91. Mytelka, Lynn K., 'The Lome Convention and a New International Division of Labour', *Revue d'Integration Europeene*, September 1977.
92. For this argument see *Europe and Africa: From Association to Partnership*, *op cit*, p. 168.
93. Wall, D., *The European Community's Lome Convention: 'Stabex' and the Third World's Aspirations*, London, Trade Policy Research Centre, 1976.
94. *Report of the ACP–EEC Council of Ministers*, 1980–81, Brussels, EEC, 1981.
95. Akinsaya, A., in 'The European Common Market and Africa', *International Problems*, 1977, vol. 16, argued that the EEC was indeed attempting with the Lome Convention to defuse demands for an equitable international economic system. For a discussion of how the Convention affected the ACP's industrial development prospects, see Mytelka, Lynn, 'The Lome Convention: A New International Division of Labour', *op cit*.
96. Galtung, *op cit*.
97. 'Claude Cheysson, Etes-Vous un Ministre des Colonies?', *Jeune Afrique*, no. 1022, 6 August 1980.
98. Ali Mazrui pointed out the importance of the racial divisions in the relationship, although it is possible to conceive of a racially mixed alliance without neo-colonialism, Mazrui, A., *The Anglo-African Commonwealth*, Oxford, Pergamon, 1967, Ch.4.
99. Pierre Boisson quoted in Deschamps, Hubert, *Methodes et Doctrines Coloniales de la France*, Paris, Armand Colin, 1953, p. 177.
100. 'Viewpoint', *Times Literary Supplement*, 1 February 1980.
101. Galtung, Johan, 'The Lome Convention and Neo-Capitalism', *African Review*, 1976, vol. 6 (1).

102. Emerson, Rupert, *From Empire to Nation*, Cambridge Mass., Harvard University Press, 1967.
103. *Memorandum on the Community's Development Aid Policy*, EEC Document Com (82) 640 final, 1982, (Pisani Memorandum), p. 1.
104. Cf. *Treaty Establishing the European Economic Community*, (1957), London, HMSO, 1962, (Treaty of Rome), Part IV, 'this association shall in the first place permit the furthering of the interests and prospects of the inhabitants of these countries and territories in such a manner as to lead them to the economic, social and cultural development which they expect'.

Selected bibliography

EEC documents

'The ACP—EEC Convention of Lome', (Preamble), *The Courier*, no. 31, Brussels, EEC, March 1975, (Lome I).
Agreement Establishing an Association Between the European Economic Community and the United Republic of Tanzania, the Republic of Uganda, and the Republic of Kenya and Annexed Documents, Brussels, EEC, 1969, (second Arusha Convention).
'Comments on the Operation of the Export Earnings Stabilization System', *Report Adopted by the Court of Auditors of the European Community*, 19 July 1979.
Comprehensive Report on Stabex 1975—9, Brussels, EEC (Sec81—1104).
Convention of Association between the European Economic Community and the African and Malagasy States associated with that Community, London, HMSO, 1965, (Yaounde I).
Convention of Association between the European Economic Community and the African and Malagasy States Associated with that Community and Annexed Documents, 1969, Brussels, EEC, (Yaounde II).
'Development Aid: Fresco of Community Action Tomorrow', Brussels, European Commission, *Bulletin of the European Communities*, Supplement 8/74, (The Fresco).
The European Community and Southern Africa, Brussels, EEC, December 1981.

The European Community and the Third World, Brussels, EEC, November 1977.
The European Community and the United States, EEC Publication, DGI, November 1980.
European Development Fund 1958–1968, Brussels, EEC Commission.
The First Stage of the Common Market: Report on the Execution of the Treaty January 1958–June 1962, Brussels, EEC, July 1962.
Harmonization and Coordination of Development Cooperation Policies within the Community, Brussels, EEC, COM (76) 358 final.
Memorandum of the Commission to the Council, April 1973, (Deniau Memorandum), Brussels, EEC, COM (73/500/fin).
Memorandum on the Community's Development Policy, (Pisani Memorandum), Brussels, EEC, 1982, COM (82) 640 final.
Rapports sur L'utilization des Fonds Transferes au Titre des Systemes de Stabilization des Recettes Institues par la Premiere Convention de Lome et par la Decision Relative a l'Association des PTOM a la CEE, EEC document SEC (81) 1751.
Report of the ACP–EEC Council of Ministers, 1976–1980, Brussels, EEC, 1980.
Report of the ACP–EEC Council of Ministers, 1980–81, Brussels, EEC, 1981.
'The Second ACP–EEC Convention', *The Courier*, no. 58, November 1979.
The Second Yaounde Convention: Great Possibilities for Private Investment, Brussels, EEC.
'Third ACP–EEC Convention', *The Courier*, (no. 89), January–February 1985.
General Report on the Activities of the Community, Brussels, EEC, (*First* to *Tenth* 1958–1967).

ACP and other documents

Draft Report on Cultural Cooperation between the ACP and European Community, Joint Committee of ACP–EEC Consultative Assembly, 5 August 1981, (Chasle Report).
Focke, Katarina, *From Lome 1 towards Lome 2*, text of the report and resolution adopted on 26 September 1980, by the ACP–EEC Consultative Assembly, (Focke Report).
The Georgetown Agreement, 1975, Brussels, ACP Library.
Presentation Notes by the Committee of Ambassadors on the Conclusions and Recommendations of the Experts' Meeting in Brussels, June 22–25, 1981, ACP document ACP/859/81.

Recommendations for the Establishment of a Trade and Development Bank, UN document TCD/int-77-RO7/1, 1977.
Report of the Meeting of Trade Operators from the ACP Group of States held at Lome, Togo in July 1981, ACP document ACP/465/81.
Report on the Fifth Annual Report of the ACP–EEC Council of Ministers, (Insanally Report), 12 October 1981, Doc., ACP–EEC 29.81/rev.
Report of the ACP–EEC Conference on the Development and Promotion of ACP Trade, ACP document ACP/810/79.
Suva Declaration, 1977, ACP General Secretariat, Brussels.

Other sources

A Correspondent, 'Guinea After Five Years', *The World Today*, March 1964.
ACP States Yearbook (1980–81) Brussels, Editions Delta, 1981.
Akinsaya, A., 'The European Common Market and Africa', *International Problems*, 1977, vol. 16.
Alford, Col. J., 'The Strategic Relationship', in *Europe and Africa*, London, ODI, 1980.
Andic, F., 'The Development Impact of the EEC on the French and Dutch Caribbean', *Journal of Common Market Studies*, vol. 8, no. 1, 1969.
Anyadike-Danes, Monya, 'Regional Cooperation and the ACP Group', *Lome Briefing*, no. 19.
Arnold, Hugh, 'Africa and the New International Economic Order', *Third World Quarterly*, April 1980.
Asante, K.B., 'The African Attitude Towards Europe', *Europe and Africa*, London, Royal Africa Society, 1978.
Axline, W.A., *Caribbean Integration: The Politics of Regionalism*, London, Frances Pinter, 1979.
Barnes, William, *Europe and the Developing World: Association Under Part IV of the Treaty of Rome*, London, Chatham House, February 1967.
Baynham, Simon, 'Equatorial Guinea: The Terror and the Coup', *The World Today*, February 1980.
Berg, Eliot, 'The Economic Basis of Political Choice in French Africa', *American Political Science Review*, June 1960.
Betts, R., *Assimilation and Association: French Colonial Theory*, New York, Columbia University Press, 1961.
Blaug, M., 'Lenin and Economic Imperialism Reconsidered', in Winks, R. (ed.), *British Imperialism*, New York, Holt Rinehart Winston, 1964.

Bozeman, Adda, *Conflict in Africa*, Princeton, Princeton University Press, 1976.

Bretton, Henry, 'United States Foreign Policy Toward the Newly Independent States', in Judd, P. (ed.), *African Independence*, New Jersey, Dell, 1962.

Brinkhorst, L.J., quoted in Alting von Geusau, F.A.M. (ed.), *The Lome Convention and a New International Economic Order*, Netherlands, A.W. Sijthoff, 1977.

Brunschwig, Henri, *French Colonialism 1871–1914*, London, Pall Mall, 1966.

Carrington, Edward, 'The Renewal of the Lome Convention', Lecture to the University of Antwerp, 12 February 1980.

Chaffard, Georges, *Les Carnets Secrets de la Decolonisation*, Paris, Calmann-Levey, 1967.

Cheysson, Claude, 'Europe and the Third World After Lome', *The Relationship Between the European Community and Africa*, London, Royal African Society, 1978.

Cheysson, Claude, 'Security and Development, A View from Europe', address to a World Bank Seminar, Annapolis, 1981.

Cheysson, Claude, 'An Agreement Unique in History', *The Courier*, no. 31, March 1975.

Cosgrove, C. and Twitchett, K., 'The Second Yaounde Convention in Perspective', *International Relations*, May 1970.

Cowan, L., 'Guinea', in Carter, G. (ed.), *African One Party States*, Ithaca, N.Y., Cornell University Press, 1962.

Curzon, G. and V., 'Neo-Colonialism and the European Economic Community', *Yearbook of World Affairs*, 1971.

de Gaulle, Charles, 'Memoirs of Hope', in Smith, Tony (ed.), *The End of the European Empire*, Lexington, Mass., D.C. Heath, 1975.

de Koster, H.J., former Netherlands Secretary of State for Foreign Affairs, in *Revue du Marche Commun*, May 1969.

de Schacht, F., 'Le Contexte Politique de L'Association', *Revue du Marche Commun*, May 1969.

Deschamps, Hubert, *Methodes et Doctrines Coloniales de la France*, Paris, Armand Colin, 1953, 'Preface'.

Dodoo, C. and Kuster, R., 'The Road to Lome', in Alting von Geusau, F.A.M. (ed.), *The Lome Convention and a New International Economic Order*, Leyden, Sijthoff, 1977.

Dolan, Michael, 'The Lome Convention and Europe's Relationship with the Third World: A Critical Analysis', *Revue d'Integration Europeene*, I(no.30), 1978.

Dolan, M. and Caporaso, J., 'The External Relations of the European Community', *Annals of the American Academy of Political and Social Sciences*, November 1978.

'France's New Role in Africa', *The World Today*, September 1964.

Frey-Wouters, Ellen, *The European Community and the Third World*, New York, Praeger, 1980.

Galtung, Johan, *The European Community: A Superpower in the Making*, London, Allen and Unwin, 1973; also 'The Lome Convention and Neo-Capitalism', *African Review*, 1976.

Gavshon, Arthur, *Crisis in Africa*, London, Penguin, 1981.

Ghai, D.P., *Asian Commonwealth Countries and the EEC*, London, Commonwealth Secretariat, Commonwealth Economic Papers, no. 2, 1973.

Grabendorf, Wolf, 'The United States and Western Europe in Latin America', *International Affairs*, vol. 58, no. 4, 1982.

Green, R.H., 'The Child of Lome: Messiah, Monster or Mouse', in Long, F. (ed.), *The Political Economy of EEC–ACP Relations*, London, Pergamon, 1980.

Gruhn, I.V., 'Inching Towards Interdependence', *International Organization*, vol. 30.

Hewitt, A., *The European Development Fund and its Function in the EEC's Development Aid Policy*, London, Overseas Development Institute, Working Paper no. 11, 1982.

Hewitt, A., 'The European Development Fund as a Development Agent: Some Results of EDF Aid to Cameroon', *Overseas Development Institute Review*, no. 2, 1979.

Hewitt, A., 'Stabex: Analysing the Effectiveness of an Innovation', *EEC and the Third World: A Survey 3*, London, Hodder and Stoughton, 1983.

Hewitt, A., *Malawi's First Eight Years of Cooperation with the EEC: The Results of the Lome Conventions*, London, Overseas Development Institute Working Paper no. 12, 1983.

Hewitt, A. and Stevens, C., 'The Second Lome Convention', in Stevens, C. (ed.), *EEC and the Third World: A Survey 1*, London, Hodder and Stoughton, 1980.

Jenkins, Roy, 'Europe and the Third World: The Political Economy of Interdependence', *Round Table*, October 1978.

Jones, David, *Europe's Chosen Few: Policy and Practice of the EEC Aid Programme*, London, Overseas Development Institute, 1973.

Kahler, M., 'Europe and its "Privileged Partners" in Africa and the Middle East', in *The European Community*, ed. Loukas Tsoukalis, Oxford, Blackwell, 1983.

Kazakevicus, V., 'The Common Market and the Developing Countries', *International Affairs*, (Moscow) 1979.

Khan, H.H. the Aga, 'The Great Gamble in Africa', *The Commonwealth Journal*, July–August 1962.

Kissinger, Henry, 'Britain and the United States: Reflections on a Partnership', in *International Affairs*, Autumn 1982.

Kitzinger, U.W., *The Challenge of the Common Market*, Oxford, Blackwell, 1961.

Kreinin, Mordechai, 'European Integration and the Developing Countries', in Balassa, Bela (ed.), *European Economic Integration*, Oxford, North-Holland, 1975.

Kuhne, W. and von Plate, B., 'Two Germanys in Africa', *Africa Report*, July—August 1980.

Lawrence, R., 'Primary Products, Preferences, and Economic Welfare: The EEC and Africa', in Robson, P. (ed.), *International Economic Integration*, Harmondsworth, Penguin, 1972.

Lemaignen, Robert, *L'Europe au Berceau*, Paris, Plon, 1964.

Lipset, S.M., *The First New Nation*, London, Heinemann, 1963.

Lister, M.R., 'The Functioning of the Second Lome Convention', *Journal of World Trade Law*, September—October 1982.

Matthews, J.D., *The Association System of the European Community*, New York, Praeger, 1977.

Mazrui, Ali, 'African Attitudes to the European Economic Community', in Krause, L. (ed.), *The Common Market: Progress and Continuity*, 1964.

Mazrui, Ali, *The Anglo-African Commonwealth*, Oxford, Pergamon, 1967.

Moss, J., *The Lome Conventions and their Implications for the United States*, Boulder, Westview, 1982.

Moss, J. and Ravenhill, J., 'Trade Between the ACP and EEC during Lome I', in Stevens, C. (ed.), *The Atlantic Rift, EEC and the Third World: A Survey 4*, London, Hodder and Stoughton, 1983.

Mower, A.G., *The European Community and Latin America*, Westport, Greenwood Press, 1982.

Muniz, Blanca, 'EEC—Latin America: a Relationship to be Defined', *Journal of Common Market Studies*, September 1980.

Mytelka, L., 'The Lome Convention and a New International Division of Labour', *Revue d'Integration Europeene*, September 1977.

Ndegwa, Philip, *The Common Market and Development in East Africa*, Nairobi, East Africa Publishing House, 1965.

Ndongko, W.A., 'The Economic Origins of the Association of Some African States with the EEC', *African Studies Review*, September 1973.

Nkrumah, Kwame, *Neo-Colonialism: The Last Stage of Imperialism*, London, Heinemann, 1965.

Nye, J., *Pan-Africanism and East African Integration*, London, Oxford University Press, 1966.

Okigbo, P., *Africa and the Common Market*, London, Longmans, 1967.

Olu Sanu, E., *The Lome Convention and the New International Economic Order*, Lagos, Nigerian Institute of International Affairs, 1977.

Ouattara, Alassane D., 'Trade Effects of the Association of African Countries with the European Economic Community', International Monetary Fund, *Staff Papers*, 1973.

Pearson, S. and Schmidt, W., 'Alms for AAMS: A Larger Flow?', *Journal of Common Market Studies*, vol. 3, 1964.

Persaud, B., 'Export Earnings Stabilization in the ACP—EEC Convention of Lome', in Long, F. (ed.), *The Political Economy of ACP—EEC Relations*, Oxford, Pergamon, 1980.

Persaud, B., 'Industrial Cooperation in the Lome Convention', in *The Renegotiation of the Lome Convention*, London, Catholic Institute for International Relations and Trocaire, 1978.

Pisani, Edgard, Speech to ACP—EEC Consultative Assembly, Strasbourg, 24 September 1981.

Rabemanjara, J., 'L'Organization des Dix-Huit, Leur Coordination, Leurs Rapports avec les Autre Pays Africains', *Revue du Marche Commun*, May 1969.

Ramphal, S., 'South—South: Parameters and Pre-conditions', in *South—South Strategy*, A. Gauhar (ed.), London, Third World Foundation, 1983.

Ravenhill, Frederick John, *'Asymmetrical Interdependence: The Lome Convention and North—South Relations'*, University of California, Berkeley, PhD., 1981.

Rivkin, A., 'Lost Goals in Africa', *Foreign Affairs*, October 1965.

Rothstein, R., 'The North—South Dialogue', *International Affairs*, Spring—Summer 1980; also *The Weak in the World of the Strong: the Developing Countries in the International System*, New York, Columbia University Press, 1977.

Rubin, Abby, *The Renegotiation of Lome II*, London, Catholic Institute for International Relations and Trocaire, 1978.

Sekou Toure, Ahmed, 'The Republic of Guinea', *International Affairs*, April 1960.

Shaw, T.M., 'EEC—ACP Interactions and Images as Redefinitions of EurAfrica: Exemplary, Exclusive or Exploitative?', *Journal of Common Market Studies*, 18 (12), December 1979.

Smith, Arnold, *Stitches in Time: The Commonwealth in World Politics*, London, Andre Deutsch, 1981.

Stevens, Christopher, 'An Economic Overview of Lome II', lecture to the University Association of Contemporary European Studies, 11 November 1979; also, 'Prospects for Lome III', lecture at Overseas Development Institute, London.

Stibbe, P., 'French-Speaking Tropical Africa', in Judd, P. (ed.), *African Independence*, New York, Dell, 1962.

Swann, Dennis, *The Economics of the Common Market*, 2nd edn, Harmondsworth, Penguin, 1972.

Twitchett, Carol Cosgrove, *Europe and Africa: From Association to Partnership*, Westmead, Saxon House, 1979; also, *A Framework for Development: The EEC and the ACP*, London, Allen and Unwin, 1981; also, *ACP Foreign Trade*, Brussels, ACP Group, 1979.

Twitchett, K., 'Yaounde Association and the Enlarged European Community', *The World Today*, February 1974.

Zartman, I.W., 'Europe and Africa: Decolonization or Dependency', *Foreign Affairs*, vol. 54, no. 2, January 1976.

Zartman, I.W., *The Politics of Trade Negotiations Between Africa and the EEC*, Princeton, N.J., Princeton University Press, 1971.

Zischka, Anton, *Afrique, Complement de l'Europe*, Paris, Laffont, 1952.

Index

Abidjan meeting (1973), 69–70, 76
ACP
 aid results, 131–42, 145–54
 –EEC negotiations, 69, 74–89
 exports to EEC, 110–17
 industrial cooperation, 89–95
 interdependence, *see* Lome entente
 Lome institutions and, 96–102
 Lome provisions for, 58–61, 63–4, 103–5
 negotiations (intra), 69–70
ACP unity
 cooperation (history), 169–74
 cooperation (in practice), 174–82
 General Secretariat, 174–9
 problematical nature, 167–8, 183–4
Ad Hoc Assembly, 14
Africa
 anglophone states, 64, 69, 70, 211, 219
 colonial legacies, 1–31
 francophone states, 62, 64, 66, 69–70, 101, 136, 202, 211, 212, 219
 solidarity, *see* pan-Africanism
 see also ACP; Association of African and Malagasy States; EurAfrican relations; South Africa

African, Caribbean and Pacific Group of States, *see* ACP
African Development Bank, 69
Agency for International Development, 146, 147
agriculture, 134, 159
 Common Agricultural Policy, 43, 76–7, 82
 Lome projects, 142–3, 213
aid, *see* emergency aid; financial aid; food aid
Algeria, 3, 17, 18
alliance concept, 104
Alliance for Progress, 104, 186
Amin, Idi, 133, 134, 153, 156–7, 197–8
anglophone states, 64, 69, 70, 211, 219
Angola, 11n, 195–6, 202, 206
apartheid, 157–8, 199, 201n
Arab Development Bank, 146
Arab Monetary Fund, 128
Arusha Convention, 47, 48, 76
Asian Commonwealth, 68, 92, 132
Assembly (of French Union), 4, 5
assimilation policy, 2, 3

233

Associable countries, 63–4, 66–8, 85, 96, 103–4, 153
Associate–EEC trade, 22–5
association (colonial legacies)
  French Community, 6–10
  French Union, 3–6
  policy (role), 1–3
  Treaty of Rome Association, 10–31
Association of Africa, 2–3, 71, 155, 156, 157, 209
Association of African and Malagasy States (AAMS), 36–55 *passim*
  on Lome Convention, 63–8, 77
Association Council (Yaounde), 41–3, 99
Association of South East Asian Nations (ASEAN), 128

Babacar Ba, 90
balance of payments, 73, 129
  support, 125–6, 154–5, 173, 174
banana trade, 15, 114
banks
  European Investment, 42, 49, 50, 91, 95, 141, 149, 150, 177
  intra-ACP development, 179–81
beef and veal trade, 115, 136
Berlin Clause, 194–5
Berlin Treaty (1885), 208
Berlin West Africa Conference, 14, 69
bilateral aid, 25–7, 29, 51, 88, 132–3, 139, 149, 153, 196
bilateral trade agreements, 207, 212
bloc politics, 192–4
Brandt Report (1980), 188
Briggs, Federal Trade Commissioner, 75
Britain, 2
  EEC entry, 37–8, 60, 61–4, 66–7
Buenos Aires Declaration, 207

Caribbean Associables, 67
Caribbean Common Market, 69
Caribbean Tourism Association, 150
Carter, Jimmy, 204
Casey–Soames Understanding, 205
Castro, Fidel, 190
Central African Customs Union, 40

Central African Empire, 153
Centre for Industrial Development, 90, 91, 94–5, 100, 102, 141, 173, 213
chambers of commerce, 182
Cheysson, Claude, 59, 77, 93–4, 97–8, 102, 159, 186–90, 192, 202–3, 210, 213, 215
civil rights, 199
co-financing (aid), 135, 146–7, 151, 206
colonialism
  legacies of, 1–31
  see also neo-colonialism
co-management (aid), 87, 88, 105
co-management (industrial co-operation), 89–95
Committee of Ambassadors
  ACP, 170, 171, 175, 176
  Lome, 5, 96, 99–100, 102, 120
Committee of Association, 40–41
Committee of Coordination, 36
Committee of Industrial Co-operation, 90, 95
Committee of Permanent Representatives, 100
commodity prices, 46, 54, 77, 173, 174
Common Agricultural Policy, 43, 76–7, 82
common external tariff, 16, 20, 21, 22, 43
Commonwealth, 37–8, 62
  Asian, 68, 92, 132
  Associables, 63–4, 66–8, 85, 96, 103–4, 153
  Sugar Agreement, 82, 83–5, 155
communications (intra-ACP co-operation), 172
communism, 191, 204
Compensatory Financing Facility, 79, 80, 120, 126, 128
Conference on International Economic Cooperation, 128
consultation (on aid projects), 88–9
Consultative Assembly
  of Council of Europe, 14
  EEC–ACP, 170, 171, 200
  Lome, 62, 96–7, 100–102, 170

234

continental bilateralism, 193, 204, 206, 207, 208
contractual arrangements, 97–8
Cot, Jean-Pierre, 202
Council of the Association, 40–41
Council of Coordination, 36
Council of the Entente, 9
Council of Europe, 14
Council of Ministers
  ACP, 170, 178
  ACP–EEC, 102, 128, 138, 140 200
  EEC, 20, 63, 100, 152, 197, 210
  Lome, 5, 96, 99, 100, 102, 103, 120, 122, 128
Council for Mutual Economic Assistance, 195
Courier, The, 100, 103, 148, 158, 160, 179, 181–2, 197
Court of Arbitration, 6, 7
Court of Auditors
  EEC, 118–20, 122, 126, 129, 133, 135–6, 140–45, 148, 152, 154
  Yaounde, 40, 41
cultural issues, 2, 39, 160, 174
customs duties, 43, 44, 92
customs unions, 21, 22, 40
  ECOWAS, 10, 69, 73, 168, 211

De Gaulle, 7, 8, 9, 30, 38, 71, 73
de Schacht, F., 191
decolonization theory, 46, 211–13
delegates (role), 139–41, 214, 216
Deniau Memorandum, 78, 82, 85, 90, 104
dependence threshold, 118–19, 127
desertification, 161
development policy, 4, 12, 153, 173, 201
Dillon round, 21
Diori, President, 45
donor agencies, 146–7
Dos Santos, President, 196

East–West relations, 194–6, 200–204, 206
East African Community, 48
Economic Community of West African States, 10, 69, 73, 168, 211

Economic and Social Committee, 101 –2
education policies, 144, 174
emergency aid, 121, 188, 213
Emerson, Professor, 217
energy projects (Lome), 145
equality concepts, 6, 97–8, 104–5
Equatorial Guinea, 133, 156, 157, 197, 198, 210, 212
Ethiopia, 205
Ethiopian summit (1973), 69–70
EurAfrican relations, 3n, 12–14, 17, 37–9, 159, 183–4
  Association, 2–3, 71, 155–7, 209
  interdependence, *see* Lome entente
  negotiations, *see* Lome I; Lome II; Lome III; Treaty of Rome Association; Yaounde I; Yaounde II
European Coal and Steel Community, 14
European Community's Association, 62–4
European Defence Community, 14, 15
European Development Fund
  Lome, 65, 73, 78–9, 86–9, 91–2, 95, 102, 117, 133, 140, 173
  Lome (management), 141–7, 212, 214
  Lome (objectives), 134–9
  Lome (results), 147–56
  Treaty of Rome, 19, 26–9
  Yaounde I, 37, 41–3, 49
  Yaounde II, 46, 49, 50, 51–2
European Economic Community
  ACP exports to, 110–17
  –ACP negotiations, 69, 74–89
  association policy, 1–4, 10–31 *passim*
  British entry, 37–8, 60, 61–4, 66–7
  Latin American relations, 206–8
  Lome Convention, *see* Lome Convention; Lome entente
  Lome II, 103, 156–9, 196
  Lome III, 156, 158, 159–62, 196
  Yaounde I, 35–44, 55
  Yaounde II, 45–55
European Economic Conference (1949), 13

235

European Investment Bank, 42, 49, 50, 91, 95, 141, 149, 150, 177
European Political Community, 14
Executive Council (French Community), 6, 7
exports, 44, 52–5
  ACP to EEC, 110–17
  Associate–EEC trade, 22–5
  earnings, see Compensatory Financing Facility; STABEX system
  sugar, 82–5
  textile, 92, 115–16

federation of chambers of commerce, 182
Ferrandi, Jacques, 102
financial aid, 19
  bilateral, 25–7, 29, 51, 88, 132–3, 139, 149, 153, 196
  East–West relations and, 194–6
  Lome, 60, 85–9, 131–56, 160
  multilateral, 26, 29, 132–3, 139, 149
  STABEX system, 149–50, 154, 197, 202, 213
  suspension (human rights clause), 197–8
  Treaty of Rome Association, 25–9
  Yaounde, 42–3, 48–51
FitzGerald, G., 75
Foccart, M., 73
Focke Report (1980), 90, 94, 124, 128, 136, 150–51, 154
food aid, 48, 130–31, 140, 161, 197
Food Aid Convention, 48
franc zone, 11, 15, 16
France
  association policy, 2–3, 14–18, 104, 201
  policy issues, Lome and, 201–3
  see also French Community; French Union
francophone states, 62, 64, 66, 69, 70, 101, 136, 202, 211, 212, 219
free entry, 19, 76–7, 158
free trade areas, 20, 21–2, 40, 54
freedom of movement, 21–2
French Community, 5, 6–10, 12, 62, 72

French Union, 3–6, 12, 201
'Fresco' document, 4, 12, 201
Frey-Wouters, E., 70
friendship concept, 104
friendship treaties, 194, 195
fuelwood energy, 145

Galtung, Johan, 215
Gavshon, Arthur, 202
General Agreement of Tariffs and Trade, 20, 21, 23, 76, 84, 205
generalized system of preferences, 45, 48, 52, 55, 63, 68, 110, 211, 213
geopolitical system, 193, 204
Georgetown Agreement, 12, 169–71, 175, 177, 182
geothermal energy projects, 145
Germany (East–West relations), 194–6
Giscard d'Estaing, 73
Gleita Dam, 146
Grenada, 205
  airport, 87, 98, 135–6, 138, 206
Group of 77, 178, 189
Guinea, 8, 9, 18, 30
  Democratic Party, 73
  EEC and, 68, 70–74

Hallstein Doctrine, 194
Harmand, Jules, 2, 3, 13
health projects (Lome), 144
Heath, Edward, 38
Hewitt, Adrian, 126, 132, 137, 144
High Council (French Union), 4, 5
House of Lords Select Committee on the European Communities, 92, 136, 140, 152
human rights, 73, 157, 158, 159, 196–201
hydro-electricity projects, 145

imperialism, 208, 209
  cultural, 2
  Lome neutrality and, 189–90
Implementing Convention, 18, 19–20, 29, 38

imports
  common external tariffs, 16, 20, 21, 22, 23, 43
  customs duties, 43, 44, 92
Indian Ocean Commission, 168
indirect rule, 2, 5, 208
industrial cooperation, 89–95
inequality concept, 6, 97–8, 104–5
inflation, 139
Insanally, S.R., 176
inter-Associate trade, 21
interdependence, 186–9
International Development Agency, 139
international division of labour, 213
International Monetary Fund, 21, 79, 126, 128, 154
International Sugar Agreement, 77, 82, 84
International Trade Organization, 77
intra-AAMS trade, 54
intra-ACP cooperation, 168, 172, 174
intra-ACP development bank, 179–81
intra-ACP negotiations, 69–70
investment guarantees, 93, 161

Jackman, Ambassador, 85
Jenkins, Roy, 186
Joint Committee of Ambassadors, 90
Joint Consultative Assembly, 100, 161
joint financing, 146–7
Jones, David, 50
Jones, Roy, 181

Kahler, Miles, 193
Kennedy round, 21
Kingston Conference (1974), 75, 76, 81, 86, 90
Konate, Tieoule, 177
Kreditanstalt fur Wiederaufbau, 146

Lagos Convention, 47–8, 76
language factor, 103–5, 170
Latin America, 20–21, 204, 206–8
legitimacy (Lome Convention), 105
Lemaignen, Robert, 22, 27–8, 30, 37
Lewis, Ambassador, 178
Lima Conference (1975), 90
littoral states, 189, 93

Lome I, 35, 48
  AAMS view, 64–6
  ACP–EEC negotiations, 69, 74–89
  ACP cooperation, 167–73, 175, 177, 183–4
  aid results, 60, 131–56
  British EEC entry, 60, 61–4, 66–7
  colonial foundations, 1–2, 4–6, 10–12, 55–6
  Commonwealth, 66–9
  Guinea and EEC, 70–74
  industrial cooperation, 89–95
  institutions, 96–102
  intra-ACP negotiations, 69–70
  terminology, 103–5
  trade results, 110–31, 155
Lome II, 73, 103, 123, 156–9, 196
Lome III, 156, 158, 159–62, 196
Lome entente
  French policy and, 201–3
  interdependence, 186–9
  neo-colonialism and, 208–16
  political issues, 192–201
  political neutrality, 97, 98, 189–92, 202–3, 206, 217
  prospects, 216–19
  superpower attitudes, 203–8
Lome Industrial Development Information System, 95
Lusaka Council, 179
lusophone states, 211, 212
Luxembourg Compromise, 170

Machel, President, 196
Macias Nguema, F., 133, 157, 198
Macioti, Manfredo, 191
MacMillan, Harold, 37–8
Madagascar, 9, 10, 35–6
Malagasy, *see* AAMS
Malawi, 137, 139
Mali Federation, 9, 10
managed market schemes, 15
Mano River Union, 73
Matthews, Jacqueline, 11
Mazrui, Ali, 62
Meyer, Klaus, 94
microprojects, 152–3, 156, 161
mineral products, 159, 186, 187, 201
  support scheme, 123, 158, 161, 202

237

Mogwe, Archie, 131
Monroe Doctrine, 207
Montego Bay meeting (1980), 182
Monyake, Ambassador, 178, 182–3
Mopti health centre project, 150
Morocco, 48
Moss, J., 190
Mozambique, 11n, 195–6, 202
multilateral aid, 26, 29, 132, 133, 139, 149
multilateralization of relations, 212–13, 218

Naipaul, V.S., 216
Nairobi Conference (1979), 178, 182
nationalism, 7, 71
 see also pan-Africanism
NATO, 203
Ndongko, W.A., 16
neo-colonialism, 47, 55, 60, 65, 67, 71, 105, 133, 160
 Lome entente and, 192–3, 208–17, 219
new international economic order, 59, 60–61, 65, 79, 81, 90, 103, 156–7
Niger, 8, 64
Nigeria, 47–8, 64, 68–9, 168
 as aid donor, 86–7
Nkrumah, Kwame, 30, 71, 208, 210–11
non-alignment, 71, 72, 74, 178, 190, 203, 217
non-political alliance (Lome), 189–92
non-tariff barriers, 77, 92
North–South relations, 60, 85, 110, 155, 160, 178, 216
North West Integrated Agricultural Development Project, 134

OCT Associations, 47, 50, 51, 86, 121, 210
oil industry, 79, 111, 178
Okelo Odongo, Thomas, 177, 182
Olu Sanu, Edward, 67, 158, 167
OPEC states, 61
Organization of African Unity, 69–70, 104
Organization for European Economic Cooperation, 13–14

Ouattara, A.D., 21
Overseas Countries and Territories, 47, 50, 51, 86, 121, 210
Overseas Development Administration, 139
Overseas Development Institute, 136, 156

pan-Africanism, 9, 10, 65, 68, 70, 72, 73–4, 151, 167, 187
parallel financing, 146
Parfitt, Trevor, 134
Parker, Geoffrey, 188, 193
Parliamentary Conference, 40, 41
Parti du Regroupement Africain, 9
partnership concept, 3, 4, 104–5, 186
 see also Lome entente
patronage, 49, 176, 212–13, 219
Patterson, Percival, 178
Pisani, Edgard, 131, 134, 151, 159n, 160, 187, 196, 201, 206
political factors
 Lome entente, 192–201
 Lome neutrality, 97, 98, 189–92, 202–3, 206, 217
 Lome II negotiations, 157–8
Poniatowski, Michel, 181
Portugal, 195, 207, 212
Prebisch, Secretary-General, 20–21
President (French Community), 6
President (French Union), 4, 5
prices, 15, 17, 20, 81
 commodity, 46, 54, 77, 173, 174
 stabilization, 42, 43
 sugar, 82, 83, 84–5
product-by-product approach, 127, 128
programme aid, 154
protectionism, 91–2, 94, 117
Protocol 22, 63, 77, 82

quasi-federal institutions, 5

Ramphal, S.S., 60, 62n, 158, 178, 209
rapprochement policy, 73
raw materials, 60, 81, 116, 186–7, 188, 189, 202, 208
reciprocal preferences, 52, 59, 60, 76

regional development banks, 181
regional development funds, 138, 177
regional organizations, 9—10
regional projects, 150—52, 156, 161
regionalization, 192—4, 196
reverse preferences, 34, 44, 54, 55, 205, 213
rights of establishment, 15, 21, 22, 48, 60, 69
Rivkin, Arnold, 188
Rockefeller Report (1969), 104
rules of origin, 55, 92, 94
rum trade, 114—15, 136
rural development projects, 142—3

St John, Bernard, 199
scientific cooperation, 174
Sekou Toure, Ahmed, 8, 30, 70—72, 73, 74, 210
Senate (French Community), 6, 7
Senghor, President, 14, 192, 210
'sickness benefit', 121, 188, 213
Smith, Arnold, 92, 191
socialism, 17, 72, 196
solar energy, 135, 145
solidarity
  Third World, 65—6, 69, 151, 167, 169
  see also ACP unity; nationalism
South Africa, 157—8, 199—200, 201, 218
South Pacific Bureau for Economic Cooperation, 168
South Pacific Forum, 168
Southern African Development Co-ordination Conference, 158
Soviet Union, 72, 190—91
  attitudes to Lome, 203—4
Spaak Committee Report (1956), 15
Spain, 195n, 207, 212
STABEX system, 46, 139
  advantages, 127—9, 149—50
  aid mechanism, 149—50, 154, 197, 202, 213
  Lome, 58—9, 61, 77—82, 85, 90, 92, 136—7, 158—9, 160, 161, 214
  results, 118—27
  structural problems, 129—31

STABEX system (cont.)
  as 'unemployment benefit', 121, 188, 213
Standard Bank, 67
Stevens, C., 132, 136, 156
Strasbourg Plan (1952), 13
Sugar Protocol, 82—5, 88, 114, 139, 155, 202
superpowers, 190—91, 193, 203—8, 210
Suva Declaration, 171—4, 179, 182
SYSMIN, 123, 158, 161, 202

tariffs, 19, 44, 92
  common external, 16, 20, 21, 22, 43,
  GATT, 20, 21, 23, 76, 84, 205
Technical Centre for Agricultural and Rural Cooperation, 159
technology, 173, 186—7, 188
terms of trade, 46, 83
textile exports, 92, 115—16
third world, 1
  North—South relations, 60, 85, 110, 155, 160, 216
  solidarity, 65—6, 69, 151, 167, 169
tomatoes (quota), 115
trade
  EEC—ACP, 110—17
  free entry, 19, 76—7
  intra-ACP, 172—3
  see also individual commodities
trade preferences
  EEC programme, 16—17, 19, 22—5, 29, 38, 40, 86
  generalized system, 45, 48, 52, 55, 63, 68, 110, 211, 213
  margin of, 52, 53—4
  reciprocal, 52, 59, 60, 76
  reverse, 34, 44, 54, 55, 205, 213
trade results
  Lome, 76—85, 110—31, 155
  Treaty of Rome, 20—25
  Yaounde, 43—5, 52—5
TransCameroon railway, 135, 144
transport projects, 135, 143—4, 172
Treaty of Brussels, 61, 63—4, 65, 67, 75, 77, 82

239

Treaty of Rome Association
  colonial foundation, 2, 5—6, 10—13, 208, 209—10
  major provisions, 19—20
  negotiations, 13—18
  objectives, 18
  results, 20—31
trigger threshold, 118—19
Tunisia, 48
'turn-key' project, 148
Twitchett, Carol Cosgrove, 93, 209, 211

Uganda, 133, 134, 153, 156, 157, 197—8
'unemployment benefit', 121, 188, 213
United Nations, 9, 128
United Nations Conference on Trade and Development, 20—21, 23, 45, 48, 52, 79
United Nations Department of Technical Cooperation for Development, 179
United Nations Development Programme, 176
United Nations Economic Commission for Africa, 69
United Nations Food and Agriculture Organization, 77
United Nations General Assembly, 81
United Nations Industrial Development Organization, 90
United States, 76, 190—91
  Agency for International Development, 146, 147
  attitudes to Lome, 203, 204—8

voluntary export restraint, 116

Wall, David, 15, 86, 214
water supply/sanitation projects, 145
welfare neo-colonialism, 105, 213—14, 215, 216—17
West Africa, 66, 74
West African Customs Union, 40
Westminster Conference (1949), 13
women (role enhancement), 160
Working Party on Intra-ACP Co-operation, 178
World Bank, 74, 133, 135, 139, 146, 147

Yaounde I, 103
  aid provision, 34, 42—3
  colonial foundation, 5, 6, 21, 27, 30, 188
  major provisions, 40—42, 55
  negotiations, 35—8
  objectives, 34, 38—9
  trade provision, 34, 43—5
Yaounde II, 103
  aid provision, 34, 48—51, 86—7
  changing context, 47—8
  negotiations, 46—7, 55
  objectives, 34, 45
  trade provision, 34, 52—5, 77—9
Young, Andy, 204

Zartman, William, 36, 209, 211—12